PRAISE FOR *The Sc*

Maria Banerjee provides an elegant, Dostoevsky's masterworks, *Notes from Underground* and *The Brothers Karamazov*. Her theme is the harm that reason can do to the human soul if it is divorced from the higher spiritual powers within it. The separation of reason from the other human faculties is a fundamental theme of Russian religious philosophy. Thus her understanding of Dostoevsky's worldview is formed by the philosophical commentaries of Solovyov, Ivanov, and Berdiaev. In passing, she gives us a panorama of Russian intellectual life of the nineteenth century, showing how Dostoevsky was influenced by and reacted against such figures as Belinsky, Bakunin, Chernyshevsky, and Herzen. Banerjee has successfully accomplished what should be the final goal of such a work: to send us back to the masterworks themselves, which we will now re-read with a deeper comprehension.

—BORIS JAKIM, preeminent translator of works by S.L. Frank, Pavel Florensky, and Sergei Bulgakov

Professor Banerjee looks at 'Dostoevsky's novelistic world as an intellectually coherent, spiritually integral whole' in a brilliant attempt to provide a rational indictment of reason itself that complements Dostoevsky's message of love. Students and scholars of Russian and Comparative literatures will find here a compelling case for Dostoevsky's embrace of Christianity as his rebuttal to rationalist philosophy.

—THOMAS R. BEYER, Middlebury College

This work is based on Maria Banerjee's many years of teaching and reflecting on the meaning of Dostoevsky's novelistic world and world-view. Her grasp of his religious imagination is firm and her interpretations are challenging. Professor Banerjee is a trustworthy guide in analyzing *Notes from the Underground* and *The Brothers Karamazov*.

—GEORGE A. PANICHAS, editor of *Modern Age: A Quarterly Review*

Facsimile of a letter from Dosteovsky to his brother Mikhail, written
from the Peter and Paul Fortress, October 22, 1849.

DOSTOEVSKY
The Scandal of Reason

DOSTOEVSKY
The Scandal of Reason

Maria Nemcová Banerjee

Lindisfarne Books
2006

© Maria Nemcová Banerjee 2006

Published by Lindisfarne Books
610 Main Street
Great Barrington, MA 01230

www.lindisfarne.org

First Edition

LIBRARY OF CONGRESS CATALOGING-IN-PUBLICATION DATA

Banerjee, Maria Nemcová.
  Dostoevsky : the scandal of reason / Maria Nemcová Banerjee. -- 1st ed.
    p. cm.
  Includes bibliographical references.
  ISBN 1-58420-041-3
  1. Dostoyevsky, Fyodor, 1821-1881. Brat'ia Karamazovy. 2. Dostoyevsky,
Fyodor, 1821-1881. Zapiski iz podpol'ia. 3. Reason in literature. I. Title.
  PG3325.B73B353 2006
  891.73'3--dc22
                                          2006016258

All rights reserved. No part of this book may be reproduced in any
form without the written permission of the publisher, except for brief
quotations in critical articles and reviews.

Published in the United States of America

Contents

Acknowledgments

I wish to thank my editor Christopher Bamford for being such a good reader; his assistant Mary Giddens and all the staff of Lindisfarne Books for their attentive treatment of my manuscript; Ms. Elizabeth Applegate for her patient retyping of my original text, which brought it into the electronic age; and, last but not least, I thank my husband Ron D.K. Banerjee for being the indispensable interlocutor throughout it all.

Introduction

SHORTLY after his release from the Siberian prison camp, in a letter from Omsk dated February 20, 1854, Dostoevsky wrote to N.D. Fonvizina: "...if someone proved to me that Christ is outside the truth and that in reality, the truth were outside the Christ, then I would prefer to remain with Christ rather than with the truth."[1] On the face of it, a profession of faith that affirms the Christ by separating him from the truth is provocative to the point of unseemliness. While the proposition is offered in hypothesis, Dostoevsky has upped his stakes by inserting the phrase *in reality*. With this qualifier, the idea of a Christ outside of the truth gains a concrete, material dimension.

Stripped of his divinity, the historical Christ may still command the respect of unbelievers with his noble dream of human brotherhood, but as God Man he is a delusion, the promise sealed on the Cross a lie.

In emphasizing the irrational core of his faith, Dostoevsky aligns himself with the tradition of early Christian apologists, from St. Paul to Tertullian and, to a lesser degree, Augustine, who dwelt on the opposition between human reason and Revelation. Among Dostoevsky's contemporaries, Kierkegaard matches his radicalism in pushing the clash of faith with reason into the realm of absurdity and paradox. Like Dostoevsky himself, Kierkegaard had assimilated the Left Hegelian onslaught on Christianity, countering it by defining his faith in dialectical fashion, as subjective certainty made objective by passionate inwardness. Similarly, Dostoevsky's assertion of his will to believe in Christ embraces and overrides the contradictory proposition advanced by his reasoning mind.

In Russian, the philosophical term for the truth, *istina*, derives from the Scriptural lexicon, where it defines the absolute ontological value of divine revelation. Dostoevsky clearly appreciates the original, religious significance of the word, having reached for it in the same letter to describe the rare moments of illumination when his faith broke through his doubts. He writes: "In such moments when, thirsting for faith like 'withered grass,' you find it, because in sorrow 'the truth' (*istina*) is unveiled into light."[2] But in the sentence that relegates Christ "outside the truth," the secular meaning of the same word comes into play, *istina* as *veritas*, to signify a categorical statement that stands or falls by virtue of logical argument.

In the essay "Philosophical Truth and the Moral Truth of the Intelligentsia" (1909), the Christian existentialist thinker Nikolai Berdiaev criticized the culture of Russian radicalism for elevating the imperative of social justice, truth as *Pravda*, above and beyond the criteria of intellectual integrity associated with truth as *veritas*.[3] Dostoevsky's defiance of *istina-veritas* uncovers his roots in the moral maximalism of the oppositionist Russian intelligentsia. As an idealist of the forties, a rightful member of the founding generation that counted Belinsky, Herzen and Bakunin in its ranks, he had paid the price of martyrdom for the dream of human brotherhood inspired by the secular ideology of Utopian Socialism. His quest for *Pravda*, as expressed in his commitment to the liberation of the Russian peasants from serfdom, led him to join the Petrashevsky conspiracy and eventually took him to the Siberian prison camp (*katorga*) and the brutal squalor of convict life. There, in the enforced company of violent criminals, he understood that reason was powerless to control the wayward, convulsive impulses of human will. Throughout the four-year-long ordeal, he was sustained by his daily reading of the New Testament, in the book given him and all the other Petrashevtsy by the Decembrist wives who came to meet their convoy in Tobolsk. Nadezhda Dmitrievna Fonvizina was one of these women. In the most intensely personal part of his confession, Dostoevsky addresses her as a fellow believer: "This *Credo* is very simple, here it is: to believe that nothing is more beautiful, profound, sympathetic, reasonable, manly, and more perfect than Christ; and I tell myself with a jealous love not only that there is nothing but that there cannot be anything."[4] This passage, leading directly to the agonistic formula of faith, reveals the spiritual meaning of the choice Dostoevsky proposes. He knows that the deadlock of faith and reason in which his mind is trapped cannot be loosened by mind alone. Only a free commitment of will, his wayward will, can affirm the spiritual truth of the radiant image of Christ the Son of God and Man in an ontological act of love—"I am and I love"— that Father Zosima will teach in *The Brothers Karamazov*.[5] In the Dostoevskian version of Pascal's wager, faith consorts with freedom, while reason, Pascal's *esprit de geometrie*, is bonded to the rigor of logical necessity.

As a child of the century that his underground man will dub "this negative age,"[6] Dostoevsky can only experience faith *per negationem*, by drawing strength out of the power of contradiction. He explains this to Fonvizina: "As a child of the century, a child of disbelief and doubt, I am that today and (I know it) will remain so until the grave. How much terrible torture this thirst for faith has cost me even now, which is all the stronger in my soul the more arguments I can find against it."[7]

Ten years later, keeping vigil at the bier of his first wife, Maria Dmitrievna, he will affirm his faith in Christ's promise of individual resurrection in spite of the material evidence of death. Each time, his act of faith hovers over the abyss of his doubt, suspended in the void with nothing to support it except the example of Christ's love.

In December 1880, in the penultimate month of his life, Dostoevsky jotted down in his Notebook the main points of his ongoing argument with the secular jurist K.D. Kavelin: "Turn the other cheek, love more than yourself not because it is useful, but because it is pleasing, to the point of passion. Christ made mistakes—it has been proven! This burning feeling says: It is better for me to stay with a mistake, with Christ rather than with you!"[8] Once again, generating fervor from the heat of opposition to Kavelin, a Westernizer who had been tutored by Belinsky in his youth, Dostoevsky pits Christ against the power of logical reasoning. Written within the aura of the recently completed "Legend of the Grand Inquisitor," this imaginary dialogue casts Kavelin in the role of Christ's accuser. In that context it is easy to intuit that the mistake imputed to Christ is his mysterious gift of freedom that humankind find so difficult to accept.

Like threads running crosswise on a taut loom, warp and weft, the conflict between faith and reason weaves the strong fabric of Dostoevsky's spiritual life. That perennial struggle, as encoded in the letter to Fonvizina and the note on Kavelin, finds a more ample and dramatically intricate expression in the great novels.

The design of *The Scandal of Reason* is shaped by my understanding of Dostoevsky's novelistic world as an intellectually coherent, spiritually integral whole. I consider his major fiction as the unfolding of a vision born of two moments in his passage from youth to maturity: the collapse of secular time in the countdown to death of his mock execution and later, in the Siberian prison camp, a crisis of faith that forged his love of the Russian people in the crucible of doubt.

As a literary critic devoted to the art of close reading, I approach each of the three Dostoevskian texts included here as a unique imaginative unit. But viewed through a philosophical lens, the creative sequence initiated by the two *Notes* discloses a deeply embedded pattern of large themes with variations. The critique of reason, the theme I chose to explore, informs everything

Dostoevsky wrote after Siberia. It is the reverse side of his belief in the messianic, Christ-bearing role of the Russian people and as such, fundamental to his consciousness.

The title of my book encapsulates Dostoevsky's formula for demystifying the hegemonic impulse he finds lurking inside reason. The multilayered meaning of the word scandal (*skandalon* in Greek) as a snare, a trap for the human will and a cause of moral stumbling, harks back to St. Paul, in I Corinthians 2:22: "But we preach Christ crucified, unto the Jews a stumbling block, and unto the Greeks foolishness." But in the Dostoevskian world scandal, with all the gamut of its interlocking connotations, attaches to the antagonistic principle of human reason. The phenomenon can be observed in its historical ascendancy as it powers the Titanic drive of unleashed humanity from revolt to self-apotheosis, as well as in the explosive effect attending its unraveling. The scandal of reason resonates most dramatically in *Notes from the Underground* and *The Brothers Karamazov*, the essential works framing Dostoevsky's great creative series. Like the twin tablets of a diptych, the two parts of my study are hinged together by the lead theme, reflecting on its variations within the psychological codes of the underground man and Ivan Karamazov.

The diptych form is inherent in Dostoevsky's conception of *Winter Notes on Summer Impressions* (1863) and *Notes from the Underground* (1864), two works of dissimilar genre linked by the philosophical theme embodied in the symbol of the Crystal Palace. In the travelogue, Dostoevsky's persona stands in front of John Paxton's pavilion in London with dread and awe, groping for the act of spiritual negation to dispel the thrall of deified materialism. In the Petersburg fiction, the acutely thinking mouse undermines that citadel of rational progress from within, matching diatribe with gestures of willful spite. In my reading of the twin texts, I pursue other, less obvious links between Dostoevsky's rejection of Western Europe and the underground man's assault on reason.

In London that summer of 1862, Dostoevsky met with Alexander Herzen, the legendary Russian exile whose analysis of the terminal illness of bourgeois Europe served Dostoevsky as his Baedeker through Paris. But while both men agreed on this diagnosis, Dostoevsky went to the roots of the historical phenomenon to attack the banner values of the French Revolution that Herzen had made his own. In my essay on *Winter Notes*, the voices of Herzen and Dostoevsky are pitted dialectically against each other, as if in a live debate. Herzen was a master of metaphoric thinking, and Dostoevsky's writing echoes some of his brilliant formulations. Beyond alluding to Herzen directly, Dostoevsky sometimes converts his conceptual tropes to his own purposes, as in the coinage of the underground man's image of the stone wall.

For Dostoevsky, European civilization was doomed by its commitment to the supremacy of rationalism, which kept it trapped within the sterile opposition between Catholic authoritarianism and rebellious Protestant individualism. Like Kireevsky, from whom he derived that dialectical model of Western thought, Dostoevsky identified reason with will to power.

In the image of the underground man, emerging from his monologic discourse, Dostoevsky has projected his meditation on the French bourgeoisie into the alienated consciousness of a contemporary Petersburg intellectual. A survivor of the waning generation of Romantic idealists, the underground man lives in spiteful isolation from real life and lashes out at the rising tide of Chernyshevsky's ideology of moral determinism. Herzen may have praised Hegelian logic as the algebra of revolution, but Dostoevsky shows it can also operate as the engine of evil necessity. The grotesque image of the underground man trapped on the treadmill of perpetual contradiction reduces the vitality of the moment of negation into inertia and debases the Hegelian mole of freedom into a mouse.

In the confessional narrative "A Propos of the Wet Snow," the underground man reveals several incidents from his youth, all of which amount to one serial act of failed self-assertion. Choreo-graphed to imitate the glamour of the Romantic duel, these con-frontations inevitably collapse into parody. But in the encounter with Liza, at the turning point of his life, his inability to recipro-cate her gift of love spells out his existential failure in the tragic mode. In that scene, Dostoevsky has inscribed the philosophical meaning of his deconstruction of individualism as *obosoblenie*, a principle of covetous isolation that condemns the self to spiritual impotence.

If "The Mouse in the Crystal Palace" depicts the terminal situa-tion of the Romantic idealist of the 1840s, Ivan Karamazov repre-sents the rebellious sons who pushed their fathers off the histori-cal stage. Conceived in the last decade of Dostoevsky's life, Ivan, in "The Russian Oedipus," is the retrospective image of the radical Russian rationalist of the 1860s, with tyrannicide in his heart. His Euclidean mind arbitrarily confines reason to the geometry of the finite world to suit a will that craves the rigorous symmetry of the act of retribution. Ivan's impeachment of the Creator echoes Voltaire's indignant cry of protest against the presence of evil in the divine handiwork, but the quality of his mind is untempered by the skepticism of his French mentor. Instead, his distinctly Russian version of rationalism mimics the pseudo-theological sys-tem he has invented for the Grand Inquisitor's trial of Christ.

After a brief consideration of the Freudian paradigm of the Oedipal scenario in *The Brothers Karamazov* my essay focuses on Ivan as the protagonist of the tragedy of reason. His ordeal of pride and guilt, entangled with the parricidal plot that drives his fate, parallels the tragic destiny of Sophocles' king. But as I follow both heroes step by step on the intellectual course each pursues on the trail of parricide, the two parallel lines do not meet at the end. Oedipus, having claimed responsibility for what he did unknow-ingly, stands on the stage with blood oozing from his empty sock-ets, an object of scandal in men's eyes. But in scapegoating himself, he has fulfilled the kingly task of his chosen identity by bringing to light the truth about the murder of Laius. Thebes is once again clean and Oedipus has reconciled the chorus's trust in the resourcefulness of the man of reason with their need to believe in divine oracles.

Dostoevsky's resolution of the tragedy of reason illuminates all that separates him from classical European humanism. Scandalized by the suffering of innocents throughout history, Ivan initiates an intellectual experiment in the form of a hypothetical theodicy. Snared by the deadlock of the either/or logic of Ivan's Euclidean mind, the divine creator is judged guilty on the mutually contradictory counts of sadism and impotence. For his next trial, Ivan dons the authority of the Grand Inquisitor to expel Christ from his rationalist revision of Christianity.

After Fyodor's murder, which turns the parricidal script from desire to deed, Ivan's questioning recoils back on him. When his interrogation of Smerdyakov yields the conclusive proof of his own direct complicity in the crime, Ivan's quest for the truth unravels into nightmare. At the trial of his brother Dmitri, who stands in as a scapegoat, Ivan's formal admission of guilt cannot stave off the miscarriage of justice. As Ivan's reason lapses into impotence, he walks out of the courtroom in the exploding scandal that leaves the public deeply divided but locked in mutual moral censure.

To preserve the fluidity of the essay form, I have separated scholarly documentation and debate from the main text. Among the many scholars I refer to in my notes, Joseph Frank was invaluable in helping me clarify Dostoevsky's prison camp conversion and its relation to the problem of parricide. Jacques Catteau and Robert Louis Jackson, who share my sense of the underlying unity of Dostoevsky's creation, are often cited for their insights. I particularly appreciate Jackson's nuanced conception of Bakhtin's poetics of Dostoevsky's novels.

My understanding of Dostoevsky's worldview was formed by the philosophical commentaries of Vladimir Soloviev, Viacheslav

Ivanov and Nikolai Berdiaev. On the specific question of reason, Lev Shestov's essays and I.I. Golosovker's study of Dostoevsky and Kant, as well as Anthony J. Cascardi's comments on Descartes, have been most useful. The notes accompanying G.M. Fridlender's edition of the Collected Works of Dostoevsky in thirty volumes, which I use for the Russian text, are a mine of information. So are Ralph E. Matlaw's Norton edition of *The Brothers Karamazov* and Victor Terras's *A Karamazov Companion*.

My interpretation of Dostoevsky has benefited from exchanges with fellow scholars and critics too numerous to name here. But beyond this audience, my essays also address readers at large and, in particular, the gifted students of Dostoevsky I have taught over the years. To them this book is dedicated, in gratitude for many inspiring hours in the classroom and in the hope that it will enhance their own reading of Dostoevsky's novels by illuminating some of the passionate ideas that drive the destinies of his memorable characters.

NOTES

1. F. M. Dostoevskii, *Polnoe Sobranie Sochinenii v tridtsati tomakh*, vol. 28, p. 176: *"Malo togo, eslib kto to mne dokazal, chto Khristos vne istiny, i deistvitel'no bylo by chto istina vne Khrista, to mne luchshe khotelos' by ostavat'sia s Khristom, nezheli s istinoi."*
2. Ibid., *"... v takoe minuty zhazhdesh', kak 'trava issokhshaia,' very, I nakhodish' ee, sobstvenno potomu, chto v neschast'e iasneet istina."*
3. Berdyaev and others, *Landmarks: A Collection of Essays on the Russian Intelligentsia, 1909,* ed. Boris Shragin and Albert Todd, trans. Marian Schwartz (New York: Karz Howard, 1977), 3–22.
4. F. M. Dostoevskii, *Polnoe Sobranie Sochinenii v tridtsati tomakh*, op. cit., 176: *"Etot simvol ochen' prost, vot on: verit', chto net nichego prekrasnee, glubzhe, simpatichnee, razumnee, muzhestvennee i sovershennee Khrista, i ne tol'ko net, no s revnivoiu liuboviu govoriu sebe, chto ne mozhet byt'!"*
5. "Fathers and teachers, I ponder 'What is hell?' I maintain that it is the suffering of no longer being able to love. Once in infinite existence,

XVIII   THE SCANDAL OF REASON

immeasurable in time and space, a spiritual creature was given on his coming to earth, the power of saying, 'I am and I love.'" Quoted from Fyodor Dostoevsky, *The Brothers Karamazov*, ed. Ralph E. Matlaw (New York: Norton, 1976), 301.

6. *Notes from the Underground*, Part I, vi.
7. F. M. Dostoevskii, *Polnoe Sobranie Sochinenii v tridtsati tomakh*, op. cit., 176: "*ia-dit'ia veka, dit'ia neveriia i somneniia do sikh por i dazhe (ia znaiu eto) do grobovoi kryshki. Kakikh strashnykh muchenii stoila i stoit mne teper' eta zhazhda verit', kotoraia tem sil'nee v dushe moei, chem bolee vo mne dovodov protiv nikh.*"
8. Quoted by Joseph Frank in *Dostoevsky: The Mantle of the Prophet (1871–1881)* (Princeton, NJ: Princeton University Press, 2002), 712.

PART ONE

A Mouse in the Crystal Palace

Winter Notes on Summer Impressions

DOSTOEVSKY saw Western Europe for the first time in the summer of 1862. A middle-aged man stamped by the ordeal of Siberia, with a terminally ill wife back at home, he was intent on playing his second chance from across the threshold of forty. In *Winter Notes*, written after his return to Russia, he reflects back on the journey to "the land of sacred wonders," that Europe of the mind for which, he says, "I have been languishing for so long, in which I have believed so staunchly."[1]

In spite of its provocative excess, the declaration can be taken at face value. It is true that Dostoevsky's imaginative entanglement with European culture reaches deep into his boyhood, at least as far back as that evening in 1831 when, as a ten-year-old, he watched with fascination a performance of Schiller's drama *The Robbers* in a Moscow theater.[2]

The image of Schiller's rebel-hero, inflated by the utopian rhetoric of the French social novelists, lived on in the heart of the bookish adolescent in the School of Engineers.[3] At twenty-five, in his first published fiction, he gave a Russian voice to this blend of sentimentalism and social protest. *Poor Folk* won Dostoevsky instant literary fame under the patronage of the arch-Westernizer Belinsky. But four years later, as European ideals collided with the realities of Russian politics, the young writer was arrested for conspiring with the radical Fourierists of the Petrashevsky circle. Like the Decembrists before him, Dostoevsky soon learned that under Nicholas I's regime, an intellectual pilgrimage to the Holy Land of the West could lead to a death trap in a Petersburg square. Within the magnetic field of Dostoevsky's mind, actual experiences often double up with images drawn from art or literature. The resulting take on reality has the fantastic intensity and the symbolic texture of a dream. Nothing illustrates this better than the psychodrama in Semenovsky Square on December 22, 1849. The Tsar staged the mock-execution of the Petrashevtsys as an allegory of death and rebirth, delivering his lesson of obedience in a drill of terror climaxed by a crushing clemency.[4] Dostoevsky, who had read Victor Hugo's *Le dernier jour d'un condamné*[5] (Last Day of a Condemned Man, 1829) at the School of Engineers and could cite from it by memory, did not bend under the ordeal. The Tsar's punitive script could not stifle the echo of Romantic indignation in a mind stretched to the maximum by the agonizing countdown to death. But no imaginative leap could have anticipated the stunning beauty of Dostoevsky's spiritual apocalypse as his consciousness, nearing its limit, sensed the throb of secular time about to explode.[6]

After returning to the Peter and Paul fortress, the death sentence commuted to eight years of hard labor and an indefinite term of service as a common soldier, Dostoevsky borrowed Hugo's words, "*on voit le soleil*",[7] (one can see the sun) to signify the joy of being alive in a letter to his brother Mikhail. In an account written between 1859 and 1861, F.N. Lvov, one of the fifteen who faced the firing squad, remembers that Dostoevsky had excitedly recalled *Le dernier jour d'un condamné* as they awaited death. They all kissed the Crucifix held up for them by the officiating priest and then Dostoevsky went up to Speshnev saying, "*Nous serons avec le Christ,*"(We shall be with the Christ) to which the latter replied with a twisted smile: A handfull of dust "*Un peu de poussière*)."[8]

Twenty years after the event, Dostoevsky used the mode of higher realism to reveal the Christological meaning contained in

Lvov's factual narrative, where he himself plays the evangelical part of the believing thief on the right hand of the Savior. In Prince Myshkin's three versions of the condemned man's last moment, the execution scene is viewed within the sacred frame of the Crucifixion. The scandal of earthly injustice is thereby superseded and transfigured by the mystery of Christ's promise of eternity.

In the brutality of the Siberian labor camp, Dostoevsky suffered the torment of being isolated in the midst of a crowd of criminal convicts. This separation from human fellowship was rendered more painful by the awareness that his own physical and moral revulsion from his lowly brethren had contributed to the barrier of class hatred in which he was trapped.

In the fictional account of his Siberian prison life, *The Memoirs from the House of the Dead* (1861), Dostoevsky dons the narrative persona of a non-political prisoner, a member of the aristocracy doing time for the murder of his wife. The focus of observation is turned away from himself to the criminals around him. But in the autobiographical tale "The Peasant Marei," published much later in *The Diary of a Writer* (1876), he dramatized the Siberian psychomachia that pits his belief in the nobility of the Russian people against the cruel facts of prison life. In his compelling analysis of the experience that inspired the tale, Joseph Frank characterizes it as an authentic "religious conversion"[9] that shattered Dostoevsky's secular dream of popular emancipation and gave birth to a new, mystical faith in the Christ-bearing soul of the Russian people.

When the text of "The Peasant Marei" is examined under the lens trained on the execution scene, the basic configuration of the two great transformational moments of Dostoevsky's life emerges with striking clarity. In both instances, a dramatic situation leads up to the characteristic Dostoevskian crisis of faith, best described in the "Cana of Galilee" chapter of *The Brothers Karamazov*. As the narrator tells us, Alyosha's collapse into cynical doubt before Zosima's dead body was not caused by disbelief in eternal life but by an excess of naive faith. The young novice fully expected God to suspend the laws of physical decay in honor of the Elder's radiant spirit. Under the taunts of the impious Rakitin ("Your elder stinks"), the insistent grievance in Alyosha's mind festers into open rebellion against divine justice. Likewise in "The Peasant Marei," Dostoevsky, sickened by the profanities of prison life, experiences the loss of illusions about the nobility of the victimized Russian people (*narod*).[10] Suffering in secret, his ache erupts into a public scandal when the Polish officer voices his own inadmissible thought, "*Je hais ces brigands!*" (I hate those brigands!)[11]

Aloysha, in his turn, hears the words of the Gospel being read by the attendant monk. Suddenly, from somewhere beyond the grasp of his unhappy consciousness, his soul takes in the story of water changed into wine at the wedding feast in Cana and he understands the meaning of Christ's first miracle as a gratuitous expression of compassion for the earthly joys of that human body whose corruption had been a stumbling block to his faith. Similarly, in "The Peasant Marei," a pastoral image from a forgotten childhood experience at Darovoe cuts through the odium of the convict's revelry, revealing an old, strangely maternal *muzhik*. When he opens his sheltering arms to the nervously excited boy who imagines himself threatened by a wolf, his earth-stained finger on the terrified childish mouth stills the ugly discord in the grown man's heart.

In both situations, the crisis of faith turns into an ordeal of growth, a testing of the spirit in a crucible of doubt. Pitting reason against the will to believe, in a conflict that blights the heart, it results in an act of affirmation where faith triumphs in spite of contradictory material evidence.

Dostoevsky came out of the *katorga* with his commitment to the Russian people renewed. Even if some Polish officer, arguing his historical case, could prove to him that the Russian peasants were not worth the price he and others of the intelligentsia had paid for their emancipation, he would not abandon them. The

Russian people might be unreformable, but they would surely be redeemed by their love of Christ, whose image was imprinted in their sinful hearts.[12]

When he returned to Petersburg in December of 1859, restored to his status as a member of the nobility and ready to resume his writing career, Dostoevsky was received as a bona fide political martyr. While not averse to displaying the charisma of his hard-earned identity, he prided himself even more on his firsthand knowledge of real Russian folk.

Next spring, with the help of his brother Mikhail, he secured the license to publish *Vremya*, a journal of opinion and literature that rallied to the banner of *pochvennichestvo*.[13] The theoretical assumption behind his political "tendency," as Dostoevsky liked to call it, is summed up in the form of a rhetorical question in his *Winter Notes*: "Can there perhaps be a kind of chemical combination between the human spirit and its native land, so that you cannot tear yourself away from it, and even if you do, you come back?"[14] The fashionable scientific metaphor, which purports to derive mystical values from chemical analysis, may be an ironic barb thrown at the gentlemen from *Sovremenik*, whom *Vremya* had contested throughout the year 1862. Even so, Dostoevsky's question raises the memory of Marei, the gentle ploughman of Darovoe, with his arcane magic. Dostoevsky's collaborators on *Vremya's* editorial board, which included the polemicist N.N. Strakhov and the literary critic Apollon Grigoriev, as well as his brother Mikhail, all shared his conviction that the time was ripe for advocating a fusion of the intelligentsia with the people.

In the early years of Alexander II's reign, when wounded national pride was reviving in the enthusiasm generated by the projected reforms from above, the alliance of Slavophile belief with progressive thought was in the air. Herzen himself wrote from London in 1861: "And like Janus or the two-headed eagle, they and we looked in different directions, while one heart throbbed within us."[15] In the euphoria that preceded the emancipation of the serfs, it seemed possible for the Westernizers to embrace the Slavophiles as the guardians of a shared dream under the double-headed eagle of the Russian Empire.[16]

This was a novel turn for Herzen, who, in the pamphlet *The Russian People and Socialism* (1851), had drawn a sharp distinction between the Russian people and that "official Russia" which he defined as "the Empire of façades, the Byzantine-German government."[17] But even then, as he took it upon himself to respond to Jules Michelet's well-publicized scorn for the works of the Russian *gendarme*, Herzen was already sounding a prophetic call for a uniquely Russian path to Socialism. The theoretical basis for his hopes had been laid out four years before that by Haxthausen,[18] whose observations about the peasant *mir* and *obshchina* soon became a staple of the Slavophile doctrine. In his desire to defend the Russian spirit against Michelet's contempt, Herzen grafted the Slavophile theme onto his beloved legend about the Decembrists, whose sacrificial rebellion in behalf of liberal ideas his French addressee could easily recognize and endorse. "Young Russia," for whom Herzen claimed to speak, was the latest shoot to grow out of the seeds of freedom planted in the blood of martyrs. Its radicalism, he foresaw, would soon outdo its Western mentors.

Having framed his decision to remain in exile as a vocation to serve as "Young Russia's" untrammeled voice, Herzen settled in London. From 1852 onward he devoted himself to publishing the periodical *The Bell* and the literary almanac *The Polar Star*. On the eve of the new decade of the sixties, when Dostoevsky returned from Siberia on the crest of a wave of good feelings, Herzen's journals could be found in every intellectual's study, including, it was rumored, the Tsar's.

During the 1862–63 season, a year after the long-awaited Emancipation Decree, *The Bell* carried Herzen's *Ends and Beginnings (Kontsy i nachala)*.[19] Written in the form of open letters, the series of essays delivers a harsh judgment on the terminal ills of bourgeois Europe, while prognosticating a revolutionary future for Russia as the cradle of Socialism. The ink had not yet dried on Herzen's last installment when the Russian government was caught, once again, in the act of suppressing another Polish revolt. The bloody events in Poland, which erupted in January 1863, doomed the brief idyll of reconciliation between the liberals and the Tsar. That violent rupture still lay months ahead when Herzen and Dostoevsky met cordially in London in July 1862. Even though his *Vremya* was already engaged in fierce polemics against the "nihilists" encamped in the hugely popular *Sovremennik*, (The Contemporary)[20] Dostoevsky himself was still counted among the progressives. In March of that year in Petersburg, he had shared the stage with N.G. Chernyshevsky at a literary and musical benefit for striking University students.[21]

The July encounter in London was based on the solid ground of mutual respect. Herzen gave a signed photograph to his guest, and Dostoevsky reciprocated by autographing a copy of *The Memoirs from the House of the Dead* for his host. But while Dostoevsky could not fail to appreciate Herzen's spirited championing of the Russian people against their European detractors such as Michelet, he knew how divergent were their hopes for the motherland. Whether or not they discussed their differences during this visit can only be conjectured from Herzen's comment in a letter to Ogarev, dated July 16, 1862: "I had a visit from Dostoevsky. He is a naive man, not too clear, but very sympathetic. He has an enthusiastic faith in the Russian people."[22]

Herzen admired *The House of the Dead* and dubbed it the *"carmen horrendum"*[23] of the Nicholaevite epoch in appreciation of the haunting, Dantean effects of certain scenes from the *katorga*. But he had little use for anything Dostoevsky wrote after that. Dostoevsky for his part would remain an assiduous and remarkably creative reader of Herzen's writings.[24] His major novels are dotted with more or less direct allusions to Herzen's ideas and expressions. Both shared an uncanny gift for turning thought into metaphor. They were poets of ideas whose writings illustrate Belinsky's dictum about art as "thinking in images,"[25] which the Russian critic derived from Schelling. In *The Diary of a Writer*, three years after Herzen's death, Dostoevsky said: "He was an artist, a thinker, a brilliant writer, an extraordinarily well-read man, a wit, a wonderful conversationalist (he spoke even better than he wrote), an excellent reflector."[26]

On that July day in London, Dostoevsky was coming to pay his respects to the man who had taught him how to think about contemporary Europe. Herzen's masterful vivisection of the civilization of bourgeois France in *Letters from France and Italy*[27] was written in the thick of events from 1847 to 1852, just like its brilliantly evocative companion, *From the Other Shore*.[28] Both sound the funereal dirge for Paris, the once noble theater of modern revolutions. These two texts served as Dostoevsky's philosophical Baedeker during his grand tour of Europe.

Dostoevsky's posture of a pilgrim about to enter the Holy Land of his dreams, which he assumes at the beginning of *Winter Notes*, is adopted from Herzen, who wrote in June 1848: "The name of Paris is joined with all the best aspirations of contemporary man. I entered it with a trembling heart, with humility, like one used to enter Jerusalem, Rome."[29] Dostoevsky's introductory formula for Europe, "the land of sacred wonders,"[30] suggests the obligatory Russian bow toward the events of 1789 and 1793, a gesture required of anyone seeking to enter the church of the liberal intelligentsia. In *Winter Notes*, Dostoevsky used it as a dramatic ploy to usher in the caricature of the Russian European, a ghostly companion on his grand tour, whom he dissolves in the acid of irony.

Herzen's pronouncements about the terminal exhaustion of the European civilization had been wrenched out of him in bitter disappointment from the sights and sounds of the June 1848 days in Paris. More than a decade later, as Dostoevsky reenacts the ritual crossing into the land of the West, the old agony shows up only as a smirk of Schadenfreude.

Dostoevsky's itinerary that summer took him not only to Paris but also to Berlin and Cologne, Geneva, London, Genoa, Florence and Vienna. Yet in *Winter Notes*, the traveller's mind remains fixed in the attitude he struck when his train rolled into Germany. "What kinds of Russians are we?" he asks, implicating an imaginary addressee. "How is it that we have not been transformed into finished Europeans?"[31] He proceeds to explain that "we" refers to the one hundred thousand Westernized Russians who define their moral and social values in terms of European concepts and ideals.

Ten years earlier, Herzen had written to Michelet that a tiny vanguard of that one hundred thousand, namely "Young Russia," was made up of "the most independent creatures in the world," possessing "a ruthlessly logical mind" and "a new and tragic sense of right and wrong, an implacable spirit of negation, a bitter irony, a tortured self-questioning." He added that "the history of Europe provides us with certain lessons, but no more: we do not consider ourselves the legal executors of your past."[32]

Dostoevsky takes his cue from Herzen's declaration of independence. Europe, in *Winter Notes*, figures as the polar opposite of Russia in the dialectical game set up by the sly pilgrim whose persona he has assumed. In that spirit, the narrative voice engages the reader in a meditation about "our Russian Europe," just as the traveller is about to enter Paris. "We Russians love the West," he declares, "we love it and when the going gets rough, westward we go."[33] The first Frenchmen he describes turn out to be four police spies who boarded his train at the Swiss-French border. Instantly, he converts the four individuals into types: "Although they had no facial resemblance, they were much alike,"[34] he comments, involuntarily raising an uncanny echo from Gogol's Russia.

In the next chapter, "Baal," where the focus is on London, he confides that his purpose in Paris had been to observe and define the inner essence of that city's life. The process of defining Paris in the heyday of the Great Man's Nephew's reign occupies the three last chapters of *Winter Notes*. Together, the "Essay on the Bourgeoisie"

(Ch. 6) and "Sequel to the Foregoing" (Ch. 7), followed by "Bribri and Ma Biche" (Ch. 8), constitute the *pièce de résistance* of the immovable Russian feast Dostoevsky serves to his readers in the guise of the travelogue. By placing the discussion of Paris after London, in a reversal of the actual sequence of his travels, he effectively imposes a dialectical grid on the flow of experience. In this scheme, London configures the thesis of European modernity in its maximal development, while feckless Paris, no longer the home of the ideally negative thought, displays the historical doom of the materialist doctrine in the shabbiness of its social life.

Moreover, this order of presentation allows for a retrospective judgment on Paris from the vantage point of London-Baal: "I have defined Paris, found an epithet for it, and stand solidly behind that epithet: namely that it is the most moral, the most virtuous city in the whole wide world. What orderliness!"[35] The heavy-handed irony leaves no doubt about the speaker's intent. Paris is being set up for the kill. For the purpose of my argument, I take the liberty of redirecting Dostoevsky to Paris and turn now to his "Essay on the Bourgeoisie."

In 1862, Dostoevsky spent a month exploring Paris. France stood politically quiescent in ostentatious prosperity, halfway between the *coup d'Etat* of December 2, 1851 and the defeat at Sedan, which led to the convulsions of the Commune. Herzen, one recalls, had anticipated the Napoleonic power grab against the Republic as early as June 27, 1848, when he commented that Paris "liked to play at soldiers; she made an Emperor out of a lucky soldier."[36] By then Herzen already knew that the liberal republicans, high-minded men like Lamartine who had proclaimed the ideal of a new social Revolution in February, cringed in fear and called for Cavaignac's guns as soon as the real "worker with his axe and his blackened hands"[37] appeared on stage. After the June standoff, Herzen concluded: "The people no longer believe in the republic, and that's excellent. It's time to stop believing in one, sole, saving Church. The religion of the republic was in place in '93; then it was colossal, great. It produced the noble line of giants with whom the long era of political revolutions comes to an end. The formal republic appeared in its true colors after the June days. *The incompatibility of fraternity or equality with the snares called assizes of freedom or the slaughter-houses that go by the name of military tribunals, is beginning to dawn upon many"* (emphasis mine).[38]

In November of 1848, shortly after the Second Republic had been officially installed, Herzen stood on the Parisian square, now named Place de la Concorde, where Louis Capet was guillotined. "No, it was a January 21st," he reflected, "not for the King, but for the people, for the revolution of February 24th was being buried." Observing the procession of parliamentarians coming from the Palais National to meet the clergy half-way on its march from the church of the Madeleine, he deconstructs the allegory of repentance as a farcical ceremony of betrayal and notes that only "the small shopkeepers, pedlars, salesmen, concierges of the neighboring houses, waiters and people like us, foreign tourists"[39] are following the compromised republican flag. For his part, Herzen, a lone figure on a square voided of its great past, armed only with the ruthless logic of Young Russia, executes a rational act of terror by ripping out the blue swath of the *Tiers Etat* from the tricolored banner.

Elsewhere, Herzen wrote that "growling shopkeepers" had proven themselves more bloodthirsty than imperial reactionaries like Radetsky and Paskevich.[40] With that damning comparison, he relegated the "men elected by universal vote, the chosen deputies of the land of France"[41] to the temporal hell where Nicholas I presides as Satan Incarnate. The era of European Enlightenment, whose gift of a Universal Declaration of the Rights of Man and Citizen had been the primer of Herzen's humanism, was thus pronounced dead, giving way to an age of bourgeois meanness. Henceforth, Europe would be governed by the new, pitiless science of economics rather than by ideas.

Deprived of moral legitimacy, the victorious bourgeoisie as Herzen viewed it had no historical future. "Bourgeois Europe will live out her miserable days in the twilight of imbecility, in sluggish feelings without convictions, without fine arts, without powerful poetry,"[42] he prophesied from Zürich in 1849. A half year later, back in Paris, he noted that he himself had grown old as the world went grey before his eyes. "What have we seen since the February revolution?" he asked. "All we can say is that two years ago we were young, and now we are old." Having rehearsed in his mind Europe's great crossing of the river of death, he found himself standing on the yonder side of his own temporal journey, wiping the cobwebs of senility from his eyes and thoroughly determined not to linger "at the bedside of the dying like an eternal mourner."[43]

"The French Revolution and German science are the pillars of Hercules of the European world," he wrote in 1849.[44] Beyond that fabled gateway lay mankind's future. Herzen could sense it glimmering in the distance, huge with expectancy, generous with fraternity in freedom. As he trained his eyes on it he recognized the familiar features—not of America, but of Russia.

Stripped of all illusions, Herzen nevertheless made the decision to remain in Europe. Spiritually divorced from the sordid, transitional reality around him, he would live in his private hope, like the Nazarene once did inside the belly of pagan Rome. Such an alienation was the historical portion allotted to the critically thinking individual in the twilight of a tumultuous era, he reflected. His only reward would be a "autocratic independence" and the "consciousness of unlimited freedom" in the acceptance of his task as the executioner of all "canonized truths."[45] For all the pain such an existence entailed, Herzen was enough of a Romantic to savor its generational pathos. "We shall be the last links joining two worlds, belonging neither to the one nor the other; men severed from our kind, divided because we can share neither the senility of one side, nor the infancy of the other side."[46]

Herzen's psychodrama in Paris is hauntingly reminiscent of Dostoevsky's agony of disassociation amidst the monstrous convicts in the Siberian prison camp. Herzen's solution was to recommit himself to the emancipatory mission of Young Russia. "For the sake of this open struggle, for this free speech, this right to be heard, I stay here,"[47] he explained in an open letter to his Russian friends. In spite of the aggressively secular thrust of his self-definition, Herzen's metaphors reveal the irreducibly spiritual, if not religious core of his being, which he shares with all the other idealists of the forties. When he says that the modern intellectual is a "melancholy Pontifex Maximus" who "only builds a bridge"[48] for the unknown man of the future to pass over it, he expresses the congenital sense of historical impotence that could only be redeemed, never cured, by the poetry of self-sacrifice imbued by the great example of the Decembrists.

Herzen's traumatic exposure to the West highlighted the Faustian duality of this quintessential Russian European, the child of a Muscovite nobleman and a plebeian German mother. The recognition of the prerogatives of the human individual was a founding principle of European life, he proclaimed to his friends. Individualism as a signal value was the one legacy of the dying Europe he would not renounce, not even for the sake of a future brotherhood. That is why he could never side with those he called the "communists," in contradistinction to the "socialists," even though he suspected that the masses might choose otherwise. "People, the masses, are elemental. They are oceanic, their path is the path of nature; they are her nearest heirs."[49] There was no point in blaming them, nor in patronizing them, as the liberals tried to do by inventing the fiction of a people in their own image.

Man was not born free, but only made himself so, slowly and painfully through the trials and errors of history, explained Herzen, in the persona of the ironic doctor accompanying a Romantic lady on her pilgrimage to Rousseau's cottage in Montmorency.[50] Even as the lady railed against the persecutions that Rousseau and other lovers of humanity had to suffer from the vulgar crowd, the doctor remonstrated that in the current stage of human evolution liberty, like reason, was the privilege of the conscious elite. The masses were moved by instinct and by their needs, such as hunger. For her part, Nature, was merciless to individuals and masses alike.

"*L'athéisme est aristocrate,*" Robespierre, that disciple of Rousseau, liked to say, and he promulgated the cult of the Supreme Being as a means of holding the people to the path of virtue.[51] The paradoxical Herzen retorted that "the writings of the egoist Voltaire did more for liberation than those of the loving Rousseau did for brotherhood."[52] In defending individual freedom Herzen was willing to defy any label that might be stuck on him. Passionate and skeptical by turns, he tempered the Hegelian mysticism of ideas with Voltaire's keen scent for the demystifying fact. Herzen was the most protean thinker in a generation of Romantic ideologues, a master of irony adept at intellectual provocation. He could soar like Faust and grouse like Mephisto and argue on both sides of the great Nature/History debate that engrossed his age.[53]

In *Winter Notes* Dostoevsky appropriates Herzen's analysis of bourgeois France for his own ideological needs. Later, in *Notes from the Underground*, he will subvert some of Herzen's metaphors and co-opt his dialectical, ironic voice in an ungrateful act of filial self-assertion. In Paris during that summer of 1862, he found Herzen's bourgeois to be a strangely timorous creature, almost a mouse cowering among the monuments of his own historical triumph. The bourgeois "hides behind Emperor Napoleon," being afraid to remember "the olden days for revolution," Dostoevsky writes. The love of order has displaced the old habit of criticism. In the season of Napoleon III's adventure by proxy in Mexico, even "the elevated style of which the bourgeois had been so fond,"[54] in the Chamber of Deputies and on the legitimate stage, has been ruled out of fashion.

In January of 1789, at the cutting edge of historical time, the Abbé Sieyès had posed the leading question "*Qu'est-ce que le Tiers Etat?*" (What is the Third estate?) His pamphlet answered it by welding the formula of analysis, "rien du tout," (nothing at all) to the formula of desire, "*Le Tiers Etat, c'est tout.*" (The Third Estate is all)[55] Sieyès' self-defining question rattled inside Dostoevsky's mind as he contemplated the tawdry cityscape of bourgeois fulfillment. Everywhere he looked in Paris, he found fresh evidence that the satiated bourgeois of the 1860s no longer aspired to the noble universality of the banner values of 1791, *Liberté, Egalité, Fraternité.* The dream of reason that the tricolored flag once evoked in the doctrinaire hearts of the men and women who rallied behind it on the parade grounds of Revolution had taken on too much flesh. As the age of greed superseded the age of ideology, a new *parole d'ordre* dispersed the old solidarity. *Faire fortune* was a command meant to be taken to heart by every man and woman for him- or herself alone.

"What is the bourgeois afraid of?" Dostoevsky keeps probing. Could it be that he fears "the arguments of pure reason?"[56] But then he notes how lately the learned men of Paris have begun teaching that there is no such thing as pure reason in matters of human concern. The universals coined by abstract reason were good enough for the eighteenth century. They served Carnot well in his geometrical reorganization of France and even later, when Bonaparte ensconced the meter as the measuring rod of all values. But these standards could not be applied to the Johns, Peters and Gustaves who now occupied the *piano nobile* of the old *hôtels particuliers* and who were anxious to isolate themselves from the motley crowds under their windows. Reason, the vehicle that the *Tiers Etat* rode to power, was no longer the convenience of choice. Money was. "Do the bourgeois still fear the workers?" Dostoevsky wonders, immediately closing off with the retort: "But the workers themselves are proprietors in their hearts."[57]

This Dostoevskian theme echoes the observations Herzen had made much earlier in his fourth letter from Avenue Marigny, in September of 1847. Herzen wrote that the revolutionary impulse of the *Tiers Etat* had expired with the last moan at Waterloo.[58] And yet, his pessimistic prognosis could not deter a submerged hope from flaring up briefly when Paris hoisted the tricolor in February of 1848. After the ravaging storm had blown past, Herzen recalled how he stood on June 23rd at four p.m. and "gazed avidly at this panorama of Paris," suddenly illumined by a flash of lightning above the Pont Neuf, as the tocsin rang from Saint Sulpice. "I loved Paris passionately. It was my last tribute to the great town." Later, after having seen omnibuses full of corpses returning from the workers' quarters, he finally ripped the lyricism of Parisian revolutions out of his heart. "Paris grew hateful to me," he wrote.[59]

Dostoevsky, beating the pavement of the new boulevards around the Opera in 1862, felt no such love and no such passion of betrayal. For him, Herzen's judgment on the French bourgeoisie, which "conceived of itself as an end" while being no more than "a mere hideous intermediate link," and his prognostication that "the world of the bourgeoisie has exhausted itself so soon and has no capacity for self-renewal,"[60] had the value of a cold axiom. Herzen's wrenching conclusions were serviceable as a theoretical premise for his own ruminations about a human phenomenon he despised. In Dostoevsky's essay on the bourgeoisie, jaundiced psychological observations replace Herzen's drama of ideas, and the details he picks on aim at creating the effect of grotesque banality. Nothing illustrates this better than the last chapter, "Bribri and Ma Biche," which is a lampoon on Parisian melodrama. It is best read as an appendix to Herzen's discussion of French theater in the second letter from Avenue Marigny.[61]

At a distance of fifteen years from each other, both Russians view the Parisian stage as a display window of bourgeois manners and morals. Both proceed from the ingrained assumption that, along with all its other social misdeeds, the bourgeoisie stood guilty of the metaphysical crime of killing poetry. While Herzen nostalgically remembers the charm and wit of Figaro before he put on the mask of fat, Dostoevsky remains unmoved by what he sees as rank hypocrisy parading on painted boards. And what he observes in the gardens of Palais Royal mirrors that which he detests in the theater. In the melodrama of her life, the bourgeois woman has achieved the exemplary status of a pet canary. Her marriage to the prosperous and tender "Bribri" is a deal whereby she receives, in exchange for the surrender of her mind and body (not to forget her hefty dowry), "the legitimate pleasures of trips to the sea shore, and stately walks in city parks, with gurgling fountains."[62] Bribri always politely looks the other way whenever Gustave appears, cloaked in romance to catch *"ma biche's"* fancy.

The debasement of the cult of virtuous domesticity confirms the degradation of values that Herzen associated with the historical triumph of the bourgeoisie. In the days of Diderot, *la vertu* had been the rallying cry of the not yet franchised *Tiers Etat* against the licentious nobility. During the Revolution, draped in a Roman tunic, Virtue paraded with the people on the Champs de Mars. Robespierre, overstepping allegory, deified her in a baptism of blood. By the time Dostoevsky trained his eyes on the former goddess, she had been reduced to a sham metonymy to serve as the esthetically offensive fig leaf for bourgeois covetousness.

The charge of hypocrisy had been levelled at the victorious bourgeoisie by many others besides Dostoevsky and Herzen.[63] Marx linked it with the reflex of frightened guilt caused by the historic betrayal of the proletariat.[64] In his fourth letter from Avenue Marigny Herzen anticipated Marx's arguments even before the events of 1848. He suggested that in denying the workers the benefit of the same logic it had used for itself in 1789, the bourgeoisie was fundamentally in bad faith.

Dostoevsky too, holds the bourgeois in contempt as the imposter of our time. But he interprets the phenomenon of bourgeois anxiety in a way that puts into question the very principles from which modern France derived its course. He thinks it naive for the socialists to shout betrayal. It appears to him that Sieyès, whose programmatic dictum of 1789 helped unleash the power drive of an oppressed and as yet undifferentiated majority, has been well served by the Future.

The great mystification of the French Revolution, according to Dostoevsky, came in 1791, when the logos of its origins was encoded in the seductive triad of *Liberté, Egalité, Fraternité*. History records as blissful the moment when the well-heeled delegates to the Constituent Assembly pinned on their hats the tricolored cockade, so popular in the Parisian streets. But in 1862, as Dostoevsky notes with undisguised malice, *Liberté* only sprang out of the box once a citizen had amassed his first million, and the idea of equality before the law worked like a "personal insult"[65] aggravating the condition of the poor who found themselves subjected to French justice.

But it is *Fraternité*, this "very curious item," that proves to be the stumbling block for Dostoevsky's mind. He knows, of course, that Western socialists contemplate fraternity in its ideal form as "a great motivating force of humankind."[66] It is the alpha and omega of this historical process that culminates in the happy confluence of freedom with equality. But no sooner has Dostoevsky hoisted the tricolored balloon of social harmony than he punctures it: "What, then, can the Socialist do, if there is no principle of brotherhood in the Westerner but, on the contrary, an individualist, isolationist instinct which stands aloof and demands its rights with sword in hand?"[67]

Stripped of its historical pathos, Sieyès' *Tiers Etat*, which, being nothing, wanted to be all, stands trapped by the violent logic of its self-definition. As Dostoevsky reads it, the dialectic of negation through which the humiliated non-being (*rien du tout*) asserts its will to be, by cancelling out all that is not itself, is a formula inscribed at the entrance to the hell of bourgeois Europe.

In his 1842 pamphlet written under the revealing pseudonym of Jules Elysard, Bakunin extolled the creative power of negation.[68] Herzen, though weary of Hegelian mysticism, promptly identified the new dialectical logic as "the algebra of revolution."[69] But now, Dostoevsky, surrounded by the loud prosperity of bourgeois Paris, undermines the procedures of armed reason by translating them into concrete psychological terms. He notes that the orators in all the official chambers of the Second Empire can still swell the air with the echoes of a revolutionary past.[70] But through the white noise, he hears only the insistent, jealous cry of self assertion: *"Ôte-toi de là, que je m'y mette!* (Get out of there, let me step in!)"[71] Dostoevsky's bourgeois, like his twentieth-century heir who confesses in Camus' *La Chute,* is congenitally afflicted by *"la vocation des sommets,"*[72] But Jean-Baptiste Clamence, unlike Bribri, belongs to the thinking breed of the underground, with the fatal Dostoevskian strain in his blood.

In 1862, when Dostoevsky scrutinized the fear written on bourgeois faces, Europe was still haunted by the specter of the defeated proletariat. Sensing the impending nemesis, Dostoevsky expected no new revelation. While the Socialists promised brotherhood, he saw them leading the way to the antheap of coercive Communism. "The frantic Socialist sets desperately to work on the future fraternity, defining it, calculating its size and weight, enticing you with its advantages, explaining, teaching, telling of the profit each stands to gain from the fraternity and just how much each will win...."[73] he writes.

The language of this passage, with its implied allusion to the calculating merchant, is key to its message. By converting the semantics of fraternity to the market jargon of the class the Socialists seek to dispossess, Dostoevsky has driven home the fundamental lesson of his essay on the bourgeoisie. His judgment goes to the root of the phenomenon. Western Europe will never create a society of brotherhood because the logos of its origins is infected by militant individuation, a principle of isolation (*obosoblenie*) that thrives on the divisive lust for property.

Dostoevsky's vision of Socialism for Russia, forged in the crucible of his Siberian ordeal, rests on the dialectic of self-sacrifice. As in the evangelical parable about the grain, the I must die by surrendering to otherness, thereby creating the community of human brotherhood. Everything he saw in Paris merely reinforced this fundamentally religious conviction.

As for Europe, it seemed to be moving toward the anthill. But the making of the anthill required the constructive skill of ants. Looking around in Paris, Dostoevsky found no evidence of such intelligence. "In short, man is still a long way from the anthill!"[74] A few pages earlier, he had written: "...in French nature, and in Occidental nature in general it (fraternity) is not present; you find there instead a principle of individualism, a principle of isolation, of intense self-preservation, of personal gain, of self-determination of the I of opposing this I to all nature and the rest of mankind as an independent autonomous principle entirely equal and equivalent to all that exists outside itself."[75]

These ruminations come from a mind not content to dwell on surface phenomena, as the common realists do, "who do not see further than their nose" and who cannot understand "how for another person the future results of present events can be crystal clear."[76] I imagine Dostoevsky sitting gloomily in the Café de la Paix, at an angle from the new temple of the Opera. As he surveys the life around him with his prophetic eyepiece, the Parisian bourgeois assumes an apocalyptic dimension. No longer a shabby, transitional creature without historical legitimacy, he now appears to him as the penultimate link in a long chain of logical necessity. Another Russian thinker, not Herzen but the Slavophile Ivan Kireevsky, had codified the evolution of European civilization as a struggle between the assertion of Reason, made manifest in the Roman Church, and the contradictory force of rebellious Protestant individualism.[77] Caught in the deadly grip of this violent dialectic, the bourgeois and his nemesis of coercive socialism are locked together in the last spiral of the descending vortex of negation.

Individualism plays the villain in Dostoevsky's libretto for the salvation of humanity. On that point, he and Herzen decisively part company. Herzen agreed that the age of human brotherhood would dawn in Russia rather than in the West, but he nevertheless valued European history as the school of individual freedom. Even the Third Estate's *démarche* of 1789, "this semi-liberation, this impudent onslaught on the past, made with the desire to inherit its power..."[78] had been a step toward this cherished goal. Where Herzen saw human progress, Dostoevsky detected only a futile running in place in the vicious circle of false principles.

Gradually, but with increasing intensity, Dostoevsky began to regard coercive socialism as a modern spiritual twin of Catholicism. During the seventies, he would develop this thought in his novels and in *The Writer's Diary*, where he prophesied: "Catholicism will surely rush to the demos. It has tens of thousands of tempters, wise and clever psychologists and seers of the human heart...."[79] He feared the Pope more than he feared the Communists. His imagination was obsessed by the specter of a barefooted Pontiff descending into the streets to lead the masses in the last apocalyptic act of European history.[80]

While Paris was a prop for Dostoevsky's entrenched views, London shocked him by the raw power of its materialism. His initial panoramic description of the city, all in broad strokes, created a mythical image that inspires dread rather than mockery:

> A city as unfathomable as the ocean, bustling day and night; the screech and roar of machines; railroads passing over the houses (and soon under them, too); that boldness of enterprise; that apparent disorder which is actually bourgeois orderliness in the highest degree; that polluted Thames; that air saturated with coal dust; those splendid columns and parks; those terrible sections of the city like Whitechapel with its half-naked, savage, and hungry population. A city with its millions and its worldwide commerce, the Crystal Palace, the International Exposition....
>
> Ah, yes, the Exposition is astonishing. You sense the terrible force which has drawn these people without number from all over the world into a single herd; you become aware of a colossal idea; you sense that here something has been

achieved, that here there is victory and triumph. You even begin vaguely to fear something. However independent you may be, for some reason you become terrified. "For isn't this the achievement of perfection?" you think. "Isn't this the ultimate?"

Could this in fact be the "one fold?" Must you accept this as the final truth and forever hold your peace? It is all so solemn, triumphant, and proud that you gasp for breath. You look at these hundreds of thousands, these millions of people humbly streaming here from all over the face of the earth. People come with a single thought, quietly, relentlessly, mutely thronging into this colossal palace; and you feel that something final has taken place here, that something has come to an end. *It is like a Biblical picture, something out of Babylon, a prophecy from the apocalypse coming to pass before your eyes. You sense that it would require great and everlasting spiritual denial and fortitude in order not to submit, not to capitulate before the impression, not to bow to what is, and not to deify Baal, that is, not to accept the material world as your ideal*[81] (emphasis mine).

By placing a Scriptural frame on this Hobbesian picture of the modern metropolis as a place where matter rules with untrammelled authority and where cannibalism is the law of social relations, Dostoevsky has moved the discussion from historical analysis to the sphere of spiritual revelation. Overarching the explicit references to the Old Testament and to the Apocalypse is the hidden allusion to Satan's temptation of the Christ in the wilderness, which Ivan Karamazov would appropriate in his poem about the Grand Inquisitor. By opening his travelogue to the sacred moment of Christ's choice, Dostoevsky has created an existential subtext for himself, where he stands before London as Christ stood before the dread spirit. The "you" form of address adds urgency to the message and implicates all of us in the drama of confrontation.

The Crystal Palace, turned into the temple of the Antichrist in the false Jerusalem of the industrial age, was a pavilion of glass and steel built by the renowned architect Sir John Paxton to house the main exhibit of the London World Fair of 1851. When Dostoevsky visited in 1862, another world exhibition was being staged in London and the Crystal Palace once again became the focus of discussion. A critic in the Parisian journal *La Revue des Deux Mondes* referred to it as a "*caserne-prison*, (barracks-prison)"[82] in an expression of contempt that was picked up in Petersburg by a reviewer for *Otechestvennye Zapiski*.

Dostoevsky was a regular reader of both journals. The comparison of the showpiece of modern industry to a barrack or a prison must have appealed to him. It fitted in with his dismissal of European utopian schemes as nothing more than anthills of soulless regimentation. Already in *The House of the Dead*, meditating on the fundamental human need for freedom, he had suggested that even "a palace of marble and gold" would soon grow hateful to the occupant if a barrier were to be erected around it.

On the desirability of freedom, Herzen could not agree more. In a 1853 correspondence with Pecherin, a Romantic poet in exile from Russia who became a Catholic priest, he used the term "*kazarma*" (barracks) for Fourier's phalanxes. He admitted that all the utopian projects of European socialism, from St. Simon to Proudhon, were no more than primitive sketches of the great dream. Nevertheless, he defended science (*nauka*) and its technological benefits against Pecherin's attack, as the only instrument capable of freeing humanity from its ancient bondage to nature. When Pecherin countered that technology terrified him, because it contained the seed of the tyranny of materialism, Herzen turned aggressive: "What is there to fear?" he asked. "Could it be the rumble of the cartwheels bringing their daily bread to the hungry and half-naked masses?"[83]

Almost two decades later, the rumbling cartwheels found their way into Dostoevsky's novel *The Idiot*. In the prologue to the symposium on Nature, improvised on the eve of Prince Myshkin's birthday, Lebedev appropriates Herzen's expression in developing his paradox about progress as the beginning of the end. In his parodistic excursion into the themes that divided the two exiles, Lebedev sides with Pecherin's pessimism about the benefits of technology, stretching his warning to assert that human history is ruled by the devil. To make his case, he cites anecdotal evidence drawn almost exclusively from Western Europe, as in the claim that cannibalism was commonly practiced in the Swiss mountains during the famines of the Middle Ages, to the fatal detriment of portly bishops. Lebedev's philosophical buffoonery plays with the proposition that humankind, in all its efforts to escape from the nightmare of nature, only ends up entrapping itself in a nightmare of its own making. To bolster this conundrum, Lebedev quotes "that lover of humanity" Malthus, whose calculus demonstrated that fatal disproportion between the ratio of demographic growth and the increase of food supply.[84]

In London that year Dostoevsky was shocked to see how many of those "hungry and half-naked masses" lived in the vicinity of the Crystal Palace. His description of the workers' joyless Sabbath orgies echoes Engels' observations about the proletarian life in Manchester of 1844: "I have been told, for instance, that on Saturday nights a half-million workers, male and female, together with their children, flood the city like a sea, flocking especially in certain sections, and celebrate the Sabbath all night until five in the morning: that is, they stuff themselves and drink like animals, enough to last the week."[85]

As a reader of Dickens, Dostoevsky knew that women and children were the prime victims of capitalism. In his evocation of proletarian London, three female figures stand out in sharp relief. The first is a young prostitute with achingly delicate features. Next, a little girl of six appears, who "rocked her disheveled head from side to side"[86] in a gesture of despair that anticipates Stavrogin's Matroysha. Then a spectral, black-clad figure flits by, a Catholic propagandist prowling the spiritual wilderness. While respectable London worshipped its success in the Crystal Palace on Sydenham Hill, the Haymarket and Whitechapel districts were still miles away from attaining the survival benefits of an anthill. In the initial decades of the century, Hegel saw the modern metropolis as the privileged locus of freedom, a place of reflection where Spirit could achieve consciousness of itself. By contrast, in the myth of London that Dostoevsky offers, the city is a monster laboring under the sign of necessity, reducing its victims to the false choice between the order of the anthill and the violent chaos of cannibalism.[87] The panoramic description with which he opens his visit compares the city to the ocean and also to a colossal machine. With this apparent contradiction between an image drawn from nature and one from history, he has configured in an oxymoron the relentless power about to crush man with its massive force of gravity. The "colossal idea" that London tries to impose on the trembling pilgrim is the thought that matter is all and that life, in the multiple forms it assumes in nature and in human consciousness, is governed by the universal inertia of death.

On April 16, 1864 in Moscow, as the manuscript of *Notes from the Underground* lay almost completed, Dostoevsky meditated on Christ's promise of immortality and on the transfiguration of the self through love, in front of his wife's dead body. "Masha's body is spread out on the table. Shall I ever see Masha again?"[88] he begins, recording in his notebook his groping for that great act of "spiritual denial" of which he had spoken in London. As he wrote in his 1854 letter to Madame Fonvizina, he was "a child of the century, a child of disbelief"[89] and faith came to him only *per negationem*, in an *agon* with despair. In rehearsing his act of faith before the inert body of a woman he once passionately desired, his will to affirm immortality seems to draw strength from the contradictory evidence before him.[90]

As the free flow of his thought runs its course, Dostoevsky's mind is irresistibly drawn to the tangle of existential and social themes he struggled with in *Winter Notes* and all through the excruciating labor on the manuscript of *Notes from the Underground*. His reflections, caught in rapid notation, run from well-formulated questions to fractured, axiomatic affirmations wrenched from feverish arguments. By this process, Dostoevsky articulates a definition of materialism as a doctrine of death, which imposes the laws of "universal inertia and universal mechanics, meaning death,"[91] on every manifestation of life.

By contradiction, freedom and eternal life emerge as the defining attributes of the spirit. Casting for proof of their existence, Dostoevsky reaches out to the evangelical Christ whose example of love teaches the individual self, doomed to die in its isolation, how to live forever by merging with absolute otherness. In the same breath, he proclaims the eschatological Christ as the true way to the earthly paradise of human brotherhood, for which the revolutionaries were willing to spill so much blood. In his first coming, Christ ruptured forever the continuum of historical time, opening it to the prospect of eternity. Standing over the dead body of his wife, Dostoevsky chooses the Christ against the tangible arguments of mortality, just as he chose to take his place on the right hand of the Crucified on the testing ground of Semenovsky Square.

With his restless, brooding imagination forever resisting monologic thought, Dostoevsky the novelist had to find a compelling human voice for the opposite side of his own existential choice. In the symposium scene of *The Idiot*, that voice speaks to us with all the seductiveness of Romantic pathos in the person of Ippolit Terentyev. A consumptive intellectual condemned to die prematurely at age eighteen, Ippolit argues his existential despair by inverting the meaning of Dostoevsky's Christology. Using Holbein's painting of the entombed Christ as conclusive evidence of the spirit's impotence against the laws of nature, he declares his allegiance to the all-too-human Jesus in the defiant rhetoric of Schiller's rebel-heroes.

As Anna Grigorievna recounts in her *Reminiscences*, Dostoevsky himself was scandalized by the harrowing realism of Holbein's dead Christ when he first saw the painting in Basel.[92] Ippolit's reaction to this Western icon of disbelief is to rail at Nature, the ironic jade, whose gift of life is a snare of death. In his nightmare, the power of nature assumes the fantastic form of a scorpion shaped like a trident. That apparition, half beast, half "engine of the latest design,"[93] recalls the oxymoronic image of London in *Winter Notes*.

In retrospect, the confrontation between trembling pilgrim and the Crystal Palace in Sydenham Hill emerges as a defining moment in the lifelong metahistorical quest that consumed Dostoevsky as an artist and as a man.

Notes from the Underground

I.

"THE UNDERGROUND"

THE year 1863 began inauspiciously with an insurrection in Poland. While the events were gathering momentum, Dostoevsky's *Vremya* (Time) carried on as usual, featuring *Winter Notes* in its February and March numbers. The journal had enjoyed two successful seasons by holding the middle ground between the conservatism of Katkov's *Russkii Vestnik* (Russian Messenger) and the radicalism of Chernyshevsky's *Sovremennik*, (The Contemporary) and the Dostoevsky brothers had no intention of changing the editorial policy.

In London, Herzen had foreseen the outbreak of violence in Poland. On October 15, 1862, *Kolokol* (The Bell) published his open letter to the officers of the Russian forces of occupation, urging them not to shoot at the Poles, since "it is impossible to begin an era of freedom in one's homeland by tying the string around one's neighbor's neck."[1]

In spite of Herzen's appeal, the Russians fought the Poles for several months. While England and France supported the Polish demands for independence from Russia and the restoration of pre-1772 borders—inclusive of Lithuania, White Russia and much of Ukraine—the leading Petersburg journals maintained a reticent attitude to the events. Shocked to the core by a rebellion that began with a massacre of sleeping Russian soldiers in their barracks, Dostoevsky sympathized with the broad public's outrage. In his notebook he commented ominously: "The Polish War is a war of two Christianities—it is the beginning of the future war between Orthodoxy and Catholicism, in other words—of the Slavic genius with European civilization."[2]

Finally in April, *Vremya* broke its silence on the conflict with a confusing, poorly argued article by Strakhov that emphasized the irreconcilable differences between Polish and Russian cultures. The government, seething with resentment over the lukewarm support received from the journalists, struck out by closing down *Vremya*.[3] For the Dostoevsky brothers this was a calamity, effectively depriving them of their livelihood at a time of grave family needs.

Cut loose from his moorings, Dostoevsky left for Europe in early fall of 1863, in hot pursuit of his truculent paramour, Apollinaria Suslova. This return to the West had a frenzied, distinctly non-philosophical character. Dostoevsky found himself repeatedly humiliated by the "new woman" and betrayed by the roulette in Baden. At home, his consumptive wife was sinking into death.

By January 1864, when Dostoevsky returned to the public fray as the lead writer and publisher of the newly authorized *Epokha*, (Epoch) the Russian press had undergone an ideological realignment. Blagosvetlov's *Russkoe Slovo* (The Russian Word) with its nihilist critic Pisarev was now pressuring *Sovremennik* from the extreme left. Dobroliubov was dead and Chernyshevsky incarcerated in the Peter and Paul Fortress. With the same editorial board as the defunct *Vremya*, Dostoevsky's new journal would have a distinctly conservative "tendency." The strategic shift away from the edges of liberalism corresponded to his deepest convictions.

Dostoevsky had hoped to inaugurate the *Epokha* with his latest fiction. The first part, "Podpol'e" ("The Underground"), was composed between January and February in Moscow. The second part, "Povest' po povodu mokrogo snega" ("A Propos of the Wet Snow"), was written from March to May.[4] Dostoevsky's letters to his brother Mikhail during this period testify to the difficulties he had composing this text and to the value he placed on it. "It will be a powerful and frank work. It will be the truth. Even if it is bad, it will create a stir. I know it,"[5] he wrote on April 9, 1864. But the publication of both parts of *Notes from the Underground* would have to wait until June.

If it were possible to extract a central message or a singular "truth" from Dostoevsky's philosophical tale, it would have to do with the warning against relying on reason for the solution of social problems, since man is irrational and perverse to the point of self-destruction. The idea was not new to Dostoevsky. As early as 1859 in Tver, he had contemplated writing a novel in the form of a confession around it.[6] That conception travelled with him to Europe in the summer of 1862. In December, while working on the *Winter Notes* for *Vremya*, he promised his readers a new novel with the title *Ispoved'*(A Confession).[7] In place of the novel, *Notes from the Underground* appeared more than a year later in *Epokha*.

Philosophically, this fiction is a companion piece to *Winter Notes*, but it far surpasses them in imaginative and intellectual power. In this Petersburg tale the partisan theses of the Russian traveller in Europe have been transmuted into timeless paradoxes about the tragic nature of free will. Written in the form of a diptych, *Notes from the Underground* confronts the generational collision between two major decades of Russian intellectual life in a debate where argument intertwines with image. Fantastic incidents staged in the streets and the tenements of the suffering city are woven into the flood of speech spilling from a dark, subterranean place.

The voice of the underground speaker is in control throughout the text, which can be read as a singular act of verbal aggression. He manipulates the narrative material according to his momentary whims. His discourse runs at cross-purposes with itself, being simultaneously a confession and a debate. This is particularly notable in the first part, which consists of an extended monologue cast within a dialectical mode. When the speaker uses the second person—"you"—directing it at an unseen opponent, the device serves as a lightning rod for his pent-up rancor. The apparent dialogic situation masks his solipsistic exhibitionism.

The addressee at the receiving end of this willful act of miscommunication is reduced to the anonymity of the collective designation "gentlemen." Only in Chapter 7 does the antagonist emerge with a more solid identity, if not with a voice of his own:

> Oh, tell me who was it first announced, who was it first proclaimed that man only does nasty things because he does not know his own interests; and that if he were enlightened, if his eyes were opened to his real normal interests, man would at once cease to do nasty things, would at once become good and noble because, being enlightened and understanding to his real advantage, he would see his own advantage in the good and nothing else, and we all know that not one man can consciously act against his own interests, consequently so as to say, through necessity, he would begin doing good?[8]

In this passage the underground man adds insult to the injury already inflicted on the "gentlemen." In answer to his own taunting questions, he presents rational eudaemonism in a language that paints his opponents in the caricatural image of a pedantic *Fachsidiot* whose plodding, repetitive style betrays the vacuousness of his thought. It soon becomes apparent that the real target of this mockery is not the excellent Socrates but a man much closer to home. Chernyshevsky and his cohorts of young radicals are instantly recognizable when the underground man heaps derision on the naive optimism at work in the objective calculus of their social ethics. His exclamation, "Oh, the babe! Oh, the pure innocent child!"[9] brings to mind Voltaire's mockery of Panglossism as an attitude that preempts all possibility of learning from experience by appealing to an abstract philosophical reason.

Here it is useful to recall Herzen's comment about the "egoist Voltaire" who did more for liberation than "the loving Rousseau"[10] did for brotherhood. The underground man seems to have picked up the scent of Herzen's paradox in the ironic label of "lovers of humanity," under which he lumps together all the ideologues of the European Enlightenment, regardless of their mutual differences.[11] The Russian radicals of the 1860s, who adopted the utilitarian system of morality from John Stuart Mill and Bentham, are treated as the latest specimen in the long line of misguided thinkers who relied on the resources of human reason for the solution of social ills. The fool of reason in his up-to-date Petersburg incarnation is a thorough materialist schooled in the positivistic methodology of natural science. He knows how to calculate his "advantages" and his "interests" (*vygody*; *interesy*) with the precision of a stockbroker tallying his daily gains. Once again, the clue is in the malicious choice of words, which draw attention to the similarity between Chernyshevsky's radicals and the growling shopkeepers Dostoevsky and Herzen observed in Paris.

John Stuart Mill's paradox of eudaemonism poses the dilemma of ethical choice between a Socrates dissatisfied and a pig satisfied. But in Petersburg of the 1860s, Young Russia was ascendant with a new generation of ruthless logicians and a new impatience with intellectual subtleties. They favored the quantifiable, deterministic model of the utilitarian system. The underground man's caricatural image of his opponent as someone weighing happiness in terms of ounces of fat hit the bull's eye. The arguments derived from the theory of self-interest cut both ways and always lead back *ad hominem* to the dilemma with which Mill had to wrestle. In his own life Chernyshevsky exercised the Socratic option, which took him to the Peter and Paul fortress. But a Luzhin could use the same functional logic to guild his philosophical pigsty.

N.G. Chernyshevsky was the moral and intellectual leader of the social and literary critics who had gathered around the journal *Sovremennik* in the mid-1850s. When they were at the peak of their influence, N.N. Strakhov, writing for *Vremya*, engaged them in a philosophical debate about materialism. In March of 1863 *Sovremennik* serialized Chernyshevsky's novel *Chto delat?* ("What Is To Be Done?"[12]), which he wrote in prison. The novel-pamphlet, with its programmatic title and the aura of martyrdom surrounding its author, became an immediate sensation. Almost a year later, Dostoevsky attacked the novel in the inaugural number of *Epokha*, criticizing its lack of art as well as its ideas. But this was just a preview of things to come. Dostoevsky's fullest answer to *What Is To Be Done?* lies deep in the heart of his *Notes from the Underground*. It is fair to say that Chernyshevsky's provocative fiction was the catalyst he needed to shape the form and the tone of his own Petersburg tale.[13]

The dialectic between the speaker and his unseen opponent constitutes the ideational core of Part I. While it is true that the underground man remains in control of the verbal situation, the provocation works both ways. The simple fact that the "gentlemen" are abroad in Petersburg, flaunting their naive optimism about the power of reason, awakens the underground man's perverse desire for contradiction. The speaker's voice comes into being on the strength of the compounded act of negation with which he opens his confession:

> I am a sick man.... I am a spiteful man. I am an unattractive man. I believe my liver is diseased. However, I know nothing at all about my disease, and do not know for certain what ails me. I don't consult a doctor for it, and never have, though I have a respect for medicine and doctors.[14]

The three short sentences initiate the underground man's assault on the reader's consciousness. The thrice-repeated negatives, intensifying the pressure on the first person singular, encapsulate the emblematic formula of the speaker's self-definition. The statement moves on, propelled by the force of contradiction that generates momentum by feeding upon itself in an interlocking verbal chain. The circularity of the discourse where denial instantly subverts assertion heightens the obsessive, bilious tone of the voice. The substance of his self-characterization identifies the speaker with the absence of those attributes Chernyshevsky extolls in the "new" men and women in his programmatic novel. By brazenly confessing that he lacks the positive attitude and health needed to sustain productive labor, the underground man defies the values on which Russian utilitarians hoped to build the rational society of the future.

What Is To Be Done? is a large-scale prose narrative crafted with a deliberate disregard for the esthetic conventions of the novelistic form. It flaunts its artlessness with a willful bravado that matches the underground man's opening gesture. And in its own way, Chernyshevsky's highly self-conscious strategy is a literary device aimed at undermining the mythical stature Russian literature had acquired in the age of Romantic realism. The attempt to demystify the esthetic function of the novel in the author's hortatory asides to the clever reader goes *pari passu* with the systematic inversion of Romantic themes in his plot line and the construction of his characters.

The men and women embodying Chernyshevsky's ideal of a satisfied Socrates crystallize the aggressive smugness of the generation of the sixties that so offended Dostoevsky. These paragons live by the principles of rational egotism, for which they are rewarded with a personal happiness that triumphs against all odds. Vera Pavlovna, the acknowledged heroine of her fictional universe, likes to hum the *sansculotte* marching song *"çà ira"* as she sits sewing. This disinfected echo of the *tricoteuses* is a nod in the direction of the holy city of revolutions. But while Vera Pavlovna and her friends practice Westernism *à outrance*, they lean toward the English model of industrious modernity, more suitable to their middle-class origins. Vera Pavlovna organizes her cooperative of seamstresses on the model of Owen's enlightened entrepreneurship. On the personal level, she applies John Stuart Mill's criteria of feminine independence to her two marriages. Her first husband, Lopukhov, quits the scene of his own volition so as to allow her the benefits of another free union with his friend Kirsanov. To outwit the irrationality of the marriage laws, he resorts to the expediency of a mock suicide followed by escape to America. When Lopukhov returns to Russia after several years, he passes himself off as an American businessman and eventually marries the emancipated daughter of a Russian millionaire.

The novel stages incidents and turns of events whose inventiveness would do honor to a vaudeville. But the author keeps intervening to snap the reader out of his theatrical illusion. He insists that these scenes are copied from the real lives of a fast-growing elite of young Russians, whose doings will soon be routine among the intelligentsia. Chernyshevsky's portrayals inspired instant imitation by hundreds of Russian men and women. Beyond its immediate success, *What Is To Be Done?* had a lasting influence on the culture of the Russian revolutionary underground, which was just emerging as a distinctive historical phenomenon. For Dostoevsky, who had completed his shift to the right of political spectrum by this time, Chernyshevsky's success was threatening. As was his wont, he fought back by parody.[15]

Despite his professions of realism, Chernyshevsky's novel has a utopian core. The image of future perfection is presented in a dream Vera Pavlovna experiences at the summit of her happiness, as a woman fulfilled in all her sexual and intellectual needs. The curtain opens behind the closed eyes of the sleeping heroine and the stage reveals an enchanting image of Nature in full bloom. From this Edenlike landscape a palace rises to the strains of Goethe's *Mailied*. Inside it people are feasting. Approaching the banquet, Nature whispers to the crowned poet who sits at the head, disclosing to him Her idea of History. "Thousands of years of life parade by in a series of tableaux,"[16] writes Chernyshevsky, laying bare the allegorical montage of the illusion.

In the three tableaux that follow, Chernyshevsky displays his doctrine of human progress as a process of gradual emancipation. On each of the three steps of the ascending scale of development an exemplary female figure holds the center, commenting on her sisters' social condition. In the first frame, she appears as Astarte, the idol of a primitive pastoral society. Her face, marked by servile sensuality, shows that underneath her trappings she is no better than a slave girl, the objectification of male lust. The next vision shows a city on a hilltop, imaging Athens at the peak of its civilization. Aphrodite is worshipped here for her beauty. But for all her sway over human passions, she cannot raise her mortal sisters to the dignity and respect that can only be conferred by the equality of the sexes. In the third frame, the contradictions of the European Middle Ages are reflected in the figure of the Lady, adored for her chastity, which is her only escape from male domination. Meanwhile, the vast majority of her sisters, having accepted the wifely condition, languish in subjection.

The retrospect of history, with its flawed triad of partial emancipation, finally yields to the inspirational image of a future society. After centuries of work and struggle, "man became wiser; more and more, woman strongly perceived herself as a human being equal to him."[17] A woman's voice speaks these words inside a woman's dream, in a ritual of initiation that plays off against the paradigm set in Plato's *Symposium*. Like Socrates' Diotima, Vera Pavlovna's monitress proceeds from argument to revelation, but unlike Diotima, she addresses her pupil from behind a veil. Her concealed identity, which she is about to disclose with a gesture reminiscent of Beatrice unveiling before Dante at the summit of Mount Purgatory, is key to the doctrine she wishes to convey to the dreamer: "You wanted to learn my name. I have no name other than that of the person to whom I appear. My name is my name. Now you have seen who I am. There's nothing nobler than a human being, nothing nobler than a woman. I am the woman to whom I appear, the one who loves and is loved."[18]

While staging his feminist epiphany in the dialogic form appropriated from Plato,[19] Chernyshevsky's vision remains true to the principles of rational egotism. The apotheosis of fulfilled womanhood at the top of the historical ladder promotes the value of self-affirmation over self-transcendence and postulates the equality of two mutually gratified egos and bodies as the norm of the human desire for otherness.

In Vera Pavlovna's dream, Chernyshevsky projects an Earthly Paradise organized according to the formula of individual freedom, equality and sisterhood. Having upstaged *fraternité* and the "great motivating force of humankind,"[20] sisterhood too is subject to Dostoevsky's philosophical caveat against the Western principle of individualism.

From the platform of individual happiness, Vera Pavolvna's vision vaults to the tier of social harmony: "There stands a building, a large, enormous structure such as can be seen only in a few of the grandest capitals. No, now there's no other building like it!"[21] This architectural marvel emerges from Vera Pavlovna's visionary travail as the crowning symbol of Reason made manifest in History. A work of human hands in the Garden, it images the happy concord between Nature and Humanity in a new covenant unstained by guilt. A brave new humanity holds court inside this palace, celebrating itself in the chorus of innocent egotism.

The palace is located in the Middle East, a region now occupied by New Russia. This geopolitical fancy, with its backhanded allusion to the New Jerusalem of Russian eschatology, was bound to upset Dostoevsky. Adding insult to injury, Chernyshevsky's palace, with its futuristic columns of aluminum, brazenly copies the condemned temple of Baal. "What style of architecture?" asks Vera Pavlovna. "There's nothing at all like it now," is the reply. "No, there is one building that hints at it—the palace at Sydenham: cast iron and crystal, crystal and cast iron—nothing else."[22]

The Crystal Palace, the wonder of the British engineering, has now been imported into New Russia in defiance of Dostoevsky's strictures. It may seem paradoxical to find the Baal of capitalism happily ensconced in a novel that generations of Russian Socialists up to Lenin used as their social primer. Yet, as a matter of fact, Chernyshevsky never hid his admiration for the enterpreneurial spirit of industrial Britain. In his "Eulogy" of Marya Alexeevna, Vera Pavlovna's mother, he bids goodbye to that representative of acquisitive capitalism with the compliment: "We leave you after you've been made a fool of—but this in no way diminishes our view of your intelligence.... The means you employed were bad but your environment provided you with none other."[23] The tenor of his message survives the ironic burden of the vehicle that delivers it. In the ruthless struggle for survival that became Marya Alexeevna's historical lot, greed is the supreme "advantage." Only a rebellious seminarist like Chernyshevsky could have dared to break the aristocratic taboo that prevailed against it in Russian thought and literature.

Dostoevsky, as we know, considered materialism to be the common philosophical principle (*nachalo*) shared alike by capitalists and their socialist detractors. These two economic systems, as he understood them, were two faces of the same philosophical coin.[24] The acquisitive man could wear both faces at once, as did Luzhin, or alternate between them according to his convenience and the historical opportunity.

In *Winter Notes* the Russian traveller stood before the Crystal Palace momentarily cowed by the mysterious power of Matter. He sensed that its thraldom could only be dispelled by an act of spiritual denial. By contrast, the underground man in Petersburg, with Chernyshevsky's novel under his belt, treats the Crystal Palace with contempt as a sham symbol of material progress. Translocated from a real London to Vera Pavlovna's dreamland, Baal has shed the aura of metaphysical dread. As a topos for a utopian society built on the principles of economic self-interest, the erstwhile temple has assumed the questionable identity of a reified idea.

"Then the 'Crystal Palace' will be built," says the underground man. "Then ... In fact, those will be the halcyon days."[25] Confronted with this prospect, he instantly summons up the image of "a gentleman with an ignoble or rather with a reactionary and ironical countenance" about to "arise and, putting his arms akimbo, say to us all 'I say, gentlemen, hadn't we better kick over the whole show here and scatter rationalism to the winds, simply to send these logarithms to the devil and to enable us to live once more at our own sweet foolish will!'"[26]

In this vignette, the dialectical negation is expressed by deliberately crude physical gestures. Like Rabelais' learned fool Panurge, who argued with the English philosopher Thaumaste by signs instead of speech, the underground man has mastered Stultitia's occult art of translating ideas into body language. Later, in Chapter 10, having reduced the Crystal Palace to the triviality of a "henhouse," a shelter of last resort on a wet day, he gleefully sticks out his tongue at it. In another act of demystification, he points in derision at "a block of buildings with tenements for the poor on a lease of a thousand years."[27] The dismal image, which degrades Fourier's visionary barracks to the actuality of London slums, damns with equal contempt both the socialist and the capitalist versions of the human anthill.

Throughout this diatribe, the underground man's dialectical concreteness explodes core ideas into metaphors. Those pieces of free-flying mental matter hurtle and fuse with one another, forming new clusters of thought that refashion the reader's original perception of the ideas in play.

The running debate between utopian rationalists and their challenger has been transformed into a vulgar street brawl. The reactionary's provocative sortie prefigures the underground man's nasty run-in with the officer in the billiard room.[28] In both instances, the confrontation comes about as a spiteful response to smug stupidity. Beyond that, there is the underground man's gratuitous desire to assert himself. In the billiard room, he feels that the very existence of his perennially humiliated self is at stake. The officer reacts by grabbing his shoulders to remove him to another spot, as if a cumbersome object stood in his way.

But the underground man, unlike Golyadkin, will never accept his status as a Petersburg minus-ego. Not for him the dumb show of standing abject and mute, reconciled with his tormentors and silently pointing at his heart. For the underground man, a debacle in real life does not have to spell a defeat in his mind. He may be a Petersburg clerk, but he is also a critically thinking individual, a reflective man. He has shed Gogol's overcoat and acquired a voice instead. His double dealings with the outside world may have eroded his character, but a characterless person can still figure as Romantic Irony incarnate.[29]

In his struggle against determinism, the underground man uses the strategy of degradation. By turning an abstract idea into a concrete and typically trivial image, he inverts false idealization and implicitly deflates his own Romantic impulse, even as he derides the ideology of his opponents.

In the skit that features the reactionary kicking at the Crystal Palace, the value of freedom is at stake. Having defined it *per negationem* as the missing X factor that "does not fall under any classification and is not in place on any list"[30] of objective advantages that make up the sum total of the utilitarian moral account, the underground man shifts gears again. Instead of proceeding with an argumentative defense of the idea of freedom, he manifests its existence in a vital act of contradiction that disrupts his opponents' mathematical composure and translates the theoretical contest into a battle of wills.

Expanding outward from his self-centered demonstration, the underground man sets up a contrast between "the respectable race of ants"[31] and mere humans. The former are gifted with the capacity to dwell in their perfect anthill in perpetual satisfaction, while the latter have shown a singular preference for chaos and destruction in the course of their bloody history. History, with its inexhaustible stockpile of evidence testifying to the fact that human creativity comes equipped with an urge to blight everything it has built, is trotted out to contradict the fictions invented by the ideologues. Herzen's skeptical doctor had already pointed to the contrast between doctrinaire precepts and the verifiable facts of human existence, as he proceeded to demystify Rousseau's celebrated dictum, "Man is born free."[32]

Having set up history to humble ideology, the underground man proceeds to take up mathematics. "Twice two makes four seems to me a piece of insolence," he declares. "Twice two makes four is a pert coxcomb who stands with arms akimbo barring your path and spitting. I admit that twice two makes four is an excellent thing, but if we were to give everything its due, twice two makes five is sometimes a very charming thing too."[33]

Once again, a theoretical argument has been converted into a test of wills. By flaunting the capricious formula of "twice two makes five," the underground provocateur seeks to undermine the citadel of rationalism from within. But it would be a mistake to read his perverse mathematical metaphor as an attack on mathematics per se, or on its legitimate application to the natural sciences. His deliberate trespass into absurdity should be seen as a tit-for-tat blow against reason's encroachment on human subjectivity. After all, his quarrel with the worshippers of the Crystal Palace concerned the norms of man's individual and collective existence, and not the measurable phenomena of the external world. In his principled violation of the law of identity encoded in Aristotelian logic (A=A), the underground man challenges the dominance of rational analysis in the epistemological tradition that links Chernyshevsky to Socrates.

The underground man, in the manner of the philosophical fool, tests and tempers reason in the crucible of absurdity. Judged by common sense, his preference for "twice two makes five" appears a perversion smacking of an unnatural world, a world of misrule mired in caprice. But the personification of arithmetical normalcy as "the pert coxcomb who stands with arms akimbo barring your path and spitting" turns the tables on common sense, by displaying it as the attitude of one trapped in a limited but fiercely held view of reality. It brings to mind the smug insolence of the officer in the billiard room, of Zverkov at his dinner party, and of all the other "bulls" who mistake the conventions of the Petersburg power pyramid for social normalcy.

The underground man notes that these men are unstoppable when it comes to direct action: "Such a gentleman simply dashes straight for his object like an infuriated bull with its horns down, and nothing but a wall will stop him."[34] But the seeming spontaneity of the attack is a strictly choreographed business. Just as a bull in the arena charges at the red flag by virtue of a trained instinct, his Petersburg counterpart's reactions are programmed by "the deductions of natural sciences, mathematics."[35] For the human bull, the rationalistic dressage carries the authority of immutable natural law. Happy prisoners of reason, these men are prime candidates for achieving the objectified status of "piano keys" or "organ stops."[36] Under the touch of the virtuosos of utopian rationalism, they could be instrumental in producing the choral song of social harmony.

A paradoxalist is, by definition, someone who pits his insights against accepted opinions (*para-doxa*). The underground man, whom his editor calls "this paradoxalist"[37] is well practiced at that. But the art of paradoxy also encompasses a higher form of dialectic, predicated on the coincidence of opposites. The logic of *coincidentia oppositorum*, which describes a circle of meaning beyond the linear chain of rational causality, generates significance out of contraries. This paradoxical logic is implied in the underground man's notion that there is good in human evil and suffering, because they connote the possibility of moral choice. In spite of this insight, the underground man is not a mystic but a subversive polemicist.[38] Stuck on negation, his mind will not travel full circle.

A professional fool, even an unwise one, can claim the license to look at the world upside down, testing all accepted values by standing them on their heads. From this perspective, reason's claim appears grounded in nothing more solid than a convention that men find useful to get by. In human affairs, conventions that begin as conveniences often end up as authority. In the underground man's words, "reason is an excellent thing, there is no disputing that, but reason is nothing but reason and satisfies only the rational side of man's nature, while will is a manifestation of the whole life, that is, of the whole human life including reason and all its impulses."[39]

The Russian existentialist philosopher Lev Shestov was the first to point out that the underground man's assault on reason contained a brilliantly executed maneuver of demystification. In his essay on the *Notes from the Underground*, published in 1929 in Paris, Shestov asks: " 'The laws of nature' with their invincibility, the rational truths with their self-evidence, what are they but a mystification (*navozhdenie*), a self-induced compulsion, such as is experienced by a rooster around whom a circle has been drawn in chalk?"[40] Conceived within the frame set up by the underground man, Shestov's psychological insight into the spell reason has cast over the Western philosophical tradition matches the subversiveness of Nietzsche's genealogy of Christian morality. Like Nietzsche, with whom he had compared Dostoevsky in an earlier study written in 1901, Shestov speaks from the tragically liberated consciousness of a man who is "hanging in the void," after being "torn from the community (*vsemstvo*)"[41] and its collective values. But the flaw of Shestov's interpretation lies in his assumption that the underground man shares Nietzsche's (and his own) tragic sense of freedom along with his nihilism. Moreover, in both essays, Shestov fails to make the all-important distinction between the author and his character, to the point of attributing to Dostoevsky the underground man's cynicism. Yet he is right in saying that "if you want to grasp Dostoevsky, you must constantly bear in mind his basic assumption that two by two is four means the beginning of death."[42]

Since the Renaissance, European thinkers have posited reason as the supreme arbiter of the truth of Nature. Reason was the weapon of choice in their struggle against arbitrary authority. "There is nothing more contrary to authority than logic,"[43] wrote Herzen in Letter 11 of *From France and Italy*. But the underground man's paradoxes, aimed at destabilizing the privileged relationship between logic and nature, have effectively compromised reason's legitimacy. Shestov is right on that point. Stripped of its epistemological primacy and reduced to a convention, reason still plays the knave with its phantom powers. Only in the upside-down world of the philosophical fool, logical reasoning stands exposed as an arbitrary and unnatural exercise of will, open to the very same charges it had imputed to its traditional antagonists.

As befits one who has characterized himself as an "acutely conscious mouse,"[44] the underground man proceeds to undermine the claims of reason by subversion rather than by argument. His procedure is more than a key to who he is, it is the whole phenomenon. And this is where Shestov's reading of the text, which identifies Dostoevsky with the underground man, breaks down. Joseph Frank is absolutely right in insisting that the speaker in the *Notes from the Underground* is a fully developed presence, acting within his own sphere, and not a projection of the author's personality.[45]

The underground man, as Dostoevsky conceived him, is not the existentialist counterpart of the classical everyman, but a distinctive self deeply rooted in historical time and space. The authorial note to the title of Part I ("Podpol'e") makes it plain that this fictional character is a definable Petersburg type with generational and psychological traits that link him to the superfluous men of the 1840s. "Nevertheless, it is clear that such persons as the writer of these notes not only may, but positively must, exist in our society, when we consider the circumstances under which our society was formed.... He is one of the representatives of a generation still living. In this fragment, entitled 'The Underground,' this person introduces himself and his views, and, as it were, tries to explain the causes owing to which he has made his appearance in our midst."[46] With fitting irony, Dostoevsky has taken great pains to present his apologist of freedom as a creature of historical necessity. The text will show, however, that this product of a complex environment is fully conscious of the pathological causality by which he was formed.

The best existentialist readers of *Notes from the Underground*, while highlighting the underground man's defense of the value of human freedom, acknowledge the pathos of his feeling of entrapment. Robert Louis Jackson has compared him to the "despairer" in Kierkegaard's *The Sickness unto Death* (1849), characterizing his psychomania as "a tragi-comic rebellion of the ego, crazed by its impotence, against an overpowering and humiliating reality."[47] Jackson sees the essence of the underground man's metaphysical freedom in his perpetual rebellion against the "stone wall" and the laws of nature. Such an existence is absurd, in the sense in which Albert Camus defined absurdity in his *Myth of Sisyphus* (1942). It is also profoundly tragic in the Nietzschean way, as Shestov saw it, because the agon of a will pitted against a constraining force does not achieve real freedom, but merely dispels the illusions that trap "normal" men.

In an important essay published in *The Sewanee Review* in 1961, Joseph Frank contradicts the existentialists by arguing that the underground man is neither free nor antagonistic to the rules of reason. His problem, as Frank sees it, "does not arise, as is popularly supposed, because of his rejection of reason. It derives from his acceptance of all the implications of 'reason' in its then current Russian incarnation—and particularly those implications which the advocates of reason like Chernyshevsky blithely preferred to overlook or deny."[48] Understood in this way, the underground man's battles of will and wits with the determinists have to be translated from tragedy into satire. His assault on the Crystal

Palace, as presented by Frank, is not a heroic siege but a covert operation conducted from within the citadel of Reason. "Cunning is the irony of brute force," wrote Herzen, quoting from Hegel in his *Letter to Michelet*.[49] Not surprisingly, he claimed possession of it for his own side, as the historical prerogative of the long-suffering Russian people. Likewise, the "acutely conscious mouse" in its Petersburg cellar is Russian enough to know, as the underground man puts it, that it "cannot break through the wall by battering my head against it."[50] Instead, he crawls into the Crystal Palace through the basement. He sneaks in with all the rage and resentment a thinking man can secrete by living with the awareness of being nothing but a plaything of the iron laws of Nature and History.

The underground man, Frank explains, is Dostoevsky's image of what a human being might become if he fully internalized the certainty that free moral choice is impossible in a deterministic universe. Such a being might well wreak his petty revenge on the builders of the Crystal Palace. In a society regimented by reason, an individual who does not want to be an organ stop or a piano key is likely to become perversely defiant. In this scenario, the underground man's exhibitionist antics could serve as a compelling ad hominem demonstration of the inadequacy of utopian rationalism to satisfy human needs.

Frank is right in drawing attention to the overwhelming sense of impotence that fuels the underground man's reactive posture. It is notable that the underground man turns all encounters into confrontations that rehearse the paradigm of revenge. While his imagination projects him as a challenger in a duel, reality converts his aristocratic scheme into an incident of humiliating banality. Here, one must note that the psychology of the would-be avenger, paralyzed by inertia, links the underground man to Hamlet, as the Romantics saw him. Dostoevsky has alluded to the kinship between his character and Turgenev's type of a petty Russian Hamlet. In a letter to Turgenev, accepting his *Phantoms* for publication in the first number of *Epokha*, he singles out the "futile longing" (*toska*) of a fully developed and self-conscious being"[51] as the defining phenomenon of contemporary life.

In Frank's revisionist reading of *Notes from the Underground* the underground man loses the Romantic aura of his historical origins to become a smart pawn in Dostoevsky's satire against Chernyshevsky. By redirecting attention to the literary modalities of the text, this interpretation avoids the pitfall of treating the underground man as a straightforward advocate of freedom. But Frank is mistaken in assuming that the underground man accepts the tenets of determinism, which teach him that "whatever he does is inevitable and unalterable because it is totally determined by the laws of nature."[52] Surely, that is not what the thinking mouse implies when he contrasts his own complex response to the "stone wall" of necessity with the bull's elemental stolidity. "Of course I cannot break through the wall by battering my head against it," he admits, "but I am not going to be reconciled to it simply because it is a stone wall and I have not the strength."[53]

Reconciliation, in the underground man's use of the term, signifies a higher degree and a more holistic quality of assent than the factual acknowledgement of the stone wall as an immovable obstacle. Of course, he recognizes the disproportion in strength between the mouse and the stone wall. But, as he has explained at the beginning of his exposition, his mind, unlike the bull's, works dialectically, in accordance with "the fundamental laws of overacute consciousness."[54] These internal laws hold sway over his mind with the immutable rigor that the law of gravity exercises over matter. Thus, proposition A never remains an A once it has become articulate in his consciousness. An idea, once grasped and defined, is instantly propelled by the dynamic force of contradiction to assume all the qualities that were excluded by the original act of definition.

In the underground man's lexicon, the word for consciousness (*soznanie*) connotes moral as well as cognitive knowledge.[55] This has the effect of implicating the function of will in the dialectical process. He admits as much when he confesses, "The more conscious I was of goodness and all that was 'lofty and beautiful' the more deeply I sank into my mire and the more ready I was to sink in it altogether."[56]

Unable as he is to sustain a moral choice between good and evil, he is equally incapable of affirming whether or not he really accepts the stone wall of necessity. "Oh absurdity of absurdities!" he cries out. "How much better it is to understand it all, to recognize it all, all the impossibilities and stone walls; not to be reconciled to one of those impossibilities and stone walls if it disgusts you to be reconciled; by the way of the most inevitable logical combinations to reach the most revolting conclusions on the everlasting theme that *even for the stone wall you are yourself somehow to blame, though again it is as clear as day you are not to blame in the least, and therefore grinding your teeth in silent impotence to sink voluptuously into inertia*"[57] (emphasis mine).

In spite of the entangled form of its exposition, the passage makes it amply clear that the underground man knows that he is not a prisoner of the laws of nature, but a willing captive, indeed an accomplice of the laws of his own consciousness. And he knows that his self-generated mode of being induces the condition he calls *kosnost*, "the inertia that was the direct result of those laws and that consequently one was not only unable to change but could do absolutely nothing."[58]

In his meditation over the dead body of his wife, shortly after the completion of *Notes from the Underground*, Dostoevsky uses the word *kosnost'* (inertia) as the defining term for materialism.[59] A category of absolute necessity, *kosnost'* spells death and the isolation of the individual self in its transference from the realm of matter to the preserve of spirit. It describes perfectly the underground man's entrapment in permanent self-contradiction. Unable to affirm anything beyond his will to assert himself, he luxuriates in the feeling of his own impotence and projects the blame for his existence outward in the form of resentment.

Nietzsche, who valued *Notes from the Underground* for its psychological exploration of resentment, understood the phenomenon as a particularly toxic form of aggression by the weak.[60] Camus, following both Dostoevsky and Nietzsche, zeroed in on the addictive aspect of resentment which affects the self as "an autointoxication, the malignant secretion of one's preconceived impotence inside the enclosure of the self."[61]

In the underground man's life, resentment is the automatic backlash of his humiliated power drive. It is a wound his soul inflicts upon itself, like his inertia. Projected on the screen of his consciousness, resentment shows up the negative of freedom, as in an undeveloped photograph the true image is revealed in reverse.

The underground man's entrapment in self-made necessity is a condition symptomatic of the historical culture that bore him, which he dubs "our negative age."[62] His characterization of the nineteenth century evokes Herzen's conception of the emancipated modern man as a transitional being whose task is to destroy old illusions. "We do not build, we destroy; we do not proclaim a new revolution, we eliminate the old lie," wrote Herzen, in dedicating *From the Other Shore* to his son Alexander. "Modern man, that melancholy Pontifex Maximus, only builds a bridge, it will be for the unknown man of the future to pass over it. You may be there to see him...."[63] he concluded, summing up his life's work in a testament where generational pathos speaks with the intimacy of a father addressing his beloved son.

It was Herzen who called Hegel's dialectical logic "the algebra of revolution,"[64] paying tribute to the dynamic potential of definition by negation. In "The Reaction in Germany" (1842), Bakunin went even further in exalting the act of negation. With his faith in the Science he had preached to his Moscow friends rekindled by fresh contacts with the Left Hegelians of Berlin, he singled out the phase of contradiction for special praise. "Contradiction is not an equilibrium but a preponderance of the Negative," Bakunin stated,

explaining that since the Negative "alone concludes within itself
the totality of contradiction... it alone also has absolute justifica-
tion." Rising to the final exhortation, he asserted that "the inexhaustible and pregnant nature" of the Negative is revealed in "the
vital act of denial" by means of which the Negative "should lovingly surrender to the Positive in order to consume it."[65]

In Bakunin's poetic version of the Hegelian paradigm, the act of
absolute negation copies the self-surrender enshrined in the evangelical paradox of the dying grain. Dostoevsky loved this passage
from the Gospel of St. John. Twice cited in *The Brothers
Karamazov*, in the epigraph to the novel and in the text, as the core
of Father Zosima's teaching, the parable overarches the narratives
of human rebellion with its insistence that spiritual freedom is
achieved only in the disciplined practice of *askesis* from the ego.
Compared with this mystical model of the soul's liberation, the
underground man's existential routine on his dialectical treadmill,
laboring in place from attempted self-assertion to imposed humiliation, seems like a cruel parody.

The underground man is an insignificant Petersburg clerk, a
collegiate assessor by rank, whose notions about himself are
inflated by readings of Romantic literature. His unrequited sense
of his moral and intellectual superiority swells and festers with
every contact with raw reality. Contradiction works for him like a
drug does for the addict, injecting him with a momentary illusion
of power. In his state of covetous dispossession, the underground
man incarnates Dostoevsky's gloss in Sieyès' *Tiers Etat* as an entity
conscious of being nothing while aspiring to be all. The formula
of his self-definition, "I am alone and they are all,"[66] coined during his formative years in the 1840s, inverts Sicyès' will to power
into an equally aggressive expression of self-pity.

Confined to his Petersburg cellar, the thinking mouse degrades
the lofty meaning negation held for the idealists of the 1840s by
replacing the emblematic Romantic rebel with the self-referential
figure of a morally ambiguous victim. Isolated from the stream of

life, this creature never moves beyond the stage of "unhappy consciousness."[67] Hegel had used this expression to characterize the pain of isolation experienced by a consciousness emerging from the Spirit's initial grappling with Nature. The underground man provides a concrete illustration of this state of mind in the vignette of an educated man of the nineteenth century suffering from toothache. Humiliated by this reminder of his subjection to nature, this paragon of modernity creates a scandal by loudly moaning, in a malicious attempt to convert his metaphysical grievance into a pleasurable offensive against his fellow humans.

In 1864, when he wrote *Notes from the Underground*, Dostoevsky looked back at Herzen and Bakunin with eyes jaundiced by what he considered a treasonous intervention by *The Bell* in the Polish revolt. By advocating the Polish cause, Herzen appeared to Dostoevsky as the epitome of the alienated man, a man whose "last roots rotted"[68] and whose last links with the Russian soil were shaken loose, whose every act was doomed to end in futility.

Three years after Herzen's death, in an article written for the arch-conservative journal *The Citizen* (1873), Dostoevsky would pen the epitaph for his onetime mentor. Here he defines Herzen as "a product of our aristocracy, *gentilhomme russe et citoyen du monde* (a Russian nobleman and citizen of the civilized world) above all, a type that appeared only in Russia and which could appear only in Russia." Generalizing on the particulars of Herzen's life, Dostoevsky draws the most damning conclusion from his diagnostic sketch: "When they broke with the People, they naturally lost God as well."

In a vein reminiscent of the author's explanation about the underground man's origins, Dostoevsky paints Herzen as a captive of history: "History itself seemed to predestine Herzen as its most vivid illustration of how the huge majority of our educated classes split themselves off from the People." As if to complete the resemblance with the underground man, he goes on to enumerate the contradictions that characterized the great publicist's life and thought: "...he denied the family, and was, it seems, a good husband and father. He denied private property but, pending the new order, contrived to put his own affairs in good order and was pleased to enjoy financial independence while abroad. He worked to foment revolutions and incited others to them, and at the same time he loved comfort and family peace.... Self-reflection—the ability to make of his own deepest feelings an object which he could set before him, pay tribute to and, in the next breath perhaps, ridicule—was a thing he had developed to the highest degree."[69]

In this posthumous sketch of the brilliant intellectual whose writings had taught him how to read contemporary Europe, Dostoevsky has drawn Herzen as the underground man's successful double. But neither the glamour of aristocratic identity nor the charisma of a leading role played on the grand stage of history could mask the sickness inscribed in the genetic coding of the Russian Europeans.

The underground man and Herzen are Romantics spawned in the historical matrix of the 1840s, a decade when high dreams were shadowed by a crushing sense of political impotence. Russian Romantics, the underground man notes, are quite unlike their transcendental German brethren. Always many-sided, they manage to combine a lofty contempt for society with a knack for such practical things as pensions, decorations. "And all the while, they never lose their ideal even in the depth of degradation."[70] Whether played as farce or tragedy, or—in the case of Kirilov, the latter-day, apocalyptic variant on the type of *gentilhomme russe et citoyen du monde civilisé*—as an uncanny mixture of both genres these men and all their gestures are ruled by the ineluctable force of contradiction.

In the generational battle between the idealists of the forties and the realists of the sixties Herzen and the underground man stand together. Neither of them would give up poetry for Büchner's *Kraft and Stoff* (Force and Matter, 1855). Herzen never accepted Chernyshevsky's crude form of materialism, and his position on philosophical determinism is almost as baffling as the underground man's. He approached the question dialectically, alternatively arguing that man is more free or less free than he thinks himself to be.

It is interesting to reread the exchange between the skeptic and the idealist in Chapter 4 of *From the Other Shore*. After remonstrating that "idealists are cowards about facing the truth,"[71] the skeptic compares himself with Pliny to explain his decision to stay in France despite his disillusionment. Just as Pliny sat in his boat to watch the eruption of Vesuvius, he is determined to observe the death throes of Europe from close up, with a naturalist's dispassionate curiosity.

When the idealist objects that "in the world of history man is at home, he is not only a spectator but an actor," the skeptic rejoins: "Yes, man is at home in history, but from your words one might gather that he is only a guest in nature, as though there were a stone wall between nature and history. I believe that he is at home in both, but in neither of them an absolute master."[72] Similarly, in Chapter 1, Herzen had argued that human progress was achieved through "the reciprocal action of natural forces and the forces of will."[73] In Chapter 5, he identified the masses with nature, since they were moved by biological necessities, such as hunger. Ruefully, he concluded that only the great men of ideas could attain freedom for now.

In Herzen's usage, the image of the "stone wall," which Dostoevsky appropriates for his *Notes from the Underground*, stands for the idea of a rigid separation between mind and matter that turns out to be a delusion of the mind. A stone wall, after all, is not a natural but a man-made thing. Accordingly, Herzen treats determinism as a philosophical construct, a fiction that merely inverts the error of absolute idealism. He treats both these systems as relics of a dogmatic medieval dualism and, as such, injurious to the harmonic development of human personality.

In all the protean vagaries of his cogitations, Herzen held on to the exalted vision of the critically thinking individual as the prime mover and the legitimate beneficiary of the historical struggle. This was one Western value he was unwilling to sacrifice to any Moloch, not even if it promised to fulfill his great dream of Russian Socialism. His conception of social harmony required a full acknowledgement of individual needs and prerogatives. On that he was in agreement with Chernyshevsky's new men and women, even though he stated his non-negotiable demand in the language of poetry, which they despised. As he put it, he would never consent to see living human beings turned into "caryatids supporting a floor for others some day to dance on."[74] The underground man, with characteristic pettiness, cuts down the vibrant image of human happiness to the "cup of tea" that measures his selfish whim. "Is the world to go to pot or am I to go without my tea? I say that the world may go to pot for me as long as I always get my tea,"[75] he says to Liza. To this reader his metaphoric beverage looks suspiciously like a parody of the strong tea with thick cream that Chernyshevsky's Vera Pavlovna indulged in during her blissfully purposive life.

The underground man's self-description as a "mouse" can be traced back to Herzen, just like the "stone wall" of illusory necessity he confronts. The Russian scholar A.L. Bem has drawn attention to the phrase "a mouse, born in a cellar," which Albert uses in a bitter denunciation of his father's stinginess in Pushkin's play *A Covetous Knight*: "...let them compel my father/ to maintain me as befits a son, not as a mouse/ born in a cellar."[76] The association of a cellar rat or mouse with a shabby lifestyle Albert finds contemptible, corresponds to the way the underground man describes himself when he says: "… he genuinely thinks of himself as a mouse and not a man,"[77] contrasting himself with the normal man of action. But nothing stays that simple within the purview of the thinking, if subhuman creature who is endowed with an "acute consciousness" governed by contradiction. In the uncoiling paradoxicality of his self-definition, another dimension of the mouse metaphor comes into play, implicating Herzen.

In the sixth letter of his *Ends and Beginnings*, dated October 20, 1862, Herzen analyzed the pathology of the European civilization in its exhaustion following the agonizing triumph of the bourgeoisie. Observing the phenomenon of decadence through the lens of a natural scientist, he wrote: "Work goes on within: a microscopic weaving, weathering and alluvial drift, the 'mouse's scurrying' of history, the vulcanic labor under the earth, the oozing of sap from the past autumn into the coming spring through tiny capillaries. Above it all float dreadful dreams, corpses in old armor and ancient tiaras and fantastic, luminous images, agonizing suffering, mad hopes, a bitter awareness of one's weakness and the impotence of reason. Below, the bottomless abyss of elemental passions, of a prehistoric sleep, of childish daydreams, of the *cyclop-like labor of the mole* (emphasis mine); human voices cannot reach the bottom as the wind does not reach the depth of the sea; occasionally one hears issuing from there the trumpet of war, promising destruction."[78]

In this panoramic vision of a decomposing society, death is the unseen but ubiquitous force at work. Inexorably, death creeps along by the patient and complex process of natural decay, quickened by episodic eruptions of sudden violence. The fastuous but empty dreams of towering individuals are countered by the surge of murderous instincts from the blindly elemental masses below. Two animal metaphors stand out in sharp mutual contrast—the "scurrying mouse" of History and the "cyclop-like mole" of Nature.

Herzen took the expression "the mouse's scurrying" (*myshiia begotnia*) from Pushkin's poem "Verses Composed at Night During Insomnia," 1830 ("Stikhi, sochinennye noch'iu vo vremiia bessonitsy").[79] The poet, lying alone in the dark and unable to sleep, is tormented by the monotonous "tick tock" of the clock, measuring the empty time within and around him (*"khod chasov lish' odnozvuchnyi/ Razdaetsia bliz menia/ Parki bab'e lepetan'e/ Spiaschei nochi trepetan'e/ Zhizni mysh'ia begotnia"*). The anguish of time is here experienced in a meaningless ordeal, as a tormenting cycle of repetition, rhythmed by futile remorse and premonitions of death. The living present is devalued in the sordid image of the "scurrying mouse," with its parasitical and essentially destructive activity.

Lifting the image of the mouse from Pushkin's expression of an agonizing private experience of sterility and despair, Herzen transposed it into the sphere of History. His "scurrying mouse" images a time of waning purpose, when long-held ideas have lost their vital power and the path to new beginnings seems blocked. He goes on to describe his mouse as a creature paralyzed by perpetual wavering between the stale morality of the past and the unfathomable ethos of the future. But while a phase of human consciousness winds down in a debilitating loss of freedom, Nature asserts its organic urge of seasonal renewal in the slow, half-blind labor of the mole, working underground to turn up fresh soil for another spring. Herzen's conception of a society in decadence is marked by imaginative ambivalence, revealing the poet under the mask of a natural scientist.

In 1842, when he wrote his pamphlet *The Reaction in Germany*, under the pseudonym of Jules Elysard, Bakunin was brimming with hope about the future. Having duly noted that the party of reaction was gathering momentum in German politics, he argued that the spirit of revolution had not been vanquished in Europe but was temporarily "burrowing—if I may avail myself of this expression of Hegel's—like a *mole* under the earth." Repeating the metaphor for greater emphasis, he writes: "Spirit, this *old mole*, has brought its underground work to completion."[80]

Here the specific reference is to France, where revolutionary agitation was spreading from intellectuals to workers. Having seized upon the metaphor of the mole, Bakunin endows that half-blind perpetrator of organic change at the roots with the attribute of freedom possessed by the Hegelian *Geist*. The apparent inversion by means of which an unconscious agent of Nature is converted into an embodiment of the cunning of History, is in tune with Bakunin's celebration of the negative moment of the dialectical process. A mystic of contradiction who declared that "the passion for destruction is a creative passion,"[81] Bakunin espoused the Romantic myth of the rebel-hero, which glamorized the intellectual and political "underground."

A huge gap in time and space, eventful with historical and personal disaster, separates Bakunin's mole of freedom from the thinking mouse of Dostoevsky's tale. As the voice emerges from the dark cellar, that hybrid creature is disclosed as a man on the wrong side of forty, who has spent nearly twenty years sulking inside his Petersburg funk hole. The city, which he characterizes as "the most abstract and premeditated town on the whole terrestrial globe," has become his intimate nightmare. His last comment on himself and those of his kind is: "We are stillborn, and for generations past have not been begotten by living fathers."[82]

In undergoing mutation into the thinking mouse, the mole of freedom has suffered a metaphysical collapse. Bakunin's oxymoron of a creature of nature acting as the agent of history, which encapsulates his Romantic notion of negation as the dynamo of human progress, has been overpowered by the realities of Petersburg life. With the involuntary assistance of Herzen, Dostoevsky has changed the useful rodent of the garden variety into a parasitical specimen of urban decay. Burrowing in the refuse of a noble generation of dreamers, it lives by the unnatural light of a consciousness mired in perpetual self-contradiction, wakeful but devoid of vision.

II.

"A PROPOS OF THE WET SNOW"

Notes from the Underground was conceived in the form of a diptych. Dostoevsky attached great significance to the sequence of presentation, whereby the confessional narrative of the second part emerges abruptly from the argumentative prologue. He had grave doubts about publishing "The Underground" separately as a first installment, to be followed by the conclusion in the next issue of *Epokha*. He wrote to his brother Mikhail: "Should we really publish it ("Podpol'e") separately? It will be laughed at, the more so as it loses all its impact without the other two chapters. You know what a musical *transition* is. The same thing occurs here. The first chapter resolves itself into an unexpected catastrophe in the last two chapters."[1]

The "musical transition" from the agitated philosophical *scherzo* to the more quietly paced, half-whispered *pathétique* mode of memory, is signaled by a shift back to another time. "At that time I was only twenty-four,"[2] begins the narrator, and if we take him at his word about his age ("now I am forty"), then the incidents recalled in Part II can be dated back to 1848, the cataclysmic year that ended the "marvellous decade" of Russian Romantic Idealism.

In that year, Dostoevsky published his tale about a Petersburg dreamer. "White Nights" is the story of a solitary young man who briefly ventures out of his isolation, finds love only to lose it, and then retreats into himself. A petty clerk who relies on his readings of Romantic literature to create the fantasy of a glamorous self, his delicately drawn silhouette foreshadows the underground man's endemic loneliness. Despite his gentleness, his final withdrawal from live reality is incipient with resentment.

Created almost two decades later, the underground man exhibits the terminal phase of the Petersburg syndrome. In his psyche, the formula of self-isolation, "I am alone and they are all," is entrenched at the root as the tyrannical impulse to dominate others. The narrative line of "A Propos of the Wet Snow" traces that impulse in an escalating series of aggressive gestures. In recalling these incidents, the confessor's memory paints them in the grey slush of an unhealthy urban winter.[3] It offers a contrast to the achingly pure luminosity of the Petersburg white nights that framed the dreamy season of romance in the earlier tale.

The fallen Romantic who reveals his shame after a long gap of silence, burrowing underground, has turned subversion into a fine art. His confession is also a ploy to undermine the esthetic idealism of the forties. The strategy of delayed exposure reverses chronological sequence, placing the facts of the underground man's early life before us only after we have become familiar with his ideas. By inviting a revision of the ideological combat in the light of the incidents that reveal the unappeased power drive of an unfettered ego, this presentation impresses a notion of causality on the reader. Once considered, the psychological genesis of the assault on determinism effectively undercuts its philosophical stature. For some readers, Frank being the most notable among them, this puts the underground man in the same basket with the "gentlemen" he derides.

The psycho-history that dooms the young intellectual clerk to become the underground man hinges on three episodes of conflict: the encounter with the officer in the billiard room and the confrontation with Zverkov, leading directly to the protracted combat with Liza. Each time, the clerk seeks out the confrontation, and each time his imagination shapes the situation into the formality of a duel. His script, in which he plays the aesthetically gratifying part of the challenger, imitates the models set up by Pushkin and Lermontov. He finds it easy to typify the billiard player and Zverkov as paragons of the obtuse, sword-clanking arrogance that passes for aristocratic style in the rigidly hierarchical world of Petersburg, where the uniform makes the man. To counter his opponent, the "extremely intelligent"[4] Romantic clerk wields the formidable power of the accusatory word.

It is profoundly ironic that with such a resource at his command, he should fantasize about meeting the officer on the latter's own ground with a real weapon in hand. As the ritualistic expression of manhood affected by the Byronic dandy, the duel enjoys a quasi-mythical status in the clerk's imagination. It is a gesture that choreographs the clasping of Eros and Thanatos in one masterful embrace. While he plots revenge against the billiard-playing officer, he fancies himself as the gloomy Silvio in Pushkin's *The Shot*, who cast a threatening shadow across the path of a man more fortunate than himself. And when he heaps passionate scorn on society in his sarcastic toasting of Zverkov, who has failed to invite him to his farewell dinner, his rhetoric puts him on par with Lermontov.

On both occasions, his aspiring self is brought down to reality. He is rudely forced to reassume the grotesque Gogolian identity which is the esthetic norm for those of his lowly rank in Petersburg. In lieu of a duel, he is reduced to running full tilt with eyes closed against the body of the offending officer who was ambling down Nevsky Avenue. In his highly symbolic pantomime of a clash between the thinking mouse and the unwitting bull, we are still far from the etiquette of class conflict that Chernyshevsky's Lopukhov would practice on the arteries of the same city with the onset of the brash sixties. "Except in the case of women, I will not move aside for anyone,"[5] declares that paragon of utilitarian manners in *What is to Be Done?*. He illustrates his method of social levelling by banging full force into a dignitary monopolizing the sidewalk of Kamenoostrov Avenue. After knocking him down into the gutter, Lopukhov matter-of-factly helps him to his feet, in a demonstration of common human dignity that elicits an appreciative chuckle from a peasant onlooker. Frank is right in saying that many of the situations in *Notes from the Underground* parody those in Chernyshevsky's novel. But the underground man compounds the mockery by implicating the shadow of his former Romantic self in his jaundiced laughter. The encounter with the prostitute Liza is different. What begins as parody culminates in tragedy. Unlike the underground man's two bull-like opponents, Liza, as her name suggests, is one of Petersburg's "eternal victims." The willingness to treat a woman with all the respect due to her as a fully equal human being, in the teeth of social prejudice, served as the litmus test of a man's moral development in the forties no less than in the sixties. The epigraph to "A Propos of the Wet Snow" comes from a poem by Nekrasov that features the redemption of a prostitute. Written in 1845, Nekrasov's verse narrative "O pogode" ("About the Weather") was a special favorite of Belinsky's and of the Petrashevsky circle as well.

The topos of the redeemed prostitute survived the battle of generations that swept aside so many Romantic illusions. Chernyshevsky incorporates it in his novel-pamphlet, giving it a more topical feminist twist. Nastenka Kryukova, a prostitute discovered by Kirsanov, is fully rehabilitated only after she enters Vera Pavlovna's cooperative of seamstresses. Julie Letellier, a high society prostitute, is an embryonic "new woman" who assists in Vera Pavlovna's emancipation from her petty bourgeois family. Julie justifies her profession as a relatively honest way of making a living in a fundamentally dishonest, sick society.

The underground man's visit to the brothel happens on a rebound from his humiliation in the restaurant. Having yielded to Zverkov's social status by begging pardon for the offensive toast, he now yields to Zverkov's morality by following him *"there,"*[6] where he leads his drunken crew. But even as he chases headlong after the vulgar debauchees, the underground man's mind is at work, rewriting the situation in the style of an ironic foray into "real life."[7] Nonetheless, he knows himself for a "scoundrel," and the body language of his hot pursuit of the revellers confirms that judgment. Frenzied by the slow pace of the sled he has hired, he delivers a punch to the back of his driver's neck. "What are you up to? What are you hitting me for?"[8] shouts the peasant, while proceeding to whip his nag until it begins rearing.

This vignette, which mimes the hierarchy of cruelty in the language of physical gesture, is actually drawn from a real-life incident Dostoevsky witnessed as a sixteen-year-old boy travelling from Moscow to Petersburg. He would recount the event in a January 1876 issue of *A Writer's Diary*.[9] Transposed into the underground man's life, the scene exposes the Romantic rebel in the raw as he collides with Russian life. Riding to a brothel, he briefly vaults to the top of the pyramid of power that a whipped nag carries on her back. The moment articulates the underground man's contradictions in terms that invite moral scandal. As such, it is prophetic of what will transpire in the house of ill repute.

By contrast to the crudeness of the physical pounding administered to the cabbie, the underground man's game with the young prostitute Liza is marked by a sophistication of cruelty that only an intellectual in bad faith can muster. Not content with the ordinary consummation of the sexual act he has paid for, he launches a rhetorical assault on her soul as soon as he wakes up in post-coital spite on their casually shared bed. His verbal powers serve him well that night. In order to get at Liza's submerged feeling of shame, he displays an array of literary "pictures" to her, skillfully orchestrating the grating contrast between the realism of a prostitute's funeral in the Haymarket district and the sentimentality of a family scene, with a father doting on his daughter. "Why, you speak somehow like a book,"[10] she falters, unnerved by his performance. But her untutored mind, unable to identify the echoes of Balzac's *Le Père Goriot* (Father Goriot) or the slapdash imitation of the descriptive style of the Russian feuilletons, takes his words straight to her heart. The dishonest redeemer has triumphed in spite of himself, by awakening Liza's moral sensibility. She absorbs the lesson and promises to come and see him shortly.

Liza's visit to the underground man's room, which finally unravels the quasi-comic misunderstanding between them, is one of Dostoevsky's great dramatic scenes. It takes the form of a duel of the sexes, as deadly in its own way as the tragic confrontation that will pit the psychologically abused wife against her pawnbroker husband in *A Gentle Creature* (1876). As a woman and as a prostitute, Liza carries a double handicap in a battle for human dignity, since societal rules keep encroaching on a spiritual balance of forces.

When Liza enters the underground man's room, the sensitive reader who has understood the message of the epigraph assumes the fundamental equality between the two as a moral imperative. The underground man, too, is aware of this premise. But his mind, practiced in contradiction, guards the categories of social inequality in a dark corner of his consciousness, like a concealed weapon. Standing on the threshold of emancipation, Liza stumbles into the vortex of his pride. She has caught him unprepared for her visit, in the middle of a disgraceful quarrel with his recalcitrant servant. In his humiliation, he instantly desires to show his power by humiliating her.

This inner moment triggers the psychological mechanism that was at work in the bullying of the cabbie. But this time, he reverses the sequence—first the verbal assault, and only after that the physical act of dominance. Turning confessional, he reveals to her the hideous truth about their first encounter: "I had to avenge the insult on someone to get back my own again; you turned up, I vented my spleen on you and laughed at you. I had been humiliated, so I wanted to humiliate...."[11] In his perverse game, the sincerity he assumes in owning up to the base impulses concealed behind his rhetoric is but a sadistic ploy to deny her humanity. "The cynicism, the cynicism of my words overwhelmed her...." he notes, watching her crumble under the blow "as though she had been felled by an ax."[12]

Suddenly, the unforeseen erupts, breaking into the predetermined script. Liza's compassion overcomes her sense of self-preservation. She rushes towards him with the generosity of a woman who "understands first of all, if she feels genuine love, that is, that I was myself unhappy."[13] Their tears commingle in the brief sharing of a flickering possibility. That moment, as spiritual freedom trembles in the balance, soars above the rhetoric of equality in the epigraph from Nekrasov's poem. In place of moralizing, it affirms the gratuitous miracle of love, beyond the constraining limits of gender difference.

The underground man, unable to sustain Liza's act of faith, collapses into hysteria. He weeps bitterly, knowing all the while that he weeps only for himself. "They won't let me…. I can't be good!"[14] he manages to articulate, inverting her gift of love into a resentful grievance. The fatal misunderstanding between them returns, in a grotesque *quid pro quo* of gestures and feelings, whose comic potential is overtaken by tragic intensity. Mistaking his vindictive lust for love, Liza embraces him "warmly and rapturously." When the physical transaction between them is over, "she understood it all. I had insulted her finally…."[15] And she flings back at him the five-ruble note he had thrust into her hand. He is left standing alone to savor the stale taste of a damning victory that confines him forever to his underground hell.

This duel scene, resonant with allusions to contemporary social issues, reveals the Christian conception of freedom that permeates the *Notes from the Underground*, as it will permeate everything Dostoevsky would write henceforth. What Liza experienced in the flash of an instant is the mystery Dostoevsky strove to articulate in words while meditating over the dead body of Marya Dmitrievna on April 16, 1864. Soon after, he concluded the tale of "A Propos of the Wet Snow" with Liza's gratuitous act of love that releases her humiliated self into the miraculous presence of the eternal "Other" whose name is never mentioned in the underground.

In another meditation, penned after the publication of the *Notes*—"On Socialism and Christianity,"[16] dated September 1864 —Dostoevsky developed the social and political implications of the thought that had crystallized for him on April 16, namely that

Christ represents "the highest, ultimate development of personality." Now he was ready to weigh in with his Christological reconciliation of the divide between the "I" and the "all" that no moral calculus could bridge. He wrote: "In this way, the law of the I merges with the law of humanism, and in their merging, both, the *I* and the *all* (apparently two polar opposites), each annihilating itself for the sake of the other in their mutuality, thus reach the highest degree of individual development."[17] Nearing the end of the year that had twice seared him with death, compounding the agony of his wife's prolonged dying with the loss of his brother Mikhail, Dostoevsky concluded that only this law of humanism, derived from the paradox of Christian love, could overcome the impasse between the individual and society that had perplexed Herzen and that Chernyshevsky thought to have resolved.

Dostoevsky was incensed when he discovered that the censor had deleted the passage about the "necessity of faith and Christ" that he had put into the underground man's mouth in the original version of Part I. "I am also bewailing the first part of my *Notes*," he wrote to Mikhail on March 26, 1864. "Terrible misprints, and it would have been better not to print the penultimate chapter at all (that chapter where the very idea is stated) than to print it in that form, that is with sentences left out and contradicting itself.... Those swinish censors left in the passages where I ranted at everything and *pretended* to blaspheme; but they deleted the passages where I deduced from all this *the necessity of faith and Christ*.... What are they doing, those censors? Are they in league against the government, or something?"[18]

Nevertheless, when it came to republishing the whole text in the following year, Dostoevsky chose not to restore the affirmative passage. Ralph Matlaw, who draws attention to this question, interprets the decision as one of artistic strategy: "The narrator, the strange psychological personality displayed before us, must be left in limbo. No solution is possible for him."[19] I would add that the excision is also consistent with the intrinsically Christian thrust of the text. In that sense, the psychological "limbo" of the underground represents a spiritual hell, where the will to goodness is paralyzed. Like the damned souls in Dante's *Inferno*, who can never name God, but can only refer to him indirectly, by periphrasis or parody, the underground man can only hint at the act of faith in the conditional: "On the contrary, I would let my tongue be cut off out of gratitude if things could be so arranged that I should lose all desire to put it out."[20]

The circularity of the statement reduces the desire to say yes to a tautological assertion of the primacy of will, attached to a hypothetical argument about the substance of the positive. In the last section of Part I, the underground man expresses a wish to be freed from his self, a longing for "something different, quite different, for which I am thirsting, but which I cannot find! Damn the underground!"[21] But even here, he couples his quest for affirmation with a curse on his spiritual impotence, a condition that we know to be of his own making.

As Dante knew, self-pity is the ultimate trap of the damned. The infernal nature of the underground man's condition is implied by the arrangement of the text in the form of a diptych, coupling a phony dialogue in the first panel with a confessional narrative of dubious authenticity in the second. The theme of dishonest confession links the *Notes* to Camus' novel *The Fall* (*La Chute*, 1956).[22] Camus updates the underground man as a twentieth-century bourgeois intellectual in bad faith, trapped in the hell of unappeasable guilt. Like his Russian predecessor, Jean-Baptiste Clamence personifies the moral malaise of the historical moment. The scandal of the Holocaust, witnessed by so many in willful silence, reverberates through his private situation as a man haunted by his failure to rescue a drowning suicide.

Taking a clue from Dostoevsky, Camus expands and objectifies the hellish implications of the underground man's confession discourse. Clamence speaks to us from the "soft hell"[23] of Amsterdam, a city located at the heart of bourgeois Europe, whose concentric canals evoke the circles of Dante's *Inferno*. He has chosen to move there from Paris, once he understands that his successful career as a lawyer, committed to the defense of noble causes, has been a sham. He now buries himself in a sleazy sailor's bar in the former Jewish quarter, frequented by pimps and prostitutes, as if enacting his own and the world's fall from grace.

Clamence, who notes the dual identity of the Dutch as merchants and dreamers, is fully entrenched in the awareness of his own duplicity. His self-definition as the penitent-judge (*le juge pénitent*) suggests that he has not abandoned the quest for moral supremacy ("*la vocation des sommets*"[24]) that drove his rhetoric as a Parisian tribune of victimized humanity. He deploys confessional harangue as a forensic device he has invented to exercise his subterranean need to dominate. The garrulous, seemingly improvised quality of his discourse is a snare to implicate his listener in the story of his private guilt, a power play whereby he momentarily recaptures the right to judge others. But unlike the underground man's manipulation of absent but real antagonists, Clamence's verbal entrapment of a fortuitous addressee, whom he always accosts at the bar, is clearly a rehearsed exercise.

The element of repetition in Clamence's use of the phony dialogue highlights the infernal quality of his enterprise. The recapturing of the lost innocence he craves is as illusory as Francesca's evocation of the moment of love that has damned her to gyrate forever in the embrace of the silent Paolo. And like the inexperienced Dante in the second circle of Hell, Clamence's listener is spiritually endangered by allowing himself to be lured into his confidence.[25] The contamination of the listener, first addressed with impersonal politeness as *Monsieur*, is signaled by the speaker's rhetorical shift from the first person singular "*je*" to the inclusive plural of "*nous*."[26] This discharges the guilt from his real self into the shadowy other, who has been conjured for this very purpose. Collective guilt is an abstract commodity, a hellish inversion of the love of humanity Clamence dealt in back in Paris.

The *juge-pénitent* requires the initial presence of a living interlocutor in order to practice the duplicitous verbal art that lends him
a counterfeit innocence. The underground man, for his part, stages
the mock battle of ideas in Part I and the sham confession in Part II
with the single intent of asserting himself. The resulting text is his
revenge on real life, which had always thwarted his power drive.
Unlike Clamence, he does not need a live opponent in his verbal bid
for dominance, since he writes instead of speaking. The responsibility for publishing the Notes is taken out of his hands by the editor
of the fiction, who also provides him with a collective cover with the
explanation that turns his singularity into a Russian historical type.

Along with other thematic and formal features, the *Notes* and
La Chute also share the absence of a definite closure. Clamence's
performance ends in moral ambiguity. He articulates the awareness that true innocence cannot be achieved without self-forgive-
ness. But his conscience remains in suspense, pending judicial
intervention by a discredited authority, as he passively awaits his
arrest for complicity in the theft of Van Eyck's painting. In the
underground man's case, the problem of closure is obviated by the
literary author-editor, who arbitrarily cuts him off by stating, in
an appended parenthesis: "(The 'notes' of this paradoxalist do not
end here, however. He could not refrain from going on with them,
but it seems to us that we may as well stop here.)"[27]

In both instances, the apparently inconclusive endings invite
speculation about the spiritual outcome of the confessional act.
Gary Rosenfeld, in the article "The Fate of Dostoevsky's
Underground Man: The Case for an Open Ending"[28] (1984), argues
for the possibility of the underground man's regeneration, basing it
on the fact that he tells the story of his encounter with Liza without
prevaricating, and suffers in the telling of it. He suggests that the
confession constitutes at least a partial expiation of his offense
against her.

The thrust of my essay clearly goes to the opposite side. I agree
with Robin Feuer Miller ("Rousseau and Dostoevsky: The Morality

of the Confession Reconsidered,"[29] 1979) who reads the under-ground man's manipulation of the confessional mode as a ploy to assuage a narcissistic need to glamorize himself. In an earlier essay, "Dramatization of Consciousness in Albert Camus' *La Chute* and Dostoevsky's *Notes from Underground*"[30] (1968), Irene Kirk compared the self-justificatory undertone of the underground man's account of his encounter with Liza to Rousseau's self-serving rationalization of his shameful conduct in the *"ruban volé"* episode of his *Confessions*. There Rousseau claimed that his *"faiblesse"* had led him to be an enemy of untruth.

Rousseau's example is cited in the text as a proof that truth is unattainable in a literary confession. After declaring his intent to put down his memories in writing, as a test of his ability to be absolutely frank, the underground man comments: "I will observe, in parenthesis, that Heine says that a true autobiography is almost an impossibility, and that man is bound to lie about himself. He considers that Rousseau certainly told lies about himself in his confessions, and even intentionally lied, out of vanity. I am convinced that Heine is right...."[31] He nevertheless exempts his own effort because, he notes, it is written only for himself and not for any reader.[32]

Once again, the serviceable editor has intervened and, contradicting the speaker, published his words. The artifice of an author posing as an editor of a fortuitously discovered manuscript is one of the oldest tricks in the novelistic magic, often used to enhance the credibility of the narrative. A distancing device, it plays to the value of objectivity, which the Romantics replaced with the cult of subjective sincerity. For all his jibes at Rousseau, the underground man who owns up to being a characterless person of the nineteenth century cannot deny that he is of the same lineage.

The mere fact that the underground man chooses to record the shame of his abusive conduct with Liza is anything but an act of repentance. The last words of his interrupted tale lead back to the beginning, as if to underline the deadly self-enclosure of a consciousness cut off from hope. "We are stillborn, and for generations past have not been begotten by living fathers, and that suits us better and better. We are developing a taste for it. Soon we shall contrive to be born somehow of an idea. But enough: I don't want to write more 'from the underground.'"[33]

Hiding, like Clamence, behind the collective pronoun that momentarily changes him into a victim of historical necessity, the underground man has definitively closed the vicious circle of contradiction he has been busily drawing around himself. Knowing that he will never move beyond hellish self-awareness, he is left with nothing but that empty truth to fill the abyss of his subjectivity. Such knowledge holds no vision of the future and no possibility of transcendence.

As his confession drifts into silent inertia, the underground man's condition presents the inverse side of Dostoevsky's conundrum of faith. In his letter to Madame Fonvizina, Dostoevsky wrote that "even if someone proved to me that Christ is outside the truth and that, *in reality*, the truth were outside of Christ, then I should prefer to remain with the Christ rather than with the truth."[34] The underground man too insists on the primacy of will over reason, but his preference of "twice two makes five" never adds up to an act of faith.[35] His flickering desire for faith is mired in capricious contradiction. It is meaningless without love, an endless motion without release, like the mouse's futile scurrying around a maze.

The unfinished ending of the *Notes*, which sends the reader back to the beginning, reinstates the rigor of linear time, seemingly disrupted by the sequence of presentation. But the speaker's existential here and now, sapped by the memory of twenty years ago, is ultimately unreal, like the illusory time of Dante's damned souls. They repeat their own past but know nothing of the present, even though they can foresee the distant future of the living. In the Notebook for *Crime and Punishment*, Dostoevsky reflected: "What is time? Time does not exist: time is numbers, time is the relation of being to nothingness."[36]

We recall that the devaluation of secular time had been a major part of the lesson Dostoevsky learned once and for all from his ordeal on Semenovsky Square. Without the Christ, whose love unlocked the door into eternal being, human time with all its burden of knowledge and suffering would be dead in its tracks, meaningless.

Dostoevsky's insight into the nature of human time illuminates the mysterious statement Nietzsche made about the *Notes from the Underground*. In a letter to Franz Overbeck, dated February 23, 1887, he commented on the "*very* strange, very *un*-German music" of the *Notes*, which he considered as "two novellas." Then he went on to say that the second part, "a stroke of genius in psychology," was "a kind of self-derision of the *gnosi auton* (know thyself)".[37]

The imperative to know oneself is usually associated with Socrates, who made the rational investigation of the human mind a cornerstone of his philosophy. If one accepts Nietzsche's insight into the underground man as a mockery of the Socratic example, he becomes a comic figure as the unwise fool who, having plumbed the depth of intensified self-consciousness, emerges knowing nothing. But if one allows Berdiaev his say, that "Dostoevsky knew everything Nietzsche knew, but also something that Nietzsche did not know,"[38] then another, older meaning of the formula gnosi auton comes to view. The injunction to self-knowledge inscribed above the entrance to the Delphic temple addresses man as a spiritual being. Socrates, the rationalist who listened to his inner daimon, understood the double gloss. In modern times, this harmony between secular and sacred knowledge is heard rarely. Nietzsche's ideal of a music-playing Socrates expresses his longing for a tragic art of reconciliation between the two. Dostoevsky, for his part, seems to have accepted the finality of their dissonance.

The world of Dostoevsky's novels is lacerated by the whiplash of human reason torn away from the divine core of being. The underground man inaugurates a series of major characters whose fatal passions individualize the agony of such a condition. A specimen creature conceived by Dostoevsky in anger and bitter sorrow, the acutely thinking mouse displays the phenomenon of alienated reason in its most grotesque form.

PART TWO

The Russian Oedipus

The Brothers Karamazov

I.

THE FREUDIAN PARADIGM

COMPLETED a couple of months before Dostoevsky's death on January 28, 1881, *The Brothers Karamazov*[1] was received as his philosophical testament. In this last novel, so intimately personal yet so symbolically coherent as to tempt allegorical reading,[2] the familiar theme of generational conflict is transmuted into the quintessential Dostoevskian drama of rebellion and redemption.

The rich primal matter out of which the fiction is fashioned relies on the entire spectrum of the author's life experiences and readings. Private memories, often telescoped through several temporal planes and refracted by the prism of literature or the cruder glass of newspaper reports, recombine to form the novel's archetypal characters and situations. Ironically, the Karamazov house in Skotoprigonevsk, where the parricidal plot is hatched, is modelled on Dostoevsky's own country retreat in Staraia Russa,[3] where he wrote much of the novel in the comfort of his late-blooming family happiness.

For Ivan Karamazov, that house would come alive with loathing: " 'Is it loathing for my father's house?' he wondered,"[4] about to cross its threshold. Later that night, "a sort of inexplicable humiliating terror"[5] would lurk in the shadows where the father stirs. Ivan listens from above, his imagination resonant with the hint of parricide Smerdyakov had passed on earlier, in coded words about Chermashnya.

To readers familiar with Dostoevsky's biography, the word Chermashnya signals another place and time. It is the name of a copse near the estate of Darovoe, where Dostoevsky's father, Mikhail Andreevich, was murdered by his serfs in June of 1839.[6] In the novel, Fyodor Karamazov urges Ivan to go to Chermashnya to bargain for the price of some copse land he wishes to sell. Ivan obdurately refuses to undertake this mission of greed and lust, in which Fyodor hopes "to pick up three thousand,"[7] the exact sum of money he has secreted in an envelope for Grushenka, awaiting her surrender. But on the morning after the humiliating vigil in his father's lair, Ivan wavers: "You force me to go to that damned Chermashnya yourself, then?" he snarls "with a malignant smile," only to leave his father in suspense: "I don't know whether I shall go. I don't know. I'll decide on the way."[8] Then, as Smerdyakov approaches his carriage, the words "You see ... I am going to Chermashnya" seem to "drop of themselves"[9] as he laughs nervously. Soon, however, while changing horses at a nearby station, Ivan will again reverse himself and take the train to Moscow.

In his famous essay "Dostoevsky and Parricide," Freud answers the riddle of Chermashnya by implicating the author in the psychological action encoded in the scene between the overweening, willful father and the vacillating, darkly scheming son. "The unmistakable connection between the murder of the father in *The Brothers Karamazov* and the fate of Dostoevsky's own father has struck more than one of his biographers..."[10] writes Freud. Even more forcefully, after noting Dostoevsky's empathy with the criminal mind, he concludes: "...and not until the end of his life did he come back to the primal criminal, the parricide, and use him in a work of art, for making his confession."[11] Moving in a circle between Dostoevsky's fiction and what he takes to be the facts of his life, Freud develops a psychoanalytical case history of the writer's Oedipal guilt. The substance of Freud's interpretation hinges on his unverified diagnosis of Dostoevsky's epilepsy as a hysterical phenomenon, with the siezures functioning as self-punishment for the repressed death wish against a hated father.[12]

Freud's hypothesis has now been discredited by Dostoevsky's biographer Joseph Frank[13] for failing to meet the facts and the chronology of record. And yet Freud's myth about Dostoevsky's life continues to haunt us, because it accommodates symbolic meanings beyond the scope of clinical inquiry. If nothing else, the Oedipal scenario provides a nexus between the multiple narratives of transgression, guilt and atonement in Dostoevsky's fiction and his personal journey from rebellion against the Tsar Father to reconciliation with the punishing authorities.

In a revision of Freud, Louis Breger reaffirms the thesis of rebellion against the father's tyranny as the pivotal moment in young Dostoevsky's development. More importantly, he argues that after Mikhail Andreevich's retirement to the country estate of Darovoe, where his military self-discipline and social respectability dissolved into drinking and debauchery, the adolescent Fedia displayed his aversion in numerous acts of "disidentification with his father." When the news of his father's murder, a bloody retribution by the victimized serfs, reached Fedia, "he identified with his father's murderers and was punished for this wish."[14]

In *The Brothers Karamazov* the tyrant father, who defiles everything he touches, bears the author's Christian name, Fyodor. If Ralph E. Matlaw is right that "the names of the characters always point to something significant"[15] in this novel, then this instance should give pause. In Freud's scenario, the son's identification with a hated father doomed to become a corpse is readily explained as the expression of the characteristic sexual ambivalence of the Ocdipal subject. Freud writes: "For the ego, the death symptom is a satisfaction in phantasy of the masculine wish and at the same time a masochistic satisfaction: for the super-ego it is a punitive satisfaction—that is, a sadistic satisfaction. Both of them, the ego and the super-ego, carry on the role of the father."[16]

To this reader, the above passage illustrates the philosophical divide that separates Dostoevsky's spiritual insight into the human self from the practice of mechanistic psychology, no matter how genial. The Freudian construct of the ego fails to account for the possibility of freedom, which the narrator of the novel defines paradoxically as "freedom from the self."[17] By choosing for his epigraph Christ's parable of the grain that must die to bring forth wheat,[18] Dostoevsky placed his exploration of parricidal desire under this spiritual premise. Viewed in this light, the transfer of his own name to the scandalous father figure appears as a profoundly conceived gesture of liberation from the cycle of self-inculpation and self-punishment.

In May 1878, Dostoevsky suffered the death of his beloved infant son Alyosha, who succumbed to a sudden attack of epilepsy. The suspicion about the inherited nature of the disease weighed heavily on the grieving father, instilling guilt and a yearning for expiation.[19] At the suggestion of his wife, Anna Grigorievna, he visited the monastery of Optina Pustyn', accompanied by Vladimir Soloviev, and received consolation from the elder Tikhon Zadonskii. A revisit of the paternal estate of Darovoe and the nearby copse of Chermashnya led him back to the initial point of the Oedipal trail. Here, at the crossroads of bloody retribution, I imagine the guilty father mourning the death of an innocent son come face to face with his adolescent rebellion in a tragic reversal that frees him.[20]

In the novel, Rakitin, the seminarian bent on a career as a radical journalist, discourses on the scientific riddle of heredity. Pointing to the Karamazov family as his specimen, he predicts that Fyodor will be murdered by his elder son Dmitri, a prognosis based on their untrammeled rivalry over sex and money, which has erupted in the monastery. A confirmed materialist, Rakitin subsumes the logic of motivation under the causal chain of physical heredity which, he says, the father "has handed on"[21] to all his sons.

The deterministic scenario hangs over the tangled narrative until the moment of truth when the oracle is overturned in the quick of the act. Waiting in ambush under Fyodor's bedroom with a brass pestle in his pocket, Dmitri, the preordained father slayer, experiences one last flare of parricidal desire: "The old man's profile that he loathed so, his pendant Adam's apple, his hooked nose, his lips that smiled in greedy expectation, were all brightly lit by the slanting lamplight falling on the left from the room."[22] But suddenly, the causal chain snaps, rupturing the linear narrative. The cunning narrator marks the miraculous moment with a gap in his text, a void of silence in which the arguments of necessity are stilled.

Freud, that imaginative positivist, acknowledged the artistic greatness of *The Brothers Karamazov* by counting it, alongside Sophocles' *Oedipus the King* and Shakespeare's *Hamlet*, in the triad of European dramas built around the theme of parricide, the primal crime of humanity. He notes that in all three texts, "the motive for the deed, sexual rivalry for a woman, is laid bare."[23] In Sophocles' straightforward presentation the hero himself commits, unknowingly, the double crime of parricide and incest with his mother. In *Hamlet*, the murder is carried out by Claudius, the usurping father figure to whom the forbidden motive of sexual rivalry is transferred. Dostoevsky further scrambles the psychological code of the Oedipal myth by entangling all four of Fyodor's sons in the fabric of parricidal guilt. In a notable gender switch, he substitutes three dead mothers (Adelaida, Sofia, Lizaveta) for the ghosted Laius or Hamlet's father and replaces the live Jocasta or Gertrude with the material presence of Fyodor.

The bastard Smerdyakov, who executes the parricidal act, is a sexual blank ashamed of the womb that bore him. Dmitri, a sensualist, longing for a missing mother, recklessly displays his jealousy of his father over Grushenka. He thus turns himself into the judicial scapegoat while remaining innocent of the deed. Ivan's sexual rivalry over Katerina Ivanovna pits him against Dmitri, whom he equates with the loathsome father. The formula of Ivan's parricidal desire—"one viper will devour the other"[24]—frames the murder by proxy in the impersonal symmetry of retribution. Alyosha, whom Rakitin smears with the same taint of the Karamazov sensuality, does not wish his father dead. Even so, he becomes complicit by evasion, after the fact, by deflecting the blood guilt away from both his legitimate brothers.

As Freud sees it, "It is a matter of indifference who actually committed the crime; psychology is only concerned to know who desired it emotionally and who welcomed it when it was done. And for that reason all the brothers, except the contrasted figure of Alyosha, are equally guilty—the impulsive sensualist, the skeptical cynic and the epileptic criminal."[25] But in a novel where dramatic action revolves around three great trial scenes, guilt or innocence and the act of judgment itself are prime categories. Dostoevsky plays on the asymmetry of their judicial and moral dimensions with consummate irony.

II.

THE TRAGEDY OF REASON

The hard core of the Oedipal myth encapsulates the confrontation between the masterful father and the ascendant son. Freud's interpretation of Sophocles' *Oedipus the King*, focusing on the sexual roots of the conflict, obscures the conscious mind of Oedipus and the dynamic part it plays in driving the action. Oedipus's fall is also a tragedy of reason,[26] whose powers he has invoked to dispel the darkness around his father's face and terrible authority.

In *The Brothers Karamazov* Ivan, the last of Dostoevsky's Promethean rebels, is the protagonist of the tragedy of reason. The ordeal of his doomed attempt to create intellectual order out of the emotional chaos that surrounds him warrants an in-depth comparison with the agony of the Sophoclean king.

Freud was only half right when he described Ivan as "a skeptical cynic."[27] Undoubtedly, Ivan is cynical about human nature, including his own, but his version of rationalism is ill at ease with the uncertainty and self-questioning inherent in the attitude of reasoned skepticism. His relation to the parricide is a case in point. While professing full license for his parricidal desire ("In my wishes I reserve full latitude in this case"[28]), he pins the intent to act on Dmitri, who has a judicially recognizable motive, as in his claim on Grushenka and Fyodor's money. The formula "one viper will devour the other" insulates Ivan from his own motivation, which Rakitin exposes in his analysis of the Karamazov heredity. Rakitin cynically argues that the legal consequences of Dmitri's imminent killing of Fyodor would leave Ivan in possession of an enlarged portion of his material patrimony as well as of Katerina's person. But Ivan prefers to dwell on the theoretical aspects of the case.

The pathos of Ivan's rationalism lies in his need to convert "his own ache"[29] into an objective proposition about human nature. He seeks refuge in abstraction from the ugly disorder of a life marked by parental abandonment and a humiliating dependency on distant relatives. In his displacement from a legitimate identity, a condition he shares with Sophocles' Oedipus, Ivan learned early that his intellect could serve as a protective shield.[30] In his adolescence, he hones the sharp edge of analytical reasoning as a tool in his contest with the powers that had dispossessed him.

King Oedipus, at the outset of the tragedy that bears his name, also appears as a man of reason in command of himself and his circumstances. He is confronted with a crisis in the city, a mysterious pollution that blights all sources of life. Oedipus is a self-made ruler, a *tyrannos*, confident of his own initiatives and reliant on the resources of his wit. The chorus of venerable Theban citizens addresses him as "noblest of all men," carefully marking the distinction between human greatness and divine power. "We have not come as suppliants to this altar / because we thought of you as a god, / but rather judging you the first of men / in all the chances of this life and when / we mortals have to do with more than man"[31] (31–34).

Oedipus reveals that he had anticipated his "children's" plea by initiating the quest for a solution with the dispatch of Creon, the Queen's brother, to Apollo's oracle in Delphi, "that he might learn there by what act or word / I could save this city" (72–73). Though he is quick to act in his own name, Oedipus's deference to Apollo's religious authority matches the chorus's expressions of reverence.

Apollo's message to Thebes is twofold, fashioned of both light and darkness. He has issued a clear command in asking for the banishment of the murderer of former king Laius, whose unpunished crime is the cause of infection; but he has withheld the perpetrator's identity. Faced with this call for action wrapped inside an enigma, Oedipus, the hero adept at answering riddles, proceeds to ask a series of methodical questions about the "when" and "how" of the matter at hand. Confident of the resources of his mind—"I will bring this to light again" (133)—he eagerly begins his rational quest into the facts of the case. Meanwhile the chorus, "stretched on the rack of doubt" (153), intones an ode to the Delian healer and other gods. The man of reason, who identifies himself as "the champion of my country and the God" (136), rides the crest of philosophical optimism, trusting that the process he has launched will yield the human equivalent of the healing vision which is Apollo's gift to humankind.

Like Oedipus, Ivan enters the novel in a scene that forces him to confront the blight at the roots of life in the microcosm of the Karamazov family. Even before the old buffoon displays his shamelessness inside the monastery, the narrator posing as a chronicler has established Fyodor as the rotten core of a patriarchal system of power.[32] Yet it is not the silently contemptuous Ivan but the passionate Dmitri who raises the furies with his cry: "Why is such a man alive?" and "Tell me, can he be allowed to go on defiling the earth?" Fyodor counters with the verdict: "Listen, listen, monks, to the parricide!"[33] turning the family court improvised under the aegis of the elder Zosima into a spectacle of mutual vengefulness. The verbal violence of this exchange anticipates the physical brutality of Dmitri's assault, when he bursts into his father's house and kicks him in the face with his heel.[34]

The idea of appealing to the spiritual authority of the elder to arbitrate the raging conflict between Dmitri and Fyodor had been suggested, "apparently in jest"[35] by the latter. Fyodor obviously relishes the potential for tomfoolery in the situation. The westernized liberal Miusov participates in the expedition to the monastery with a fastidious show of skepticism. But Ivan, whose reputation for intellectual superiority precedes his arrival from Moscow, appears to take the experiment seriously. He is, after all, the author of an article on ecclesiastical courts, whose prerogatives have come under question recently, in connection with the judicial reforms of 1864.

Ivan's argument, based on a categorical rejection of any compromise between the State and the Church in the matter of judicial authority, has paradoxically been applauded by exponents of both parties. The monks, however, are puzzled by Ivan's position and the learned librarian Father Iosif declares that "the argument cuts both ways."[36] Obligingly, Ivan recapitulates his opinion, based on his definition of the Church's historical role. He insists that the Church cannot surrender its vested responsibility for the reclamation of the criminal soul if it wants to remain consistent with its declared mission. "My clerical opponent maintained that the Church holds a precise and defined position in the State. I maintain, on the contrary, that the Church ought to include the whole State, and not simply to occupy a corner in it, and if this is, for some reason, impossible at present then it ought, in reality, to be set up as the direct and chief aim of the future development of Christian society."[37]

The uncompromising purity of Ivan's position, drawing fervor from opposing the minimalist thesis of his clerical opponent, seems to please the monks. Father Paissy nods in assent. But he demurs when Ivan cites the example of the Roman Church at the moment of Constantine's conversion, when it entered a pagan State with the intent of assimilating it into itself. Father Paissy faults Ivan for inverting the eschatological hope of Christianity by advocating the transformation of the Church into a socialist State, as if it were "an advance from a lower to a higher form."[38] While Miusov expresses shock at the theocratic turn of Ivan's ideas, the young intellectual avoids revealing which of the two, Church or State, he holds superior. His argument, as Father Iosif commented originally, cuts both ways. Ivan's first intellectual sortie discloses the paradox of a mind that leads with a posture of logical intransigence only to generate an equivocation tinged with scandal.

Father Zosima gently but firmly resists Ivan's rush to invest the Church with the exercise of justice. "Who has made me a judge over them?"[39] he remonstrates with Alyosha when the idea of the family court is proposed. As the heir to the spiritual tradition of the *startsy*,[40] he rests his authority on a thousand-year-old Eastern praxis rather than on an objectively defined institutional sanction. His retreat from judgment vaults over the grotesque parody of a trial that follows upon the dispute about ecclesiastical courts.

The confrontation between Fyodor and Dmitri, with its unholy trade of mutual accusations, offers dramatic proof of the intractability of human disorder. Their unbridled irreverence shocks all those who witness it, monks and laymen, and momentarily turns the monastery into a *kabak*. But as in many Dostoevskian scandal scenes, the rupture of decorum precipitates an instant of spiritual revelation. Suddenly, Zosima stuns the assembly by bowing down at Dmitri's feet, compounding the silent gesture with a plea, "Forgive me, all of you!"[41] addressed to all his guests.

That mysterious gesture, inscribing Dmitri with the *ecce homo* sign of the kenotic Christ, sends a message to Ivan as well. A while earlier, Miusov interjected that Ivan had been heard contending that "there is no virtue if there is no immortality."[42] Zosima's comment was: "You are blessed in believing that or else most unhappy."[43] The meaning of that riddling speech awaits the unlocking of Ivan's either/or logic in the instance of existential choice. Later that same day, under questioning by his father over after-dinner brandy, Ivan will categorically deny that he believes in God or in immortality. It is clear that Zosima saw that answer in Ivan's face. And, reading more deeply, he understood Ivan's despair: "But the martyr likes sometimes to divert himself with his despair, as it were driven to it by despair itself. Meantime, in your despair, you, too, divert yourself with magazine articles, and discussions in society, though you don't believe in your own arguments, and with an aching heart mock at them inwardly...."[44]

Zosima's diagnosis is reminiscent of Pascal's famous thought about "*divertissement* (distraction)"[45] as the symptomatic response to the void left within the human psyche by the departure of God. In theorizing on the Church's authority to decide between good and evil, Ivan, like Pascal's hunter, was chasing the wind. The mark of the cross Zosima has placed over Ivan's head signals the possibility of a resolution beyond the play of a mind deadlocked by its own logic. Ivan's intellect is powerless against the anxiety that frets at the conclusion inherent in his denial of God and immortality. Unlike Nietzsche,[46] who embraced the suffering entailed by the advent of nihilism as a Dionysiac experience, Ivan treats it as a hypothesis to be toyed with. His formula, "everything would be allowed,"[47] reduces tragic freedom to moral license, scripting scenarios from which he can always retreat into cynicism. "Intelligence is a scoundrel, but stupidity is honest and straightforward,"[48] he will confide to Alyosha on another occasion.

The consultation with Father Zosima, not unlike Creon's mission to Delphi, has yielded mysterious hints in place of clear answers, throwing back upon the questioners the onus for unravelling them. Oedipus, responding instantly in the name of the kingly responsibility he has won for himself, vows to bring the unknown murderer of Laius to justice. "I fight in his defense as for my father," he says (264), with massive dramatic irony. The search for evidence leads him to interrogate the blind seer Teiresias, whose knowledge, the chorus explains, comes from Apollo himself: "I know that what Lord Teiresias / sees, is most often what the Lord Apollo / sees" (283–285). When the holy man refuses to reveal what he knows, Oedipus, unable to stomach that a man possessed of light should withhold it in a crisis for the whole community, jumps to the conclusion that the priest is a fraud and implicated in the plot that killed Laius. Taunted with his blindness —"For tell where have you seen clear, Teiresias, / with your prophetic eyes? When the dark singer, / the Sphinx, was in your country, did you speak/ word of deliverance to its citizens?" (390–393)—Teiresias hurls back the mockery: "Do you know who your parents are?" (415). In the escalating quarrel, Oedipus for the first time challenges a traditional form of religious authority. He exults in his wit, which once saved the city of Thebes by solving the riddle of the Sphinx. "Mine was no knowledge got from birds" (399), he boasts. His assertive individualism scoffs at dark superstitions with reason in his grip.

In Oedipus's answer to the Sphinx's riddle, man, the creature walking on four in the morning of life, on two at noon, and on three before nightfall, affirms his will to know himself on his own terms. Prior to his confrontation with the Sphinx, Oedipus had vainly sought to wrest the hidden truth about his own identity from the Delphic oracle. But his petition, tendered in reverence for the injunction—"Know Thyself"—inscribed above the portal of Apollo's sanctuary, went unhonored. Instead, the oracle laid out for him a future cursed by parricide and maternal incest. In facing the Sphinx, Oedipus had relied only on physical sight and logic to demystify the primal terror lurking in the uncanny world of nature.

But now, Teiresias' words turn his gaze to the darkness within: "You have your eyes but see not where you are / in sin, not where you live, not whom you live with. / Do you know who your parents are? Unknowing / you are an enemy to kith and kin / in death, beneath the earth and in this life. / A deadly footed, double striking curse, / from the father and mother both, shall drive you forth / out of this land, with darkness on your eyes" (415–418).

The rift between religious and secular authority, provoked by Oedipus's charge of conspiracy against the priest, now gapes, and the king and Teiresias exit the stage separately. The hypothesis of a Creon-inspired political intrigue hangs in the air, the only rational explanation for the uncanny concordance between Teiresias and Delphi. But Creon, too, is able to summon the criterion of rational self-interest in defending himself against Oedipus's *pro cui bono* assumption. Indeed, why should Creon conspire against the king when he enjoys a full third of the royal power as his brother-in-law? When Queen Jocasta, the third power sharer, steps in to reconcile the quarreling kinsmen, the argument between them hits a standoff. Two plausible hypotheses confront each other, to the dismay of the chorus.

Once she hears from her husband's lips the story of his old fears, Jocasta consoles him by revealing a secret from her own past. When married to Laius, she sacrificed the life of her firstborn son in terror of an oracle from Apollo, which foretold that the son would kill his father. Citing the common knowledge that Lauis was killed by robbers, she denies the reliability of such prophecies. Yet, soon after, she comes onstage with garlands and incense to appease the god. Claiming disbelief in oracles, she is mired in superstitious fear and will seesaw between hope and despair with the ebb and flow of Oedipus's fortune as messengers come and go. She proposes a way out by living in darkness, as "chance is all in all" and humankind "can clearly foreknow nothing" (977–978). Jocasta will not wait to hear the herdsman of Cithaeron confirm the identity of the abandoned infant with maimed ankles, whom he had pitied and saved. Instead, she rushes offstage with one last helpless half-prayer for Oedipus's safety: "O Oedipus, God help

you! / God keep you from the knowledge of who you are!"
(1068–1069).

King Oedipus, however, will not be thrust off course in his pursuit of the truth. His commanding need to know drives him to
mentally revisit the fatal crossroads where Lauis was killed. The
agony of the intellectual process that brings his obscure past to
light matches the violence of the events that shaped it. As the
interrogation rises to its climax, Oedipus twists the arms of the
terrified herdsman to wrench the final piece of the puzzle out of
him. As the course of rational inquiry rushes to consummation,
the pulsating frenzy of questioning collapses into the panting
articulation of Dionysiac surrender. "O, o, o, they will all come, /
All come out clearly! Light of the sun, let me / look upon you no
more after today" (1183–1185).

With these double-edged words the tragic enlightener registers
the ironic reversal of fortune wrought by his mind's triumph in
unravelling the dark knot of the past.

The outcome of the inquest into the murder of Lauis has turned
the investigator into a condemned man. Reason, inasmuch as it
represents a human quest for order, has been vindicated as well as
dismayed in the enterprise. It has proven effective in implementing
the objective task of bringing the hidden criminal to justice. But in
the process, it has also brought to full view the terrible ways of the
gods with humans. The hypothesis of a malignant god plotting to
doom an innocent scapegoat had been raised by Oedipus himself
before all the evidence was in: "Would not one rightly judge and
say that on me / these things were sent by some malignant god? /
O no, no, no—O holy majesty / of God on high, may I not see that
day!" (828–831). In spite of Oedipus's rush to dismiss his paradoxical speculation, the idea of a darkly scheming Apollo remains a
cause of moral stumbling for the sympathetic spectator who, like
the chorus, wants to revere his gods. After hearing Jocasta scoff at
oracles, the chorus voiced its pious desire to see them confirmed,
so that "God's service" (910) might not perish. But in that same ode

(864–910), the chorus uttered a plea on behalf of human daring and greatness: "But I pray that the God may never / abolish the eager ambition that profits the State" (880–881). With Oedipus's downfall that cautious hope has collapsed.

Philosophical pessimism is ascendant in the chorus's great ode on mutability (1187–1223), which holds up the King, once known as the people's savior, as the paradigm of human nothingness: "O generations of men, how I / count you as equal with those who live/ not at all!" (1187–1190) ... "Oedipus, you are my pattern in this, / Oedipus, you and your fate!" (1193–1194).

And in truth, Apollo has set up Oedipus with a cruelty whose cunning outdoes the rigors of Jehovah's arbitrary testing of Job. Oedipus, who put his reason in service to a divine call for justice, has ended up on trial himself, proven guilty of crimes he has consciously sought to avoid all his life. By shattering the assumption that divine blessing flows to a human enterprise that matches reason with civic responsibility, the fall of Oedipus, the Periclean hero, strikes at the heart of the Athenian Enlightenment.

III.
Rebellious Reason

Ivan Karamazov, the young Russian radical of the 1860s, wades into the ancient contest between the divine and the human with an unambiguous intent to redress the balance in favor of the latter. A child of the century the underground man had dubbed the age of "negation," he harnesses reason to the grievances of an embattled humanity. In the pivotal "Pro and Contra" book of the novel, Ivan moves to impeach the tyranny of God the Creator and follows up by staging a full-dress trial of Christ the Savior.

In the process of writing the novel, Dostoevsky characterized Ivan's argumentation of the scandal of undeserved suffering as "the depiction of extreme blasphemy and the kernel of the idea of destruction of our time."[49] But he also held that the charge of senselessness in the suffering of innocents, documented by Ivan's dossier of cruelties to children, was "irrefutable." He chose not to answer Ivan on his own terms, "point by point." Instead, he opted for a twofold, "oblique"[50] strategy.

The affirmative answer to Ivan's rebellion is contained in the "Russian Monk" book (Part II, Book VI), where the voice of Father Zosima in live speech is heard from beyond the grave, as lovingly recollected by Alyosha. Modelled on the medieval *vita*, Alyosha's "Notes of the Life in God of the Elder Zosima" combine biographical narrative with exhortation in a text presented as the elder's spiritual testament. But in a notable departure from the hagiographical paradigm, the topos of holiness is turned upside down. Zosima speaks to his disciples as a redeemed sinner, and he teaches an anthropocentric theodicy centered on the transformational mystery of suffering. His polyphonic speech, drifting in and out of the sacred time of the Scriptures, counters the linear symmetry of Ivan's monologic discourse. His voice, always heard in dialogue, creates a verbal mosaic where all signs point to the eternal.

On the negative side, the indirect defense of God is also human-centered and existential. It takes the form of an ad hominem thrust at the accuser. Disdaining Ivan's rhetorical platform, Dostoevsky's narrator undermines his character by the cunning of psychological subversion.

Ironically, the use of psychology to subvert Ivan's ideas is a technique that mirrors the deconstructive procedures Ivan himself has devised for the improvised courtroom upstairs at the Metropolis tavern. The metaphysical trial of God the Creator resonates back to the family court in the monastery. Indeed, it is still the same case of son vs. father, but raised to a higher ontological level. In place of Dmitri, whose wrangling over sex and money erupts in scandalous speech and gesture, stands Ivan, with scandal on his mind. A Moscow-trained natural scientist and social critic he, unlike Zosima, eagerly embraces the imperative of judgment. In his patricidal fury, Dmitri always and obsessively points at Fyodor in the flesh. For his part, Ivan aims over the head of his ignoble progenitor, targeting the *arche* of patriarchal power held in effigy. But his father's face, with slack lips and goiter, hovers over the accused Creator in the dock, insinuating an intimate undertone of bitter contempt into the prosecutor's classical rhetoric. The process of abstraction cuts both ways. It raises the stakes of the indictment even as it reduces the living Fyodor to the status of a metaphysical corpse.

The mind's propensity to rise from the concrete to the idea was disparaged by Ivan's generation of Russian intellectuals, who held such philosophical levitation as fraudulent. Ivan himself appears to be keenly aware of the two-way traffic his mind conducts between the realm of concrete facts and the domain of philosophical ideas. He puts it in more contemporary terms when he tells Alyosha that "the eternal questions" about the existence of God and immortality, which the Russian schoolboys discuss endlessly, are really the same questions of socialism and anarchism "turned inside out."[51]

In playful deference to his addressee, Alyosha, who is not only his loving younger brother but also a messenger from the spiritual world of Zosima, Ivan begins his confession with a theological preamble. "Well, only fancy, perhaps I too accept God,"[52] he says. The proof of the existence of God has been a vexing problem for theologians of all times and stripes. Ivan cuts through the metaphysical knot with a decisive stroke of philosophical reductionism. Disdaining the question in its traditional form, he translates it into the linguistic code of the natural scientist. In that context, what Ivan passes off as a profession of faith, modified by the demurral "perhaps," is limited to postulating a hypothesis about to be tested.

Having witnessed Ivan's thrice-repeated denial of God and immortality in their father's house, Alyosha is baffled by the apparent reversal. But when Ivan invokes Voltaire, the "old sinner" who once stated *"S'il n'existait pas Dieu, il faudrait l'inventer,"* (If God did not exist, one would have to invent him)[53] it becomes clear that he approaches the question of God on the pragmatic level of human needs and ends. There verifiable facts speak, and not as a matter of pure speculation.

The paradoxical, ironic tone of Ivan's mock-theological preamble may be borrowed from Voltaire. But the methodology he uses to experiment with the idea of God is derived from Claude Bernard,[54] a more contemporary exponent of European rationalism. In appropriating the French physiologist's laboratory technique to deal with the central problem of theodicy, Ivan declares his intent to test the hypothesis of a just God empirically, against a rigorously defined set of data.

On the face of it, Ivan's insistence on empiricism appears like a principled challenge to the dogma of divine inscrutability. But it is also a strategy tailor-made to suit his deconstructive purpose. The more simple-minded disciples of Chernyshevsky would have ruled the question of God out of order altogether. Ivan's way is more circumspect. When he tells Alyosha: "I am trying to explain as quickly as possible my essential nature, that is what manner of man I am, what I believe in, and what I hope, that's it, isn't it?"[55] his directness is disarming. But the use of the verb "believe" in this instance is a giveaway. It turns out that what Ivan believes in, with an intransigeance that contrasts strangely with the tentative nature of his hypothetical "acceptance" of God, is his own earthly Euclidean mind. He asserts: "If God exists and if He really did create the world, then, as we all know, He created it according to the geometry of Euclid and the human mind with the conception of only three dimensions in space."[56]

Surely, this is a shaky attempt to ground his extreme subjectivism in the universality of *le sens commun*. Yet, in the same breath, Ivan acknowledges that "There have been and still are geometricians and philosophers, and even some of the most distinguished, who doubt whether the whole universe, or to speak more widely the whole of being, was only created in Euclid's geometry; they even dare to dream that two parallel lines, which according to Euclid can never meet on earth, may meet somewhere in infinity."[57]

With that admission, Ivan bares the hidden implication of his methodological choice. He may not acknowledge it, but his commitment to the procedures of his own Euclidean mind is an arbitrary act of self-limitation. This willful move partakes of the philosophical impudence in the underground man's assertion that sometimes it is preferable to resolve 2 x 2 into 5. The underground man's mathematical metaphor had been contrived as a payback to the Utilitarians, who cut down the human phenomenon to the common measure of the quantifiable. Ivan's game is very different. His insistence on representing his views in the language of geometry betrays a fear of uncertainty, a hankering for the absolute that will come back to haunt him.

Dostoevsky has a keen sense for ferreting out the madness lurking at the core of *l'esprit de géometrie*. Kirilov said all in the same breath that God must exist but he knows He cannot.[58] Thus he concluded that he had no choice but to kill himself. Alone among Dostoevsky's Promethean rebels, the honest engineer is an innocent, a quality he shares with Prince Myshkin. By contrast, Ivan is an intellectual in bad faith.[59] He is fully aware of the incongruity of applying the standards of the Euclidean mind to take measure of a universe he admits may have other dimensions. Ivan's philosophical temper has little in common with the patient empiricism of a genuine natural scientist. Instead, he resembles that philosopher from the spoof he wrote in high school: an atheist, after death, found himself at the gate of Paradise and still refused to believe in the afterlife, because its existence contradicted his principles.[60]

The authority Ivan vests in the Euclidean mind does not derive from Euclid, nor from God's cosmic blueprint, but, quite autocratically, from his own will. The laws of the physical universe are not really at issue. For Ivan, the proposition of a divinely ordered universe comes down to the simple question: how can a just God preside over the evil of undeserved human suffering? He brushes aside the ontological import of his allusion to Lobachevsky's spatial geometry with the statement: "I acknowledge humbly that I have no faculty for settling such questions, I have a Euclidean earthly mind, and how could I solve problems that are not of this world?"[61] The ironic profession of humility, led by the emphatic, thrice-repeated pronoun of egocentric particularity, sets the tone for what will follow.

Ivan's ironic tone is, of course, quite deliberate. In fact, the whole verbal sequence initialed by the provisional acceptance of God is couched in doublespeak, as Ivan articulates a ruthless methodology of deconstruction under the cover of professing his faith. His strategy of semantic conversion is highly manipulative, revealing the consummate prosecutor he is, under all his masks.

In any trial, legal procedure is a prelude to the entire event. If so, the outcome of Ivan's judicial experiment with the hypothesis of a just God in the imaginary laboratory of human history was never in doubt. The rules of engagement have been rigged; God's accuser plays with loaded dice. The facts in evidence, from the abundant record of victimized innocence, are selected to inflame to moral imagination of the humanist jury Ivan aims at, over Alyosha's head. In Ivan's kangaroo court, only two verdicts are possible. Both hinge on the determination of God's status in the case on behalf of injured innocence. If God has supreme authority, he must be held accountable for his sadistic tyranny; if he is not responsible, he can be dismissed by virtue of his impotence.

The cutting-edge procedures of experimental science and the geometrical metaphors Ivan has invoked merely update the arsenal at the disposal of the tribune of suffering humanity, with tyrannicide in his heart. The genealogy of the type reaches deep into the European past. The rhetoric of Ivan's bill of impeachment dramatizes the gesture of rejection in the dynamic phrase "I don't accept." That formula of categorical negation that Ivan keeps

repeating rises up against the deceptively good-natured prelimi-
nary concession—"I accept God simply"—with which he began.
The driving power of outrage, thus summoned, dictates the tone
of Ivan's advocacy as it unfolds inexorably, from the legal preamble in ch. iii ("The Brothers Get Acquainted") to the extended cita-
tion of evidence in the following chapter ("Rebellion"). The fury
of moral indignation reaches its climax in Ivan's summation,
coming to rest on the conclusion: "It's not God that I don't accept,
Alyosha, only I most respectfully return Him the ticket."[62]

That climactic sentence, into which Ivan pours all the passion of
offended nobility, is the live wire connecting him to another
Russian tribune. It was Vissarion Belinsky who once wrote, with
the same rhetorical fervor and the same cadence of scathing irony
wrapped in mock humility: "I thank you humbly, Yegor
Fyodorovich Gegel, and I bow down to your philosophical nightcap."[63] Belinsky's gesture of rejection, aimed at Hegel, articulates
his refusal to sacrifice the well-being of even one individual for the
sake of the overriding, abstract design of historical teleology.

Belinsky's immediate addressee was his fellow Westernizer
Botkin, and his target was not God but His surrogate Hegel, the
maître à penser of the Idealists of the 1840s. Hegel, whose dialectical logic was extolled as "the algebra of revolution" by Herzen, is
here deliberately Russified. The infliction of the suggestive but
phony patronymic "Fyodorovich" on the German philosopher
may be Belinsky's payback for his own moral stumbling under
Hegel's mesmerizing influence.

The case of Belinsky vs. Hegel is as follows. In an article published in 1839, "The Russian Nation and the Russian Tsar,"[64]
Belinsky, in a literal application of Hegel's logic, argued that the
idea of an autocratic Tsar was a necessary moment in the March
of Reason through History. This bit of metaphysical casuistry so
incensed Herzen that he refused to shake Belinsky's hand until the
latter recanted, soon after his arrival in Petersburg from Moscow.
The letter to Botkin documents Belinsky's moral reawakening to

the humbler reality of the human victims, temporarily obscured by the shadow of Hegel's Moloch. Now he lashes out against that inhuman Universal Consciousness.

The teleological argument, which explains the realities on the ground from the vantage point of infinite distance, is a perennial temptation for the apologists of divine creation. That backward logic is the kind of reasoning Ivan rejects as "utterly inappropriate"[65] for his Euclidean mind. It took the more capacious mind of Leibniz, a philosopher credited with the invention of infinitesimal calculus, to carry the defense of God into the heart of the European Enlightenment. His *Theodicée*, written in 1697 (published in 1710), is a major attempt to reconcile Christian faith with the newly assertive demands of reason. The serenity of Leibniz's comprehensive vision heralds in the spirit of rational optimism. He affirms that "the world is not only the most admirable of machines... it is also the best of republics, the one that brings men as much as possible the happiness and joy that make their physical perfection."[66]

Poised on the threshold of a new century, the darkness of the receding age of religious strife at his back, Leibniz's philosophical enterprise is rooted in the desire to justify the ways of God to men without resorting to the Augustinian dogma of original sin. Like King Oedipus, Leibniz is a champion of God who also looks out for the welfare of his fellow humans.

As Leibniz would have it, to understand the divine scheme requires a shifting of perspectives from the limited point of view of the finite individual to the theoretical overview that discloses the order of being as a whole, in the fullness of time and space. The latter is within the purview of pure reason, a category of thought he treats as distinct from and superior to the mental operations trained on the sifting of particular facts. Implicit in Leibniz's rationalist system, which postulates the *logos/ontos* correspondence, is a profoundly held belief that a benevolent Creator endowed the human mind with the capacity to make His cosmic harmony intelligible.

Ivan's brand of rationalism proceeds from the opposite assumption. His unwillingness to accept, or even to speculate about the geometrical model of a world with a dimension of infinity, where parallel lines will meet, is a shorthand for the rejection of the Leibnizian expansion of reason.

When Belinsky, awakening from philosophical philistinism, lambasted Hegel as the enforcer of Prussian order in the realm of thought, he placed himself under the aegis of Voltaire. "I now prefer the blasphemies of Voltaire to the authority of religion..."[67] he declaimed. He invoked the spirit of the philosopher who had put his wit and pen to good use in championing the causes of persecuted individuals like Calas or Sirvens. Wedded to the concrete facts of human experience, Voltaire's forensic logic could puncture every last bubble of monkish reasoning. In his public display of moral indignation, Voltaire had seized the high ground of European humanism, a position where Belinksy and Ivan chose to join him.

Ivan's tirade against God, which runs the length of an entire chapter (Chapter 4, "Rebellion"), resonates with echoes of Voltaire's philosophical sermon in verse, the *Ode on the Lisbon Disaster*.[68] A passion of reawakened outrage animates that poem, inscribed with the subtitle "Ou examen de cet axiome: *Tout est bien*,"(Or an examination of the axiom: All is well) which announces an assault on Leibnizian optimism. The occasion for this discourse was an actual event. In November 1755, an earthquake of extraordinary magnitude erupted simultaneously in Lisbon, Schezuan and Mequinez, claiming over ten thousand victims in Lisbon alone.[69] The shock of this spectacular demonstration of the presence of evil in nature (*"le mal physique"*) prompted Voltaire to turn in anger against the theses of philosophical optimism, which he himself had helped to propagate.

In his twenty-fifth Philosophical Letter[70] (1734), Voltaire had polemicized against Pascal's dark vision of the human condition, riding high in the strength of his own sanguine temperament. His confidence in the auspiciousness of human prospects had been reinforced by his reading of Pope's *Essay on Man* (1733), which he would later imitate in his "Discours en vers sur l'Homme" (1738). The English poet had declared: "One truth is clear, whatever is, is Right,"[71] in an Augustan version of the tautology of metaphysical bliss that would entice Belinsky to don Hegel's philosophical nightcap.

Voltaire, too, would be shocked back into reality by the cries of the victims in Lisbon. His reaction to the catastrophe is reported, in colorful prose, by his friend the lawyer Du Pan: *"Je n'ai pas vu ses vers sur Lisbonne, mais je sais qu'après la ruine de cette ville, le Professeur Vernet étant allé à St. Jean (Les Délices), Voltaire lui dit, eh bien, M. le Professeur, de cette affaire la Providence en a dans le cul."* (I have not seen his poem on Lisbon, but I know that after the ruin of that city, Professor Vernet went to St. Jean, Les Delices, and Voltaire said to him: So, Professor, in this business, Providence has got a kick in the ass). [72]

It is notable that all three humanists—Voltaire, Belinsky and Ivan Karamazov—are aligned in venting their moral outrage with deliberate profanity. The kick in the ass of divine Providence, the laughable reference to Hegel's "philosophical nightcap" are stylistically matched by Ivan's gesture of returning his "entrance ticket" to the divinely staged show of "eternal harmony"[73] wherein unavenged human suffering is to be appeased. Uttered in historical sequence, these three articulations can also be heard synchronically, as a single jeer of impious righteousness jubilating over the fallen Idol.

Neither Voltaire nor Ivan would seriously consider the old shibboleth of original sin to justify what they feel is an unjustifiable evil. In Voltaire's poem, that unwelcome reminder from Lisbon is named *"le mal physique."* (physical evil) Ivan draws on the case histories of suffering children he has compiled for his trial of God. But in a characteristic display of procedural rigor, he prefaces his anecdotal evidence with a reasoned explanation of why he has ruled out the cruelties inflicted on adults. "They've eaten the apple," he says, and their cases can be argued under the law of divine retribution.

Ivan proceeds to belabor his legalistic distinction: "But the children haven't eaten anything, and are so far innocent. Are you fond of children, Alyosha? I know you are, and you will understand why I prefer to speak of them. If they, too, suffer horribly on earth, they must suffer for their fathers, they must be punished for their fathers, who have eaten the apple: but that reasoning is of the other world and is incomprehensible for the heart of man here on earth."[74]

Ivan's own heart is in question in this ironic revisiting of the discredited doctrine of the Fall. After admitting that be could never understand how one can love one's neighbors other than at a distance,[75] he would compel Alyosha to shed tears of helpless anger with his stories of tormented children. Yet he remains dry-eyed, in full control of his emotional rhetoric.

The personal subtext of Ivan's reference to the sins of the fathers being visited upon their children is painfully transparent. With its glaring omission of the maternal role in the transmission of moral heredity, the statement reopens the old sore of his abandonment and inadvertently exposes the submerged memory of the vulnerable child he once was. But the masterful dialectician closes the lid on his own past self, as if the exclusive, obsessive focus on children were merely a matter of narrowing down the argument against God. The prosecutorial latitude Ivan invokes with respect to the adult part of humanity suggests a genocidal streak Voltaire would have disowned.

Voltaire can be glimpsed tottering on the brink of rebellion against the idea of God when he raises the question *"Pourquoi donc souffrons-nous sous un maître equitable?"* (Why then do we suffer under a just master?) But while he can no longer accept Leibniz's[76] a priori assumption of divine benevolence, his reason abhors the incongruity of the notion of an unjust or malignant

God at work behind the spectacular breakdown of the cosmic clockwork. As a rationalist in substance, not merely in form, Voltaire rejects the metaphysical terror implied in that hypothesis. Having discarded the futile rationalizations of God's logicians, he steers a careful course by keeping as close as possible to the solid ground of concrete facts. His unflinching empiricism leads to the unavoidable diagnosis *"Il le faut avouer, le mal est sur la terre."*(one must admit it, evil exists on earth)

At this turning point, Voltaire has reached a new level of existential maturity that prompts him to acknowledge the limitations of his reason as part of the overall helplessness of the human condition. The pathos of his cry, *"Que suis-je, où suis-je, et d'où je suis tiré,"* (What am I, where am I and where do I come from) seems to emerge from the depth of Pascal's abyss. But a plainer cadence of speech is heard in the admission *"Je suis comme un docteur, hélas, je ne sais rien."* (I am like a doctor, alas, I know nothing)The Claude Bernards of his day are implicated, along with the philosophers, in Voltaire's profession of ignorance. Voltaire's voice eventually quiets down in a conclusion that strikes a note of cautious hope, proposed as an existential necessity rather than a theological virtue. But before that sendoff into the laboratory of the future, Voltaire pays tribute to Pierre Bayle, a thinker who was great enough not to need any philosophical system. In the end, Voltaire dampens the fire of metaphysical rebellion with a dose of reasoned skepticism. With that gesture, Voltaire assumes his position in the middle of the temperate zone of European rationalism, marking the moment of equipoise between the waning of the authority of faith and the soon-to-come authoritarianism of reason.

IV.

REASON IN AUTHORITY

When Ivan tells Alyosha that "Russian boys" derive their axioms from European hypotheses, "for what's a hypothesis there, is an axiom with the Russian boy,"[77] he could cite himself as an example. Ivan, unlike Voltaire, cannot live with the existential uncertainty of skepticism. The hypothesis of a cruel God, which was unacceptable to Voltaire, fits with Ivan's maximalist temper and satisfies his craving for retribution. In defining his "essential nature," he has expressed bewilderment that "the idea of the necessity of God could enter the head of such a savage, vicious beast as man."[78]

For Ivan has no faith in man either, any more than in God. Yet he cannot accept the scenario of an evil world for which no one would be held responsible. "With my pitiful, earthly, Euclidean understanding, all I know is that there is suffering and that there are none guilty; that cause follows effect, simply and directly; that everything flows and finds its level—but that's only Euclidean nonsense, I know that, and I can't consent to live by it."[79]

With this self-contradictory explanation, which sets up the idea of an evil world abandoned to its own devices as an axiom, only to shoot it down, Ivan has stripped the Western mask from his indelibly Russian face. He worships Europe, like all the other spiritual wanderers (*stranniki*) of the aristocratic intelligentsia Dostoevsky has portrayed. He vows to visit that "most precious graveyard" of Europe and kiss its stones, which speak "of such burning life in the past, of such passionate faith in their work, their truth, their struggle and their science."[80] But that is the voice of his intellectual culture speaking, in the borrowed tone of a Romantic dandy from another generation. Ivan's essential mind is committed to the Russian *Pravda*, the revelation of righteousness in human history, not to the revelation of being, as *physis*, that was Euclid's or Lobachevsky's object and Leibniz's as well.

Like Dostoevsky himself, Ivan is rooted in the eschatological matrix of Russian spirituality, which his intellect parodies. Even in his denial of God, he does not postulate the model of a material universe without a presiding will or purpose, because it is alien to his Judeo-Christian mentality. But closer to home, Ivan requires an anthropomorphic image of the Creator as a stand-in for Fyodor. He summons the idea of a sadistic God to preside over the evils of human history because in his heart, he is neither a natural scientist nor a philosopher trying to reconcile faith and reason, but a tyrannicide.[81]

Ivan's Schillerian[82] sensibility, with its nobility and love of beauty, has been prematurely blighted by the degrading shadow of his looming father. Alyosha is deeply moved by Ivan's praise of "the sticky little leaves as they open in spring,"[83] but Ivan does not trust his thirst for life, which glows in these words like the flickering embers of a dying fire. His father will not let go of the cup of life and wants to drain it until he is eighty. Ivan has set his limit at thirty. Beyond that, he foresees no other prospect for himself than an abject surrender to the baseness of the Karamazov sensuality.

Ivan's reason, locked into the deadly presumption of his perverted heredity, is fundamentally disloyal to life. Such alienation shows as the urge to process and invert every vital impulse and emotion. Thus Ivan's passion for justice, which is real, is converted into the pitiless symmetry of retribution. When he exclaims, in the summation of his case against God, "I must have retribution, or I will destroy myself,"[84] it is the hunger of his reason he voices rather than a moral imperative. In that cry, which is a subjective reworking of the Latin phrase Belinsky had quoted in his letter to Botkin, "*Fiat justicia, pereat mundus!*", [85] the two Russian tribunes rally to the banner of revolutionary terror.

The affinity between the operations of logic and terror had already been noted by Herzen. Belinsky, with the colossal naivete of a neophyte, had declared: "I am beginning to love humanity à la Marat." Ivan's classically draped *plaidoyer* draws from the same blood-filled well. By the time we hear him echo *L'Ami du peuple*, (The Friend of the People) the metaphysical act of terror against God has been accomplished. The severed head is now being displayed, showing the death mask of a tyrant who diverted his people with sadistic games in the circus but could not give them bread.

In the same trial, Ivan has convicted God on two mutually contradictory charges: abuse of power and impotence. His judicial procedure mimics the Revolutionary Tribunal, which reduced King Louis XVI to *citoyen* Louis Capet only to saddle him with all the crimes committed by the French monarchy during its long history. In scapegoating Louis as a man for the symbolic identity that has been stripped from him, the logic of revolutionary terror has shown its duplicity. Ivan, too, plays the abstract and the concrete levels of his discourse against the middle, to implement his parricidal desire in the idealized form of a deicide.

Alyosha has suffered through Ivan's performance as if spellbound, breaking in only rarely to ask a question or to murmur a response. "To be shot"[86] was the unpremeditated verdict that escaped from his lips when Ivan described how a Russian landowner had set his hunting dog on a serf boy and watched him being torn to pieces. Confronted with the theoretical choice of "creating a fabric of human destiny with the object of making men happy in the end..." at the price of "torturing to death only one tiny creature," Alyosha replies firmly: "No, I wouldn't consent."[87] In asking the question, Ivan had wagered on Alyosha's heart to compel his solidarity with his own refusal of "eternal harmony." For the lone juror impanelled in the humanistic impeachment of God, Ivan has cunningly set up a standard of moral accounting that the Accused has been shown to have violated an infinite number of times.

Sensing the trap, Alyosha stops short of rendering judgment. Instead of returning his ticket to the divine Father, he vaults over Ivan's carefully constructed argument and names the heavenly Son, the forgotten God of compassion, as the one being who could

forgive all, on behalf of all, because of his own suffering. But
clearly Ivan had anticipated Christ's entrance. He has Christ in his
files too, and all he needs to do is delve into his memory to recite
a poem in prose about Jesus that he composed about a year before.

"The Legend of the Grand Inquisitor," in Chapter 5, stages
another courtroom drama, the third so far in the novel. In an
imaginary scene located in Seville during the heyday of the Holy
Inquisition, Ivan brings Christ face to face with the presiding
judge of that tribunal. Once again, as in the rhetorical event just
concluded, a man would appoint himself to sit in judgment over
God. But in this scene, Christ appears in the flesh, fully human,
having returned to earth for the meeting with the old cardinal of
the Church Militant who claims his authority from God.

The figure of the Grand Inquisitor, his physical presence and his
gestures, is lifted ready made from Schiller's drama *Don Carlos*.[88]
The intertextual relation carries with it the atmosphere of
Romantic rebellion that had been so formative of Dostoevsky's
youth. It also serves to reinforce the pattern of expectation set up
by the humanistic rhetoric Ivan wielded in the previous trial. Even
Fyodor, who had called his middle son "my most dutiful Karl
Moor,"[89] identified Ivan with Schiller's heroic paragon. And for
the Romantic idealists like Victor Hugo and Schiller, both of
whom Ivan quotes in his improvised literary preface to the poem,
the Spanish Inquisition was a topos of inhumanity no less powerful than the Holocaust for us.

Both Alyosha and Dostoevsky's reader have ample reason to
assume that Ivan would stand by the accused Son of Man. Yet it
soon becomes apparent that Ivan identifies with Christ's accuser,
who will eventually dismiss him from human history to implement his revisionist program of Christianity. Most of Ivan's text is
devoted to justifying that act of usurpation as the price to be paid
for human happiness.

"He was an old man, almost ninety, tall and erect, with a withered face and sunken eyes, in which there is still a gleam of light,

like a fiery spark," recites Ivan.[90] This description and the fervor with which he speaks the lines placed in the mouth of the Satanic priest betray Ivan's attitude. Above and beyond his agreement with the argument laid out by the Grand Inquisitor, Ivan conveys his awe of the figure of despair, who has dared to assume the onus of authority that the divine powers have dropped. The merging of the poem's author with the unlikely persona he has created for himself is consummated when Alyosha kisses his brother at the end of the recitation. Ivan jokingly taxes Alyosha with plagiarism. But the reenactment of the silent kiss of peace that Christ places on the Grand Inquisitor's lips at the poem's closure is a mysterious gesture imbued with power that cannot be dismissed so lightly. At this time, it is enough to note that the unmasking of the Grand Inquisitor as Ivan's fictional double considerably deflates the character's esthetic aura.

The image of the ascetic Jesuit, with contempt in his heart for the weak but turbulent creatures that make up the human herd, reflects the unnatural senescence of Ivan's spirit. The programmatic happiness he advocates is infected with a coldness at the roots that smells of the graveyard, like the Europe Ivan loves. Leatherbarrow has aptly called the Grand Inquisitor a "Shigalev in ecclesistical garb."[91] This priest, too, is an ideologue whose logic leads to an outcome that subverts the very values it pretends to serve. In Shigalev's secular utopia, happiness is procured at the cost of freedom and equality. In the Grand Inquisitor's scheme, the trade-off between freedom and happiness is offered fraudulently in the name of Christ, whom the priest has dismissed.

We already know that Dostoevsky considered Roman Catholicism and atheistic socialism as two faces of the same false coin. As Dostoevsky sees them, both systems promise an earthly paradise without freedom, cut off from eternity. The yearning for a recovered Eden haunts the alienated, Westernized humanists Dostoevsky created in the '70s. Versilov, the absentee father in the novel *A Raw Youth* (1875), called it "a lofty dream" without which he would not consent to live. In the suppressed chapter of *The Devils*[92] (1871) Stavrogin, contemplating Claude Lorrain's painting of Acis and Galatea, referred to it as the Golden Age. But in his dream revision of the image of the beautiful couple in the lap of nature, Stavrogin's attention focuses on a little red spider, a tiny blot on the canvas that grows until it covers Lorrain's idyll of human innocence.

In "The Dream of a Ridiculous Man" (1878), a companion piece to Stavrogin's Confession, Dostoevsky developed the theme of human corruptibility in the form of a mythopoetic narrative. The red spider motif reappears, clearly identifiable as the evil sign of self-conscious individuation, a flaw that the ridiculous man will introduce into his dream Eden. In Stavrogin's consciousness the red spider serves as a fixed point. It encapsulates a moment in his past to which his memory gravitates with obsessive repetition. At the instant when he knows that his child victim Matryosha is committing suicide in the next room, his mind veers away from her to observe the tiny insect crawling on a geranium leaf of a potted flower in the window.

In the motif of the red spider, Dostoevsky found a new expression for the ideas that he had begun forming long ago, during his first visit to Western Europe. Once again, reason decoupled from faith and individuation without self-transcendence are linked together by the fatal flaw of egocentrism. That theme is most dramatically displayed in the accusatory posture of the Grand Inquisitor.

In the isolation of a deserted square in Seville, the old cardinal's voice hoists logic to the seat of supreme authority. The arrogant solitude of the old ascetic deepens the emptiness around him. There is no community of the faithful, nor any representative of the human masses on whose behalf he argues. Only the silent Christ stands privy to the revelation of autocratic power unleashed by that argumentative ego, which revels in the act of judgment. But deep at the bottom of the priest's loquacious mind lies the secret of his defection to Satan. "We are not working with Thee, but with *him*—that is our mystery," he tells the Christ.[93]

The central argument of Ivan's poem inverts the outcome of the sacred drama of Christ's temptation by Satan in the wilderness, as recorded in the New Testament (Matthew 4:1–11, Luke 4:1–13 and Mark 1:12–13).[94] In Ivan's counterscript, the scene has shifted from the eternal landscape of the Holy Land to the historical montage of the Church of Rome. There, the Grand Inquisitor proudly claims, the dread spirit has prevailed over the evangelical Christ.

In spite of Alyosha's protest that "your poem is in praise of Jesus, not in blame of Him as you meant it to be,"[95] Ivan remains unswayed. He defends his Grand Inquisitor by painting him in the likeness borrowed from the sacred image of the Christ he has supplanted. He too, like the Christ, has been in the wilderness and suffered through the agony of choice between freedom and happiness. And in choosing happiness over freedom for the "specimen creatures created in jest,"[96] he has taken on the burden of human suffering upon his frail, aged shoulders.

The inversion of sacred values is the very essence of blasphemy. Ivan's entire poem is framed by desecration. Within that format, Ivan's speech alternates between the parodistic mode of pseudo-sacred discourse and the humanistic rhetoric already heard in his impeachment of God the Creator. By the Promethean code, the Grand Inquisitor is stylized as Christ's noble antagonist, a tragic hero invested with a lofty idea to benefit all humanity. But even on that level, that fantastic old man, the supreme artistic projection of Ivan's existential despair, is tainted by fraud. His compassion for "the weak, rebellious race of men,"[97] and his bartering of freedom for happiness parody the dream of human emancipation for which the Schillerian hero and others were willing to die.

Nevertheless, the dignity of the accused Christ survives intact. His silent presence, liminally poised at the two ends of the poem's narrative, radiates its charisma within and out of the blasphemous frame in which Ivan has trapped him. The Inquisitor's accusatory speech ends with the sentence "Tomorrow I shall burn thee. *Dixi*."[98] The declension of the Latin verb "to speak" to the first-person, peremptory form of the past tense, marks the Grand Inquisitor's signature on the verdict of deicide. It also rhetorically reenacts the sacred drama of Crucifixion. With that marker, the Grand Inquisitor's monologic discourse ends, followed by the heated debate between the two brothers.

"How does your poem end?" asks Alyosha," Or was it the end?" With these two questions, the suppressed voice of the witness to faith opens the way for Christ's kiss. Even though it is Ivan who reports it, "He suddenly approached the old man in silence and softly kissed him on his bloodless aged lips,"[99] the miraculous gesture explodes his script. Suddenly, the condemned man is restored to his sacred being as Son of God and Man.[100]

In the brotherly exchange that follows, Christ's unseen presence is kept alive by Alyosha's faith. Ivan's gentle mockery of Alyosha's act of plagiarism cannot obscure the spiritual meaning of his *imitatio Christi*, which transforms Judas's signal of betrayal into a sign of healing. Within the poem the effect is felt in the Grand Inquisitor's commutation of Christ's death sentence to permanent exile from the workings of human history. "Go, and come no more," he says, "come not at all, never, never!"[101]

With this shift, the arguments of certainty mellow into psychological ambivalence.[102] Having stopped short of a second killing of the Christ, the humanist without faith is bidding a nostalgic farewell to the gentle Nazarene, whose memory has lingered on in the socialist dream, surviving the collapse of the Church's intellectual prestige.

"The Legend of the Grand Inquisitor" has raised the power of Ivan's reason from rebellion to the assertion of its authority. At first glance, the sequence runs counter to the chronological evolution of the Roman Idea, as Kireevsky had outlined it. But Ivan's biography, as distinct from the dramatic order of its novelistic representation, shows otherwise. The Legend was written at least a year prior to the session in the Metropolis tavern, possibly in tandem with the article on the Ecclesiastical courts. Both texts address Ivan's systematic quest for a moral order in the absence of God. But now, in the dialogic sequel to the poem, Ivan tells Alyosha that he has given up on order in favor of license.

In retrospect, the Grand Inquisitor's pseudo-theological system, based on his manipulation of miracle, mystery and authority, shows up as the same coin of moral nihilism Ivan now circulates. The priest had said: "We shall tell them that every sin will be expiated, if it is done with our permission, that we allow them to sin because we love them...."[103] Such jesuitism, even draped in the cowl of asceticism, could not cohabit too long with Ivan's trenchant need for radical simplicity and coherence. He now waves aside the Legend as "a senseless poem of a senseless student, who could never write two lines in verse."[104]

V.

THE NIGHTMARE OF REASON

In spite of the fullness and complexity of Ivan's intellectual articulation, the unresolved question about human freedom hangs over him as he exits from the tavern. "The formula, 'all is lawful,' I won't renounce," he says squarely to Alyosha, and then more softly, "will you renounce me for that, yes?"[105] Oscillating between cynicism and hope, Ivan's mind cannot find the fixed point of his identity.

The uncertainty of Ivan's mind parallels the objective perplexity of King Oedipus, under the challenge of Teiresias' barbed questioning: do you know who you really are? Oedipus will find the answer by unravelling his knotted past, mentally retracing the path of his free will, step by step. For Ivan, the answer lies in the future, trembling in the balance of his vacillating will.

The night after his meeting with Alyosha leads Ivan into the heart of his own darkness. To his horror, that corner is in the keeping of Smerdyakov. The lackey not only knows the secret signals to gain access to Fyodor's bedchamber, he also seems to have the power of compelling Ivan to respond to him in coded speech.

In that "ambiguous game of signs and signals," as Robert Louis Jackson has called it, the lackey is the one who leads and the master follows. Jackson is particularly acute in drawing attention to the degradation of language that transpires in this conspiratorial exchange: "Language loses its function as a direct communication of thought and is transformed into a series of signs and signals whose function is not to convey thought clearly but to obfuscate or mask it."[106] For Ivan, this humiliating loss of control over his power of articulation also signals his mind's impending collapse into nightmare.

Smerdyakov is the unacknowledged son of Fyodor Karamazov, conceived in the rape of the village idiot, Stinking Lizaveta. In spite of her nickname, *Smerdyaschaya*, Lizaveta was treated with tender compassion by the peasant folk, who revered her innocence. That is why Fyodor's offense against her, committed on a dare after a drunken spree, was remembered with outrage. Baptised as Pavel, the bastard bears the civic identity of his mother's shame in his surname, to which the patronymic Fyodorovich was soon added. Born out of Fyodor's obscene experiment, Smerdyakov fits Ivan's category of a "specimen creature created in jest."

That definition of humanity, coined within the aura of the Grand Inquisitor, is not the only marker of the illicit, subconscious link that bonds Ivan's mind with Smerdyakov's person. "Am I my brother's keeper?" Ivan snaps in the tavern meeting, irritated by Alyosha's anxious question: "What of Dimitri and father, how will it end?"[107] And then, smiling bitterly, Ivan instantly acknowledges his Biblical source as Cain's answer to God about his murdered brother. What he fails to acknowledge, however, is that he is also echoing Smerdyakov's words to him a while earlier: "How am I to know about Dimitri Fyodorovich? It's not as if I were his keeper."[108] In this particular instance of the verbal game, the sign of Cain passes from Smerdyakov to Ivan, contaminating both. It also binds all four brothers together in the fraternity of crime and innocence.

Fyodor may be Smerdyakov's "natural" father, but it is Ivan he chooses for his mentor. In an attempt to voice his loathing of his birth, Smerdyakov imitates Ivan's legalistic thinking. "I would have sanctioned their killing me before I was born, that I might not have come into the world at all, ma'am,"[109] he explains sententiously. Jackson is quite right in noting that Smerdyakov's intellectual process "resembles the rigid rules of grammar."[110] Fyodor, who refers to Smeryakov as "Balaam's ass,"[111] suggests that he is not only semi-literate but also not fully human. Ivan, too, insults his illegitimate half brother as "a lackey and a mean soul," ominously adding, "a prime candidate, however, when the time comes."[112]

In its immediate context, Ivan's prognosis about Smerdyakov alludes to a future revolution that could find good use for the servant's impious rage. Typically, Ivan's speculation dwells on history, glossing over the immediate and personal target for retribution available to Smerdyakov. On the subject of his father, the bastard son, relegated to the servant's quarters, keeps silent. He makes up for it by his loquacious pursuit of Ivan's approval.

If parody were a form of flattery, Ivan should have declared himself pleased with his half brother's intellectual performance on the subject of Christian faith. Smerdyakov boasts that he can deny the Christ at will and still remain blameless before the eternal judge. "With what sort of justice can I be held responsible as a Christian in the other world for having denied Christ, when, through the very thought alone, before denying Him I had been relieved from my christening?"[113] This piece of casuistry, which creates a legal loophole out of the ambiguity between the institutional and the spiritual definition of the Christian identity, draws only a thin smile from Ivan. But old Grigory, the peasant who served as Smerdyakov's substitute father, is driven to fury by such blasphemy. In trying to imitate Ivan, the aspiring lackey has given birth to a quibble worthy of Dante's false counselor Guido da Montefeltro, in Canto XXVII of the *Inferno*. Guido too was caught in the trap of his spiritual duplicity, and it was the devil who had the last laugh by pointing out, as he dragged Guido to hell, that he too was a master logician.[114]

Smerdyakov caps the demonstration of his rational acumen with a seemingly self-contradictory disquisition on faith. He believes that "one man in the world, or at most two, and they most likely are saving their souls in secret somewhere in the Egyptian desert"[115] have the power to move mountains. Fyodor and Ivan agree that Smerdyakov's need to believe in miracles is characteristic of the people's faith. Alyosha counters firmly that "Smerdyakov has not the Russian faith at all."[116]

While pretending to Ivan's intellectual mantle, Smerdyakov really is a secret sharer of his teacher's baser will. With his ambiguous game of signs and signals and his coded message about Chermashnya, Smerdyakov tests the limits of Ivan's parricidal wish. The implied conspiracy between them is above all else a compact of two wills locked into a single purpose. In that shadowy partnership, there is a mutual transference of responsibility. Smerdyakov solicits Ivan's sanction for the idea of parricide while simultaneously offering to distance him from the act. By his passivity, Ivan effectively allows Smerdyakov to be a master of his fate.

Fyodor's murder is enveloped in darkness, as the action in Part III of the novel moves between the spiritual chaos in the monastery and the cruder chaos in town. The narrator, who knows the events from the panoramic perspective of hindsight, deliberately holds back the moment of truth, allowing for a cloud of doubt to drift briefly over the killer's identity. The narrator's default at the pivotal moment in Chapter 4, "In the Dark," of Book 8, when Dmitri pulls the brass pestle out of his pocket, is much more than a device to generate dramatic suspense.[117] The reader, who has been drawn along to witness Dmitri's frenzied chase after Grushenka and the jealous watch under his father's bedroom window, is cut loose at the crest of Dmitri's parricidal rage. By drawing a suspension line in the text, over the gap between the proven intent and the putative act, the cunning narrator has plunged us into the perplexity of the Sophoclean chorus contemplating the murder of Laius.

Immediately after the dotted line we read: " 'God was watching over me then,' Mitya himself said afterwards."[118] The narrative has resumed, but at second hand, effectively shifting focus from the dramatic action to its interpretation. It is on Dmitri we now must rely to fill the mystifying blank that no subsequent judicial narrative would account for adequately. Dmitri thanks God for the unmerited act of grace that foiled the blow about to fall on Fyodor's head. But since God cannot be summoned to testify, Dmitri's credibility hinges on our acceptance of a chain of coincidences that began when Grigory roused himself from his sickbed and came out just in time to absorb the fury of Dmitri's raised pestle that stuns but does not kill him.

As the judicial process is unleashed against Dmitri and the action hurtles toward a spectacular miscarriage of justice, Ivan steps forth on his own to exercise his forensic logic in his brother's case. His three interviews[119] with Smerdyakov take place between the first day of his return from Moscow after the murder (ch. vi, Book 11, Part IV, "The First Interview with Smerdyakov") and the eve of Dmitri's trial (ch. viii, Book 11, Part IV, "The Third and Last Interview with Smerdyakov"). In these three meetings, Ivan thrice revisits the facts and circumstances of his night vigil at his father's house, relentlessly probing the meaning of the words exchanged between the lackey and himself.

The first time, five days after Fyodor's death, Ivan tracks Smerdyakov to the hospital, where he is still recovering from the epileptic fit into which he fell on the night of the crime. Troubled by the way the events have duplicated Smerdyakov's hypothetical scenario, and remembering the latter's boast about his ability to feign such attacks, Ivan presses the sick man with questions. He is met with the mask of winking complicity that seems to echo the words he had heard at the gate, before his departure for Moscow: "... it's always worthwhile speaking to a clever man."[120] Once again, the lackey is offering Ivan the security of a mutually understood collusion to avoid responsibility. He glosses over Ivan's promise of going to Chermashnya as no more than an attempt to run from sure trouble. "Forgive me, sir, I thought you were like me,"[121] he whispers, still respectful of the mentor in whom he has put his whole trust, "as in God Almighty."[122] Ivan is loath to assume the cowardice implied in the evasion. Something dark and reckless within him prompts him to say before taking leave of Smerdyakov: "But I won't say anything of your being able to sham a fit, and I won't advise you to, either."[123] The deal struck, Ivan experiences a humiliating mixture of relief and repugnance.

Two weeks later when Ivan, driven by his need for certainty, returns to question Smerdyakov, the latter wears an expression of malicious haughtiness. Infuriated by his lack of cooperation, Ivan strikes Smerdyakov on the shoulder and sends him reeling against the wall. Under that blow, Balaam's ass speaks out at last. Like Teiresias, who broke his silence after being reviled by Oedipus, Smerdyakov speaks with a force not his own, hurling the questions back to ricochet against the murky surface of the questioner's consciousness. Then, plunging to the bottom of Ivan's will, which he has plumbed before, he dredges out a fully developed, legally cogent theory of Ivan's motivation with regard to his father's murder. It is a tangle of greed, lust and loathing, replicating Rakitin's prognosis, but pointing in Ivan's direction.

Ivan, who still clutches to the hope that Dmitri is the killer as a way to exonerate himself of complicity in the act, if not in intent, sets out to refute Smerdyakov's brief. The dialectician works hard to keep the encroaching monster at bay, but it is the despair of the accused one hears in his cry, "No, I swear I didn't!"[124] with its echo of Oedipus's defiance, "I'll not be proved a murderer" (576). Smerdyakov retorts that Ivan had consented to go to Chermashnya at his bidding ("simply at my word") and must have "expected something"[125] in return. Though intent on certainty, Ivan has to retrench to mere plausibility. And there, arguments cut both ways and the motives, grounded in the evil of the Karamazov heredity, are shared between the brothers.

In the Freudian paradigm, which foregrounds the psychological meaning of parricide, the actual event recedes into the shadows. But Ivan's reason craves the broad daylight of objectivity. What he needs now is not arguments but evidence. When Katerina Ivanovna shows him Dmitri's self-incriminating letter, where he swears that he would break his father's skull to get at the three thousand rubles he owes her and be free of her, this outburst instantly assumes the status of a "mathematical proof"[126] for Ivan. That contrived certainty keeps Ivan going for a month, until the eve of Dmitri's trial.

In his third and last meeting with Smerdyakov, Ivan's false security collapses in one shattering moment of truth, whose silent horror matches the effect of the cry with which Oedipus greets his blinding revelation: "O, o, o, they will all come,/ all come out clearly! Light of the sun, let me/ look upon you no more after today!" (1183–85).

With an insane terror, as if watching in a dream the slow unfolding of a monstrous image, Ivan looks on, transfixed by Smerdyakov's hands. Smerdyakov fumbles inside his stocking and pulls out three packs of hundred-ruble bills amounting to the fatal sum of three thousand. The material evidence of money, which Fyodor had secreted in the corner behind the icons, known only to Smerdyakov, is now held aloft in the murderer's hands. All doubt fades as Smerdyakov gives a voice to the silent indictment in his gesture. "You murdered him; you are the real murderer, I was only your instrument, your faithful servant Licharda, and it was following your words I did it."[127]

Charged with unbearable tension, the catastrophic moment stretches out and splinters in Ivan's mind. He inadvertently recalls a snatch of the song he had heard from the drunken peasant on his way to Smerdyakov. The drunkard had toppled over, blocking his path, and he had pushed him back into the snow. "Ach, Vanka's gone to Petersburg,/ I won't wait till he comes back."[128] So went the ditty. The trivial echo teases Ivan's mind with the thought of another Vanka's fatal departure, not to Petersburg, nor to Chermashnya, which lies nearer, but to Moscow.

As Ivan's grip on reality loosens, the phantomlike figure of the supercilious lackey before him seems to grow a double. The third presence, which now stands between the two accomplices, is named by the uncanny Smerdyakov: "The third is God Himself, sir, Providence, sir. He is the third beside us now. Only don't look for him, you won't find him."[129]

What is one to make of that utterance, at an instant so fraught with the yawn of non-being on the part of Smerdyakov, whom Alyosha himself had branded as a non-believer? Has Smerdyakov become a believer, or is it Balaam's ass that speaks so prophetically, having assumed a human voice to the dismay of the impious master who had struck him? Once again, as in other instances in this novel, this transformational moment confounds the reader's expectation with an unforeseen ambiguity.

But keeping in mind what Dostoevsky has already given us, Smerdyakov's belief in the thaumaturgic powers of ascetics in the desert does not qualify him as a man of faith. Instead, it identifies him as the ideal follower of the Grand Inquisitor's pseudo-theological system. Smerdyakov's real Idol had been Ivan all along.[130] But now he has failed him, paradoxically because he chose to be a truth seeker rather than a keeper of secrets. So, renouncing his imitation of Ivan, he has exchanged his French book for *The Sayings of the Holy Father Isaac the Syrian*,[131] a favorite text of Grigory's. But when Ivan asks him if he believes in God, since he is returning the money, Smerdyakov whispers, "No, I don't believe."[132] Indeed, he has merely transferred allegiance to an alternate form of authority. Like Ivan himself, Smerdyakov is the abandoned son of a tyrannical father. But unlike Ivan, Smerdyakov has denied his mother. In spite of the insults and injuries heaped upon him by various representatives of the patriarchal order, he emulates its ways and despises everything feminine.[133] Smerdyakov's quest for God is a sham from the start, for all he asks for is an authority to sanction his sadistic impulses and his appetite for blasphemy.

Despite his mystifying reference to the divine presence, it does not seem likely that Smerdyakov will see God. His apostasy from Ivan, whom he now accuses of being unable to see God, has not freed his soul. Rather, it has confirmed the act of usurpation already implicit in the ambiguous game of signs and signals. Having displaced his master in the seat of authority, he now assumes Ivan's despair.

Smerdyakov's suicide by hanging aligns him with Judas, the scriptural antagonist of Christ who twice rejected his divine gift of love, first with a kiss and then with the rope of despair. Smerdyakov, too, opts out of the possibility of redemption. His suicide note, which deals one last devastating blow to his failed god, illuminates the logic behind his choice. "I destroy my life of my own will and desire, not to blame anyone,"[134] Smerdyakov writes, with a cunning worthy of the devil himself. In claiming autonomy for his own will, "the faithful servant Licharda" mocks his dethroned master with exquisitely crafted double irony. The seeming neutrality of the suicide message, which neither blames nor exonerates Ivan, is a time capsule delivering revenge in the form of ultimate evasion. By the manner of his exit, Smerdyakov has effectively denied Ivan a judicial resolution of his ordeal.

"You won't dare to do anything, you sir, who used to be so bold!"[135] Smerdyakov had jeered as Ivan declared his determination to bring their complicity into the open. For the failed God, there is no forgiveness, Ivan ought to know. The following day in the courtroom, he will have to acknowledge his impotence: "I have no proof. That cur Smerdyakov won't send proofs from the other world...in an envelope."[136] The devil whose essence is mockery is the third in that last confrontation between Ivan and Smerdyakov. His likeness will be made manifest to Ivan in the wake of Smerdyakov's exit.

The devil materializes as a fantastic, but not entirely unexpected guest in Chapter 9, Book 11, Part IV, entitled "The Devil. Ivan Fyodorovich's Nightmare." The Dostoevskian atheist is often tormented by such apparitions.[137] For, as Tikhon tells Stavrogin, belief in the devil can coexist with disbelief in God. In one major way, however, Ivan's problem with the devil differs from the conundrum of the non-committal, as Kirilov had articulated it: "If Stavrogin has faith, he does not believe that he has faith. If he hasn't faith, he does not believe that he hasn't."[138] Ivan may not believe in God, or in man, but he is committed to the procedures of his Euclidean mind. He holds on to the authority of reason with a passion other men invest in their faith. Until it snaps, during the night between his last meeting with Smerdyakov and his courtroom entry next morning, Ivan wields his reason confidently, like a deft archer shooting an arrow from a tightly drawn bow.

The apparition of the devil confronts Ivan's mind with the absurdity of offering the material proof of the existence of an immaterial dimension of reality he has denied. The mysterious visitor from the world of infinity, where parallel lines meet, amiably passes off the determination of his ontological status to Ivan. He warns him, however, that "proofs are no help to believing."[139] That lesson should be familiar to Ivan, who authored the legend about the atheist refusing to believe in paradise while standing at its gate. "The other world and material proofs, what next!"[140] the devil chortles, delighting as the nemesis of Ivan's logic.

The malignant specter who derides Ivan with his babble of reason unravelling into nightmare has other torments to inflict. Apart from baiting the impotence of logic, the devil's philosophical prattle raises the two ghosted monsters Ivan loathes most. The similarities between Fyodor and Ivan's guest run the whole gamut of possible manifestations. The devil's word game with the proposition of an "ax in space"[141] echoes the conceit of "hooks in hell"[142] with which Fyodor derided Alyosha's faith in eternal life. Both share a taste for off-color anecdotes salted with French expressions, which testify to their somewhat *passé* status as aristocratic libertines. This is how the visitor's external appearance is typified: "It looked as though the gentleman belonged to that class of idle landowners who used to flourish in the times of serfdom.... Such gentlemen of accommodating temper and dependent position, who can tell a story, take a hand at cards, and who have a distinct aversion for any duties that may be forced upon them.... Sometimes they have children, but if so, the children are always brought up at a distance, at some aunt's...."[143]

The mock-typology of a phantom, with its specious generalizations à la Gogol, reads like a spoof on the ideology of "realism," so earnestly prescribed for the Russian novel by the Belinsky/Chernyshevsky school of criticism. But, as always, Dostoevsky's clever literary game is also strictly functional. The passage not only points to Ivan's intellectual lineage, it also dramatizes the fact that he has recognized his father in the nightmare.

The devil's link to Smerdyakov is less obvious, but no less humiliating for Ivan, who persists in treating his guest as a hallucination of his own. Like Smerdyakov, the devil relishes the opportunity of practicing moral license under the sanction of a religious authority. "Those Jesuit confessionals are really my most delightful diversion at melancholy moments,"[144] he gloats. As an example of praiseworthy casuistry, he cites an anecdote about a buxom Norman girl and her Jesuit confessor, who enjoys her charms under the license of the ritual of absolution.

Usurpation is the devil's operative mode. He keeps taunting Ivan by plagiarizing his thoughts and parodying his compositions.[145] This serves as the intellectual expression of the chain of

degraded filiation that binds Ivan to Fyodor and, inversely, to
Smerdyakov. Under the auspices of Ivan's mind, the unseen
ambiguous third presence that emerged in the last meeting of the
two parricides has now congealed into a three-headed monster of
mockery, made in the image of man.

As one might expect of Ivan's uncanny double, the devil's verbal pyrotechnics display a medley of distinctly European voices
and arias. France, Germany and Westernized Russia commingle
promiscuously in that performance. Like Ivan himself, the devil is
a rationalist. He has composed his philosophical libretto around
the leitmotif of Descartes' axiomatic syllogism *"je pense donc je
suis*,(I think therefore I am)"[146] which derives being from an
autonomous act of the thinking subject. With that thread he
weaves in fragments of juvenilia written by the Russian schoolboy
Ivan, which replicate the pattern of logical solipsism. The formula
of autocratic reason rules the devil's discourse. But outside the
frame of Ivan's nightmare, it is countered in form and substance
by Father Zosima's statement "I am and I love."[147] Zosima's existential dictum restores the primacy of being in an act of love,
expressed in the form of a dialogical synthesis of self with the
other.

In his literary persona, the devil offers his variations on the
moods and stylistic modes of German Romanticism. His self-definition as "the indispensable minus"[148] playfully inverts Goethe's
devil's paradox about his role in the comedy of human salvation:
"Mephistopheles declared to Faust that he desired evil, but did
only good. Well, he can say what he likes, it's quite the opposite
with me. I am perhaps the one man in all creation who loves the
truth and genuinely desires good."[149]

With its impish tone, this recitation reveals the contrarian attitude that propels Ivan's devil to formulate his ideas *per negationem*. But more importantly, the Russian version of Goethe's
text translates Mephisto into a tragic hero whose humanist strivings are foiled by a divine authority that has reverted to its gothic

form. "The ironical tone à la Heine,"[150] which the speaker disports, shows no trace of the major chords of Olympian creativity heard in Goethe's drama. Underneath the pedantic display of cosmopolitan culture, as in the Luther parallel to Ivan's gesture of throwing a glass of tea at him, this devil is incorrigibly Russian.

Trapped in the non-being of solipsistic isolation, the spectral soul of Ivan's phantom secretes an incurable nostalgia for human concreteness. He longs "to become incarnate once for all and irrevocably in the form of some merchant's wife weighing two hundred fifty pounds, and of believing all she believes."[151] With this bit of fancy, the demonic voice gives a grotesque twist to the desire for a return to the native roots that Russian intellectuals carried with them in all their wanderings. If the devil's ironic mind is indeed, as Onegin's was before him, a parody of his Western models, in his desires he imitates the vast formlessness of the Russian space. Once opened, that inner landscape invites a Gogolian swindler to sneak in and occupy the terrain. "You seem to take me for Khlestakov grown old, but my fate is a far more serious one,"[152] the voice babbles on, having discarded the Western masks for the comforts of home.

The importunate visitor, whose identity is such a fascinating puzzle for the reader, confronts Ivan with an epistemological choice. To accept him canonically as Satan, or at least as a subaltern messenger from where parallel lines meet, would be to deny the Euclidean mind's privileged claim on reality. The devil himself fails to clearly define his ontological status. A dialectician, he shows off his ability to argue both sides of the question, alternately conceding to be nothing more than Ivan's nightmare and asserting his will to convince him of his own existence.

For Ivan, his own ambivalence in interpreting this experience is a source of torment. To admit the devil as a part of himself, "an incarnation of myself, but only of one side of me ... of my thoughts and feelings, but only the nastiest and stupidest of them,"[153] as he tells the phantom, would amount to letting Fyodor and Smerdyakov penetrate inside him. The devil cynically advises him to give in, with a self-referential travesty of Terence's line: *"Satan sum et nihil humanum a me alienum puto."* (I am Satan and nothing human is alien to me)[154] That option hinges on the acceptance of the demonic as an essential core of humanity. The advice may fit in with Goethe's conception of Mephistopheles as the paradoxical agent of Faust's salvation, but for Ivan, it is problematic. On a philosophical level, it amounts to a shocking reinstatement of the theological premise of the human fall. Worse still, on the personal level, giving in means to recognize his own face held up in effigy, *imago patri*, in the crooked mirror of his demonic double.

VI.

REASON ON TRIAL

Ivan's dilemma about the devil's identity forces him to confront the question of who he really is, from inside out. He has always used ratiocination to put a distance between himself and that thing of darkness which the devil claims for his own. This time, the answer will come in the form of a dramatic revelation at Dmitri's trial.

True to the undertaking he gave Smerdyakov, Ivan does stand up to testify before the all too fallible court where men judge one another. The dramatic impact of Ivan's brief entry parallels the effect of Oedipus's last scene in Sophocles' tragedy (1297–1421). The blind Oedipus enters the stage, "a terrible sight for men to see" (Chorus, 1297). The empty sockets still ooze the blood that sprang out when he struck his eyes repeatedly, with the brooches torn from Jocasta's robe, in the dark incestuous bedroom. The chorus shudders in horror, stunned by the sight of Oedipus's self-inflicted blows. "What spirit urged you?" (1328), the old men question their king.

"It was Apollo, friends, Apollo,/ that brought this bitter bitter-
ness,/ my sorrows to completion./ But the hand that struck me/
was none but my own" (1329–1332). Oedipus's words at the end
of his journey into darkness speak with an awesome clarity, revealing self-recognition behind the deed of self-mutilation. In punishing himself so, Oedipus has proven true to his publicly declared
commitment to justice. He has now accomplished his kingly duty
and appeased the ghost of Laius. The city of Thebes, which had
placed its trust in the "great man," even though he was a stranger
of uncertain origins, is now clean. The Delphic decrees of Apollo
stand upheld. At an extreme cost to himself, the hero Oedipus has
restored the harmony between divine command and human will,
which the chorus had longed for. But in coming forth to claim, in
the eyes of men, his responsibility for the monstrous deeds he has
performed unknowingly and which his own mind abhors,
Oedipus has effectively destroyed his social identity.

Soon, Creon will step forward and urge Oedipus off the stage
where he stands, an object of scandal for men's eyes. But human
pride rides high in that great individual, who has raised himself
above the ordinary conventions societies must live by. Still, in
doing so, Oedipus's aspiring mind has always sought to measure
his acts in the light of divine purpose. Even now, his pride rides in
tandem with a renewed, hard-won reverence for the crushing
majesty of the divine will. Oedipus has accepted Apollo's cruel
design for his life, but in claiming the gesture of self-punishment
as his own, he has retrieved his moral freedom,[155] without which
men are doomed to live in darkness.

Earlier, the chorus speculated about the mystery of Oedipus's
parentage and linked him to Dionysos' mountain, Cithaeron. And
indeed, in the destiny of Oedipus, who claimed Apollo's power of
light and healing for human reason, the apotheosis is enacted in
the pathos of the Dionysiac ritual of sacrifice.

Years after completing *Oedipus the King* (c. 427 BC), Sophocles
brought the tragedy of reason to a higher resolution in the miracle

play *Oedipus at Colonus*[156] (c. 404 BCE), which completes his Theban trilogy. Here, the action takes place in a suburb of Athens, Colonus, where the dying Oedipus has taken refuge. In the expectation of his passing, the blind outcast has become a coveted prize for Thebes, which King Creon schemes to capture. But another hero, King Theseus of Athens, upholds his right to sanctuary in the grove of the Furies. Theseus' charismatic hospitality in the spirit of the Athenian Enlightenment will help mediate Oedipus's passage beyond death. Alone among men, King Theseus will witness the long-living sufferer's delivery into the kindly arms of the goddesses whose thirst for justice has now been fully propitiated. In that mystery, the agony of the human scapegoat ends in a passing beyond humanity and its pain.

It is difficult to imagine such a triumphant atonement for Ivan. In the epilogue of the novel, which looks forward to its promised sequel, Dostoevsky maintains his options about the long-term prospects of the two afflicted brothers.[157] Dmitri may find the strength to suffer through his Siberian ordeal, if he sets aside Katerina's scheme of escaping to America with Grushenka. Ivan may recover from his high fever and accept the gift of Katerina's passionate love. Somewhat ominously, the epilogue places both men's prospects in the temporary custody of that lady's imperious will.

But it is Alyosha, not Ivan, who is presented as the future hero of the drama of sin and redemption that Dostoevsky set out to write. Ivan's intellectual persona seems to have passed on to Kolya Krasotkin, the precocious adolescent who emerges into the foreground in Part IV. In the terminal scene of the epilogue, Kolya participates in the gathering of boys at Ilyusha's tombstone. Alyosha, who brought them together, transforms their grieving into a fellowship of active love, consecrated by the memory of the dead boy who suffered so much. Kolya's cry "Hurrah for Karamazov!"[158] spells out the hope that becomes Dostoevsky's farewell.

Perhaps Dostoevsky envisaged his earliest dream of Christian Socialism emerging at the end of his historical horizon.[159] A brotherhood of love would rise in the spirit of Christ, the scape-goat/redeemer, and purge the ancient wrongs of the flawed succession of tyrannical fathers and parricidal sons. Soon after Dostoevsky's death, the assassination of Tsar Alexander II tainted the Russian tribe of the primal horde with new bloodshed. In the novel, Ivan's individual destiny seems to be decided at Dmitri's trial.

Ivan enters the courtroom with his head bowed, "as though plunged in gloomy thought."[160] Resolved to bear witness to the truth he knows beyond doubt, he is stymied by the judicially inconclusive evidence he has to offer. Smerdyakov's suicide has checkmated his rational purpose. The devil's quip about the limits of medical science, "we can only diagnose,"[161] applies here as well, and Ivan knows that. No argument he can make would persuade the jury that the money he carries in his hand comes from the torn envelope that now rests on the table reserved for material evidence. The procedures of analysis and logical deduction cannot prevail if the supporting facts have disappeared into another dimension of reality.

Even within the four walls of the courtroom, Fetyukovich,[162] Dmitri's defense lawyer, would demonstrate how facts can dissolve in the acid of Pyrrhonism and meanings turn on the flip of words. By the time Fetyukovich concludes his brilliantly sophistic performance, the crime of parricide as such will be swept off the table by his deconstructive method. If Fyodor was not a real father to Dmitri, Fetyukovich argues, how can Dmitri be charged as a father killer? And that sums it up for Dmitri, whether or not Grigory was dreaming when he saw him with the brass pestle in hand. Psychological ambiguities can undermine the solidity of facts and a logical argument may serve as a knave in a rhetorical exercise.

Ivan enters the courtroom in the precarious posture of a convinced rationalist who knows that all the resources of his reason have been pulled from under him. With uncertain steps he walks in the quicksands of epistemological chaos to take his stand in front of the tribunal. There, his resolve to tell the truth collapses in a fit of capricious willfulness. "I am like the peasant girl, your excellency... you know. How does it go? 'I'll stand up if I like, and I won't if I don't,' "[163] he tells the shocked President of the Court. His babble, for all its blatant irrelevance, actually mimics the ambivalence he displayed in the coded, conspiratorial exchange with Smerdyakov about going to Chermashnya. Once again, Ivan appears unable to articulate coherently what he proposes to do.

When the President pulls him up, Ivan presents the material evidence to the bailiff, the bundle of three thousand rubles from Smerdyakov's stocking. But his accompanying words fail to compel belief. "I got them from Smerdyakov, from the murderer, yesterday ..." he mumbles, "I was with him just before he hanged himself. It was he, not my brother, who killed our father. He murdered him and I incited him to do it...." The facts are all there, but presented in a strangely fractured manner. And then, as if in response to an unvoiced query, Ivan turns to the bewildered President: "Who doesn't desire his father's death?"[164]

With that rhetorical deflection, Ivan has veered away from the existential challenge at hand and secured a footing on the high ground of theory. On that platform, the self-incrimination turns morally neutral. From there it is but a short breath to the scornful accusation Ivan hurls in words that seem to pour out of their own accord. "They all desire the death of their fathers. One reptile devours another ..." he snarls. Having raised his accusatory finger to point away from himself, Ivan recovers his verbal powers. "It's a spectacle they want! 'Bread and Circuses,' "[165] he cries in the exalted voice of the tribune. But his new gloss on the phrase about returning the ticket to God redirects the outrage at his fellow men, in an ironic recoil from his humanistic advocacy.

In contrast to Dmitri, who accepts his share of guilt in Fyodor's murder while pleading innocent of the deed,[166] Ivan has effectively cast off his responsibility in the very act of pleading guilty. By converting his confession into a sweeping indictment of humanity, Ivan has discharged his private despair over reason's failure to secure justice into a public scandal with huge philosophical implications. The cynosure in spiralling chaos, reason is revealed as a purveyor of scandal, not a healer. It sets in motion a series of events that will cause further moral stumbling in the unfolding trial.

Ivan's intervention unleashes Katerina's hysteria. Stung to the quick in her passionate admiration of Ivan, she reveals her suppressed hatred of Dmitri in a reckless testimony about their sexual duel and damns him with her shame.[167] In that pandemonium, the accused man's legal fortunes take a tumble. With his well-crafted address to the jury, the prosecutor seals Dmitri's fate. Proceeding step by step, Ippolit Kirilovich links cause to effect in a judicial narrative that reduces the complex polyphonic drama of loathing and sudden grace into a linear structure.[168] The rationalization of Dmitri's psychology carries an impressive illusion of authority. Relentlessly riding the presumption of Dmitri's culpability, the prosecutorial eloquence moves the courtroom. At the same time, it offends the moral sympathies of the reader, who knows from the novelistic narrative that the logical chain weaving the facts is contrary to truth. The jury rules Dmitri guilty of parricide, a verdict that promises a twenty-year term in the mines.[169]

As the trial ends, the gap between earthly justice and human craving for righteousness looms large. Paradoxically, Dostoevsky seems to suggest that the wrongful judgment, which condemns Dmitri for the crime committed by Smerdyakov and Ivan, could be read as a spiritual triumph. After all, the predominantly peasant jury have resisted the temptation of a facile acquittal by reason of temporary insanity, and they have stood firm against Fetyukovich's dangerous sophistries. Still, at least half of the public is revolted by the outcome, which cleaves the community into irreconcilable camps.

That dismay corrodes the trust the Russian liberal opinion has invested in the newly reformed system of justice. Zosima's retreat from the act of judgment has been vindicated. The scapegoating of Dmitri only confirms the caveat against the tribunals of this world, real and imaginary, that Dostoevsky urges on us throughout the novel. Unwittingly, with devastating irony, Ivan's intervention exposes secular justice as the devil's plaything.

As he exits the courtroom, Ivan is a diminished figure, reft of the aura of nobility he cast during his inquest.[170] Powerless to bring the truth to light, his will to reason unravels into caprice. With a cunning worthy of the darkly scheming Apollo, Dostoevsky has staged the trial scene as the nemesis of Ivan's impeachment of God. The scales of justice on which he had weighed the divine and the human have now tilted against him.

In the courtroom scandal, the rationalist's dream of human apotheosis becomes derisory. Reason itself, which drove Ivan to usurp the mantle of divine authority, is compromised in the debacle. Its tragic greatness, too, has dissipated.[171] But when at last Ivan's mind surrenders to darkness, pathos flows into the void left by his intellect's passionate vigil. And a question quickens in the silence around him. Is it the dream of reason rather than its sleep that engenders the insidious monsters of modern history?

Notes

1. Feodor Dostoevsky, *Winter Notes on Summer Impressions*, trans. Richard Lee Redfield (New York: Criterion Books, 1955), 47. The Russian text is from F.M. Dostoevskii, *Polnoe Sobranie Sochinenii v 30. tomakh*, edited and annotated by G.M. Fridlender et al., Tom 5 (Leningrad: Nauka, 1973), 46–99. Dostoevsky originally published *WN in Vremiia* 1 (1863): 289–318, and 2 (1863): 323–362. The notation "Authorized by the Censor" is dated February 6 and March 1863.

2. Dostoevsky's brother Mikhail translated Schiller's dramas *Die Raüber* and *Don Carlos*. See Joseph Frank, *Dostoevsky: The Seeds of Revolt*, 1821–1849 (Princeton, NJ: Princeton U. Press, 1976), for an authoritative discussion of Schiller's influence on Dostoevsky. Frank writes: "These themes of Schiller remained with Dostoevsky all his life, and when he came to write his own version of *The Robbers* in *The Brothers Karamazov*, the abundance of Schillerian references and quotations indicates to what extent Dostoevsky could still express his own deepest values in Schillerian terms" (p. 61).

3. Jacques Catteau, in *La création littéraire chez Dostoievski* (Paris: Institut d'études slaves, 1978), suggests that the Schillerian rebel-hero archetype assumes two distinctive and contradictory incarnations in Dostoevsky's novels—the Westernized, secular humanist, as in Raskolnikov and Ivan Karamazov, and the Russian *vsechelovek*, as in Father Zosima and Alyosha Karamazov.

   In *A Writer's Diary*, "One of Today's Falsehoods" (1873), Dostoevsky recalls the complex mix of emotional and intellectual convictions that made him embrace the Western ideas of Socialism and rebellion and stand up for them all the way to the scaffold: "There was not a single 'monster' or 'scoundrel' among the Petrashcvsky Circle.... It is really true that at the time this nascent socialism was being compared—even by some of its ringleaders—with Christianity, and was taken as merely a correction and improvement of the latter, in accordance with the spirit of the age and civilization. All these new ideas of the time had a tremendous appeal for us in Petersburg; they seemed to be sacred and moral in the highest degree and, most of all, they seemed to be universal—the future law of humanity without exception. Even well before the Paris revolution of 1848 we were caught up by the fascinating power of those ideas. Even in 1846 Belinsky had initiated me into the whole *truth* of this coming 'regenerated world' and into the whole sanctity of the future communistic society" (pp. 284–286). "We of the Petrashevsky Circle stood on the scaffold and listened to our sentences without the least bit of repentance. Obviously, I cannot testify for all of us; but I think that I'm not mistaken in saying that at that moment, if not each one of us, then the great majority would have deemed it dishonorable to renounce our convictions" (p. 288). Quoted from Fyodor Dostoevsky, *A Writer's Diary*, vol. 1 (1873–1876), translated and annotated by Kenneth Lantz, with an introduction by Gary Saul Morson (Evanston, IL: Northwestern U. Press, 1993).

4. D.D. Akhsharumov (1823–1910), a member of the Petrashevsky Circle, has pictured the scene with striking visual details: the red circle of the newly risen sun, the platform draped in black, the ravaged yellowish face of Speshnev as the Petrashevskys huddled together while their names were being read aloud, fifteen of them condemned to death, and a priest invited them to confess to their crimes and repent. The first group of three condemned men — Petrashevsky, Speshnev and Mombelli, were tied to the pillars and the order to shoot was given: *"...moment etot byl uzhasen ... serdtse zamerlo v ozhidanii i strashnyi moment etot prodolzhalsia s polminuty..."* and then the drum was heard and the guns were straightened: *"ot serdtsa otleglo srazu, kak by svalilsia tesno sdavivshii ego kamen'!"* as a messenger from the tsar galloped in with the commutation of the death sentence. Quoted from *F.M. Dostoevskii v vospominaniiakh sovremennikov*, ed. A. Dolinin, 2 Vols., Moscow 1961, Vol. 1, p. 230. Dostoevsky's account of the morning can be found in his first biography, originally commissioned and later rejected by his widow, Anna Grigorievna. See Orest Miller i Nikolai Strakhov, *Biografiia i Zametki iz Zapisnoi Knizhki F.M. Dostoevskogo*, St. Petersburg, 1883, p. 119.

5. A masterpiece of Hugo's anguished imagination, the fictional narrative is an abolitionist plea against the death penalty that reads like an authentic human document. That illusion is created by the focus of the narrative within the mind of the condemned man, a criminal who has been given paper and ink to write *"le journal de mes souffrances, heure par heure, minute par minute,"* as he registers the countdown to the moment of execution, travelling from the prison of Bicêtre to the Place de Grève. His inner time unreels in a moral agony of foreknowledge, with the certainty of death counterpointed

by the irrational hope of a reprieve. The guillotine, this *"monstrueuse charpente,"* looms large over the narrative. A death machine invented by a humane doctor to lessen the physical pain of execution, it figures in the text as the visual emblem of the scandal of technology, contriving the sham of human progress: *"Y a-t-il des morts de leur façon qui soient venus les remercier et leur dire: C'est bien inventé. Tenez-vous-en là. La mécanique est bonne"* (p. 131). Quoted from Victor Hugo, *Bug Jargal—Le dernier jour d'un condamné,* accompagné de *Claude Gueux,* Paris, 1942.
The intertextual relationship between Dostoevsky and Hugo has been explored by V.V. Vinogradov, *Poetika russkoi literatury,* Moscow, 1976, pp. 63–75, and by Natalia Babel Brown, *Hugo and Dostoevsky,* introduced by Robert Belkap (Ardis), Ann Arbor, 1978. See also "Dostoievsky lecteur de V. Hugo," in *Le rayonnement international de Victor Hugo,* edité par Francis Claudon, *Proceedings of the International Comparative Literature Association, XIth International Congress* (Peter Lang), NY, 1985, pp. 159–168, and Frank Paul Bowman, "The Intertextuality of Victor Hugo's *Le dernier jour d'un condamné,"* in *Alternatives,* edited by Warren Motte and Gerald Price (French Forum Publishers), Lexington, Kentucky, 1993.

6. Joseph Frank in *Dostoevsky: The Years of Ordeal, 1850–1859,* Princeton U. Press, 1983, emphasizes the death/rebirth quality of Dostoevsky's experience: "It is from this moment that the primarily secular perspective from which Dostoevsky had previously viewed human life sinks into the background, and what comes forward to replace or absorb it are the intimate and agonizing 'cursed questions' that have always plagued mankind—the questions whose answers can be given, if at all, only by religious faith" (p. 59). Frank compares Dostoevsky's new moral consciousness to the "interim ethics" of early Christians, who daily anticipated the Last Judgment: "...there *is* no time for anything but the last kiss of reconciliation because, quite literally, there is no time" (p. 64).

7. *Le dernier jour d'un condamné* (op. cit.), p. 110. The condemned man expresses his desperate hope for *"les galères... ou à perpetuité avec le fer rouge.... Mais grâce de la vie ! Un forçat, cela marche encore, cela va et vient, cela voit le soleil."* Dostoevsky, in a letter dated December 22, 1849 from the Peter and Paul Fortress, writes: *"...no vo mne ostalos' serdtse i ta zhe plot' i krov', kotoraia tak zhe mozhet liubit', i stradat', i pomnit', a eto, vse taki zhizn'. On voit le soleil!"* Quoted from F.M. Dostoevskii, *Pis'ma,* edited and annotated by A.S. Dolinin, 4 vols, Moscow, 1928–1959, vol. 1, Letter 58, p. 129.

8. See F.A. Lvov's account, written between 1859 and 1861, in "Zapiska o dele Petrashevtsev," *Literaturnoe Nasledstvo*, No. 63, Moscow, 1956, p. 188.

9. See *The Years of Ordeal* (op. cit.). Simultaneously, Frank also draws on neuro-pathological concepts to explain Dostoevsky's "conversion" as a collapse of old brain patterns under extreme stress and the birth of new patterns, in a violent psychic process that was accompanied by epileptic seizures. Frank categorically rejects Freud's Oedipal thesis: "But there is not the slightest evidence to prove that Dostoevsky submitted to or sought punishment from the Tsar-Father.... It was only from the people that Dostoevsky sought absolution, both because of the immediate sense of guilt engendered by the complexities of his prison-camp sentiments and, farther back, because of his acceptance of a share of guilt in his father's presumed murder. Unlike his earlier Fourierist-Socialist sentimentality towards the poor and oppressed, his new found faith in the beauty of the Russian peasant was now charged with an intense nationalism and his love of the people became intrinsically linked to his love of Orthodoxy" (p. 125).

10. Lev Shestov argues that Dostoevsky, who went through a phase of cynicism after the collapse of his youthful faith in the nobility of the *narod*, never could overcome his negative view of humanity. Shestov considers Dostoevsky's subsequent professions of love for humanity as insincere and self-deluding. See Leo Shestov, "Dostoevsky and Nietzsche: The Philosophy of Tragedy," *Essays in Russian Literature, The Conservative View: Leontiev, Rozanov, Shestov*, edited by Spencer E. Roberts, Athens, GA, 1968. Shestov thus puts in doubt Dostoevsky's declaration of 1873, when he credits "the direct contact with the People, the brotherly union with them in common misfortune" for his conversion. See *A Writer's Diary*, "One of Today's Falsehoods" (op. cit.), p. 289. I disagree with Shestov and shall return to this question in my reading of *Notes from the Underground*.

11. "The Peasant Marey," in the February 1876 issue of *A Writer's Diary* (op. cit.), p. 352. Dostoevsky calls this piece a "story," adding, "actually, it's not even a story, but only a reminiscence of something that happened long ago" (p. 351).

12. This conception agrees with the Orthodox preference for a mystical rather than an ethical approach to human evil. Ernest Benz, in *The Eastern Orthodox Church*, NY, 1963, points out that the doctrine of original sin has much less hold on the Orthodox mind than on the Catholic or Protestant mind. He argues that the Augustinian theory

of evil in man does not harmonize with the Orthodox vision of man as *imago Dei*.

13. See "Nikolai Strakhov: Memories of Fyodor Mikhailovich Dostoevsky as a Journalist," *The Dostoevsky Archive*, edited by Peter Sekirin (McFarland and Co.), Jefferson, NC, 1997 (segment translated from *Semeinye Vechera*, February 1881): "It was 1861, and the abolition of serfdom was the major event.... It seemed as if a new life had started in Russia... So new directions and literary trends appeared.... The most recent trends then were those of *Time*, and it was founded by Fyodor Mikhailovich.... Anyway, in the yearly announcement about *Time* subscriptions, it was written that both Slavophiles and the Westernizers belonged to the past, and that we had to start something new.... Then there appeared a new literary party which became known in St. Petersburg circles as 'The Soil' (*Pochva*). Fyodor Mikhailovich's favorite expressions were 'we have departed from the soil' and 'we must seek our soil' and he used them in his first article" (p. 151). For Dostoevsky's relation to *pochvennichestvo* and its leading exponents, A.A. Grigoriev (1828–1864) and N.N. Strakhov (1828–1896), see Wayne Dowler, *Dostoevsky, Grigor'ev and Native Soil Conservatism*, U. of Toronto Press, 1982.

14. *WN*, p. 49.

15. *My Past and Thoughts: The Memoirs of Alexander Herzen*, 4 Vols, introduced by Isaiah Berlin, translated by Constance Garnett (Alfred A. Knopf), NY 1968, Vol. 2, p. 549.

16. "Slavophilism attracted the entire sympathy of the most progressive elements in Russian society," is how Ovsyanikov described the mood of the late 1850s, in D.S. Ovsyanikov-Kulikovskii, *Istoriia russkoi intelligentsii*, 3 vols, St. Petersburg, 1909, vol. 2, p. 4.

17. *The Russian People and Socialism: An Open Letter to Jules Michelet*, written in French from Nice Maritime in September 1851, is a response to Michelet's scathing portrayal of Russo-Polish relations in "A Legend of Kusciusko." I quote from the English text, included in Alexander Herzen, *From the Other Shore*, with an introduction by Isaiah Berlin, Oxford U. Press, 1978, p. 165.

18. Baron A. von Haxthausen (1792–1866), a German ethnographer, published his *Etudes sur la vie populaire en Russie* in 1847. Herzen cites Haxthausen's observations as evidence that the Russian peasants' attitudes with respect to land ownership are not individualistic, but based on the fundamental assumption that every member of the village commune has an equal right to use his share of the land that is held in common. Herzen argues that the Russian peasants show

remarkable inventiveness in devising ways of distribution that are suitable to local conditions, while satisfying the moral demand of equality.

19. A.I. Gertsen, *Kontsy i nachala*, Vol. XVI, *Sobranie Sochinenii v 30. Tomakh* (Akademiia), Moscow, 1859, pp. 129–198. The eight letters were originally addressed to Turgenev, but Herzen published them in *Kolokol* (July, August, October, and November 1862; January 1863). Turgenev did not use the pages of the journal to publish his reply. Instead, he incorporated many of his ideas, previously aired in dialogue with Herzen, in the novel *Smoke* (*Dym*) (1867).

20. These polemics were primarily conducted by Strakhov, who had a strong background in the natural sciences, and who had a major influence on Dostoevsky's thinking in the period of *Vremya* and *Epokha* (1861–65). See Strakhov's entry in *Dostoevskii v vospominanii sovremennikov*, Tom 1 (*Izd. Khudozhestvennaia literatura*), 1964, edited by V.V. Grigorenko, N.N. Gudzii et al. Strakhov first met Dostoevsky in the winter of 1859–60 through the old Petrashevets A.P. Miliukov (1817–1897). While a frequent guest in the Palm-Durov circle, Miliukov had remained outside the pale of its inner conspiratorial nucleus and was not present in Semenovsky Square on December 22, 1849. He was allowed to say farewell to Dostoevsky and Durov in the Peter and Paul Fortress, and he maintained epistolary contact with Dostoevsky throughout his exile. In 1860, Dostoevsky wrote a playful narrative of his arrest for Miliukov's daughter's album. In the early 1860s Dostoevsky was at home in Miliukov's circle, which retained the tone of sentimental humanism from the 1840s. A dominant theme was compassion for the people, and any transgression against the populist credo was treated harshly, whereas weaknesses of the flesh were forgiven, in accordance with the Saint-Simonian doctrine of rehabilitation of the flesh. Dostoevsky's novel *The Insulted and Injured* (1861) was highly praised.

21. Strakhov characterized this musical evening as *"kul'minatsiia nashei vozdushnoi revoliutsii."* See *Dostoevskii v vospominanii sovremennikov* (op. cit.), p. 295.
Joseph Frank, in *Dostoevsky: The Stir of Liberation, 1860–1865* (Princeton, NJ: Princeton U. Press, 1986), points out that Dostoevsky was an administrator of the Literary Fund organized to support scholars and writers who had suffered from exile or prison. At the January 10, 1862 meeting of the Literary Fund, Turgenov read his essay "Hamlet and Don Quixote." The March 2, 1862 musical soiree was also organized by the Literary Fund, and it was conducted against

the background of incendiary pamphlets circulated by the young radicals, followed by suspicious fires in Petersburg. Frank aptly notes that Dostoevsky picked up on the highly charged, hysterical atmosphere surrounding the March musical soiree, and parodied it in the description of the benefit fête for governesses in *The Devils*.

22. Michel Aucouturier, "Herzen et Dostoievski," *Autour d'Alexandre Herzen*, Révolutionnaires et Exilés du XIXe Siècle, Documents Inédits (Librairie Droz), Genève, 1973, pp. 303–306. Aucouturier, who has reconstructed the July 1862 encounter between Dostoevsky and Herzen in London, quotes from Herzen's letter to Ogarev, dated July 16, 1862. Aucouturier sums up the length of the Herzen-Dostoevsky relationship that began as a casual acquaintance in Petersburg in 1846, around Kraevskii's journal, *Otechestvennye Zapiski*. The July 1862 meeting in London was to be the high point of the two men's relations. After that, Dostoevsky saw Herzen a few more times—in October 1863 in Naples, in August 1863 in Wiesbaden, where he unsuccessfully solicited a loan from him, and two more times in Geneva, in September 1867 and briefly, in the street, in March 1868. See also Elena Dryzhkova, "Dostoevskii, Gertsen, Londonskoe Svidanie 1862 Goda," *Canadian-American Studies*, No 3, 1983, pp. 325–348.

23. A.I. Gertsen, "Novaia faza v russkoi literature," in *Sobranie Sochinenii v 30. Tomakh* (op. cit.), Vol. XVIII, p. 219.

24. N.N. Strakhov, in *Biographiia* (op. cit.), comments that "Dostoevsky's relation to Herzen then was quite tender and his *Winter Notes* smacks of the influence of this writer." A.S. Dolinin, in "Dostoevskii i Gertsen," *F.M. Dostoevskii, Stat'i i Materialy*, Leningrad, 1935, Vol. I, pp. 275–324, demonstrates that Dostoevsky was profoundly influenced by Herzen's writings about Europe, notably *S togo berega* (1848–1852), *Pis'ma iz Frantsii i Italii* (1847–1852), and *Kontsy i Nachala* (1862–1863). Frank, in *The Stir of Liberation* (op. cit.), writes: "Dostoevsky was so steeped in these later texts (i.e. Herzen's post-1948 writings about Europe) that phrases, expressions, and allusions easily identifiable with Herzen constantly show in his prose during these years" (p. 54).

25. V.G. Belinsky, "The Idea of Art" (1841), in Vol. I, *Russian Philosophy*, edited by James M. Edie, James P. Scanlan, Mary Barbara Zeldin (Quadrangle Books) Chicago, 1968, pp. 285–303. For the Russian text see V.G. Belinskii, *Estetika i literaturnaia kritika*, 2 vols, Moscow, 1959 (vol 1).

26. I quote from Boris Brasol's translation: "Old People," *The Diary of a Writer*, by F.M. Dostoievsky, NY 1954, p. 5. The rest of the portrait,

published in 1873, after Herzen's death, is far less flattering. I shall return to it in my reading of *Notes from the Underground*.

27. A.I. Gertsen, *Pis'ma iz Frantsii i Italii Iskandera* (1847–1852)—written, as Herzen put it, *"pod shum i grom sobytii."* Four of these letters appeared in *Sovremennik* in 1847, as "Pis'ma iz Avenue Marigny." The second, complete edition of the letters was published by Herzen in London in 1859. I quote from A.I. Gertsen, *Sobranie Sochinenii v 30. Tomakh* (op. cit.),Vol. V. The translations are mine.

28. I quote from Alexander Herzen, *From the Other Shore* (op. cit.). The first full edition of *S togo berega* appeared in German, *Vom anderen Ufer*, Zürich, 1849 (and in 1850, without Herzen's name, "Aus dem Russischen Manuskript" in Georg Herwegh's edition). The second edition by Herzen himself, in Russian, *S togo berega*, London, 1855, was published under his old pseudonym Iskander. The definitive Russian edition can be found in Vols. VI and VII of *Sob. Soch. v 30 Tomakh*.

29. In Letter 9 of *Pis'ma iz Frantsii i Italii* (op. cit.), dated June 10, 1848, Herzen wrote: *"Imia Parizha tesno soedineno so vsemi luchshimi upovaniiami sovremennogo cheloveka; ia v nego v'ezzhal s trepetom serdtsa, s robost'iu kak nekogda v'ezzhali b Ierusalim, v Rim"* (p. 141).

30. *WN*, ch. 2, "On the Train," p. 47. Frank, in *The Stir of Liberation* (op. cit.), p. 234, identifies Dostoevsky's expression *"zemlia sviatykh chudov"* as a quotation from Khomiakov's poem "Mechta" (1834), in which the slumbering East is summoned to awaken and replace the dying West. The date of Khomiakov's poem suggests that Herzen's and, a fortiori, Dostoevsky's conception of the West as a civilization in decay, was hardly new. In the 1840s and 1850s, the idea was propagated by the Slavophiles, but after his disappointment with the French revolutions of 1848, Herzen, a committed Westernizer, came to share this view.

31. *WN*, Ch. 2, pp. 47–48.

32. *Letter to Jules Michelet* (op. cit.), pp. 198–199.

33. *WN*, Ch. 3, "Which Is Completely Superfluous," p. 73–74.

34. *WN*, Ch. 4, "And for the Traveller Not Superfluous," p. 80.

35. *WN*, Ch. 5, "Baal," p. 84.

36. "After the Storm," Ch. II of *From the Other Shore* (op. cit.), p. 53.

37. Ibid., Ch. III, "Year LVII of the Republic, One and Indivisible," dated from Paris, Champs Elysées, October 9, 1848, p. 60.

38. Ibid., Ch. IV, p. 84, "Vixerunt!" dated from Paris, December 1848.

39. Ibid., pp. 70–71. Earlier, in July, Herzen had written: "There is an

astonishing resemblance between the phenomenology of terror and that of logic." He goes on, arguing that the supreme test of the efficacy of reason consists in the task of destroying canonized values: "Reason is, like the Convention, merciless, severe, no respector of persons, it stops at nothing, it brings the Supreme Being itself into the dock" (Ch. II, "After the Storm," dated from Paris, July 27, 1848, p. 50).

40. "After the Storm," p. 46.

41. Ibid., p. 52: "For three months men elected by universal vote, the chosen deputies of the land of France, did nothing, and then they suddenly rose to their full height to show the world an unprecedented spectacle of eight hundred men behaving as one villain, as one monster."

42. "Epilogue," dated from Zürich, December 21, 1849, Ch. VII (op. cit.), p. 146.

43. "Omnia Mea Mecum Porto," dated from Hotel Mirabeau, Paris, April 3, 1850, Ch. VI (op. cit.), p. 125.

44. "Epilogue," p. 148.

45. "Omnia Mea Mecum Porto," p. 127.

46. "Epilogue," p. 151.

47. "Farewell" ("Addio"), dated from Paris, March 1, 1849, *From the Other Shore* (op. cit.), p. 10. Herzen placed this open letter in the preamble of his book, after the dedication to his son, "My friend, Sasha," in which he calls the book "a monument to a struggle in which I have sacrificed much, but not the courage of knowledge" (p. 3).

"This right to be heard" (*glasnost'*) was not a mean advantage for Herzen, who maintained that the power of criticism was "the force of our age, our triumph and our lot" (Letter 4, *Pis'ma iz Frantsii i Italii*, op. cit., Paris, September 1847, p. 61).

48. "Modern man, that melancholy Pontifex Maximus, only builds a bridge; it will be for the unknown man of the future to pass over it" ("To my Friend, Sasha," dated January 1, 1855, from Richmond House, Twickenham, in *From the Other Shore*, (op. cit., p. 3).

Like so many of Herzen's expressions, the formula "Pontifex Maximus" found its way into Dostoevsky's fiction. Kirilov, the mystic of double negation who defines God as "the pain of the fear of death," in Part I, Ch. III, ch. viii, p 114, of *The Possessed* (*Besy*), had been introduced by Liputin as an engineer who collects data about suicides, and who has returned to Russia in order to build a bridge. When Stepan Trofimovich Verkhovensky rejoins, "...you want to build our bridge and at the same time you declare that you hold with the principle of universal destruction. They won't let you build our bridge," his witticism aims indirectly at Herzen's metaphor, which Liputin has reduced to its literal, material level. In the process, Dostoevsky also targets the Pope, the Supreme Pontiff, who inherited the formula and the title from the Roman Emperors. Quoted from Part I, Ch. III, ch. iv, p. 94 of *The Possessed* (Modern Library), NY, 1930, translated by Constance Garnett.

49. "Vixerunt!" (op. cit.), p. 92.

50. "Consolatio," Ch. V (op. cit.), dated from Paris, March 1, 1849.

51. For his part, Herzen wrote: "...*kritika i somnenie — ne narodny, narod trebuet gotovogo uchenia, verovaniia, emu nuzhna dogmatika...*" in Letter 4, *Pis'ma iz Frantsii i Italii* (op. cit.), p. 62.

52. "Omnia Mea Mecum Porto" (op. cit.), p. 139.

53. In "Vixerunt!" (op. cit.), Herzen wrote: "If we had not learnt from the age of five that nature and history are two different things, it would not have been difficult for us to understand that the development of nature passes imperceptibly into the development of mankind, that these are two chapters of one novel, two phases of one process, very far apart at the extremities, very close together at the centre. It would not have surprised us then, that part of everything that takes place in history is influenced by physiology, by dark forces. It is true that the laws of historical development are not opposed to the laws of logic, but their paths do not coincide with those of thought, just as nothing in nature coincides with the abstract norms constructed by pure reason" (pp. 75–75).

54. *WN*, Ch. 6, "Essay on the Bourgeoisie," p. 101.

55. Dostoevsky simplified Sieyès' argument, in order to maximize the incipient power grab of the *Tiers Etat*. Sieyès' exposition is made up of three parts, imitating the classical order of a syllogism:
"1. *Qu'est-ce que le Tiers Etat?—TOUT.*
2. *Qu'a-t-il été jusqu'à présent dans l'ordre politique ?—RIEN.*
3. *Que demande-t-it ?— A ÊTRE QUELQUE CHOSE."*
Moreover, when Sieyès explains, "*Le Tiers Etat est TOUT, c'est-a-dire 'une nation complète,'* " he makes it plain that the claim to a proper share of power by the politically dispossessed majority derives from the fact that the *Tiers Etat* is that part of the French nation which, unlike the two privileged estates, is both willing and able to think and work for the benefit of the whole. I quote from Sieyès, *Qu'est-ce que le Tiers Etat?* Préface de Jean-Denis Bredin (Flammarion) Paris, 1988, p. 14.

56. "Essay on the Bourgeoisie" (op. cit.), p. 101. Svetlana Boym, in *Common Places: Mythologies of Everyday Life in Russia*, Harvard U.

Press, 1994, writes: "Dostoevsky's travel account 'Winter Notes on Summer Impressions' offers a critique of the profane trinity of Western individualism—'*Liberté, Egalité, Fraternité.*' He goes on to describe Paris, in the tradition of Fonvizin, as the capital of a people 'who have no reason' " (p. 82).

57. "Essay on the Bourgeoisie," p. 108.
58. Letter 4, *Pis'ma iz Frantsii i Italii* (op. cit.) p. 60.
59. "After the Storm" (op. cit.), p. 46.
60. "Year LVII of the Republic, One and Indivisible" (op. cit.), p. 68.
61. Letter 2, *Pis'ma iz Frantsii i Italii* (op. cit.) dated from Paris, June 3, 1847.
    Frank, in *The Stir of Liberation* (op. cit.), notes that many of Dostoevsky's comments on the French theater "coincide so perfectly with the portrait of the French given by the much more urbane and cosmopolitan Herzen in his sparkling *Letters from France and Italy*" (p. 186). Pointing to the similarity between the tone of the narrator of *WN* and the underground man's in Part I of *Notes*, Frank characterizes it as the "rhetoric of inverted irony" (p. 234).
62. *WN*, Ch. 7, "Bribri and Ma Biche," p 140.
63. In *Kontsy i nachala* (1862–1863), *Sobranie Sochinenii* (op. cit.), Vol. XVI, in Letter 6, written on October 20, 1862, Herzen concludes that there is "no freedom, no equality and no fraternity in contemporary France or Europe" (p. 179). He damns the parliamentary forms of government as sterile, devoid of the seeds of liberation or redemption.
64. Karl Marx's (1818–1883) post-mortem reflections on the Parisian revolutions of 1848 are contained in *The Eighteenth Brumaire of Louis Bonaparte*, a virulent political pamphlet written in 1852–53. In a companion piece, *The Class Struggles in France*, which consists of a series of articles written in 1850 and published by Engels after his death, Marx analyzes the stratification of class interests within the bourgeoisie and their political configurations. He concludes that *Fraternité*, the rallying cry of the February Revolution, was no more than a catchword in the doomed attempt to paper over the irreconcilable conflict of interests that pitted the matured bourgeoisie against its temporary ally, the proletariat. See *The Marx-Engels Reader*, edited by Robert C. Tucker (Norton), NY, 1972.
65. "Essay on the Bourgeoisie," p. 109.
66. Ibid., p. 110.
67. Ibid., p. 114.
68. Mikhail Bakunin, "The Reaction in Germany," in *Russian Philosophy*

(op. cit.), Vol. I, pp. 385–406. The article was originally published in German, "Die Reaction in Deutschland," in *Deutsche Jahrbücher für Wissenschaft und Kunst*, edited by Arnold Ruge, Leipzig, October 1842.

69. "The philosophy of Hegel is the algebra of revolution; it emancipates a man in an unusual way and leaves not one stone upon another of the Christian world, of the world of tradition that has outlived itself. But, perhaps with intention, it is badly formulated." Quoted from *My Past and Thoughts: The Memoirs of Alexander Herzen*, "Moscow, Petersburg and Novgorod (1840–47)," p. 237, U. of California Press, 1982.

70. In Ch. 7 of *WN*, "Sequel to the Foregoing," Dostoevsky reports on his visit to the *Palais de Justice*, where he listened to an inheritance case pitting the heirs of a pious bourgeois woman against a congregation of hermit priests. Thanks to the eloquence of a lawyer (Jules Fabre), who deployed all the commonplaces of the revolutionary tradition in order to secure the blessing of the capitalist succession for the legitimate heirs, the priestly money grab was quashed.

71. The phrase "*ôte-toi de là, que je m'y mette!*" figures in Dostoevsky's "Musings about Europe," in the March 1876 issue of *A Writer's Diary* (op. cit.), p. 402.

72. Albert Camus, *La Chute* (Gallimard), Paris, 1956, p. 32.

73. "Essay on the Bourgeoisie" (op. cit.), p. 114.

74. Ibid., p. 116. The "anthill" is Dostoevsky's choice metaphor for a social order of regimented equality, without freedom.

75. Ibid., p. 110.

76. "Realism is the mind of the crowd, of the majority, who do not see farther than their nose, but it is cunning, and keen, quite adequate for the present moment" (From Dostoevsky's Notebook, written in the mid-1860s. See *Polnoe Sobranie* (op. cit.), Vol. 20, p. 182). In various statements dispersed throughout his career, Dostoevsky sought to distinguish his visionary approach from a mimetic realism that limits itself to describing the appearances of phenomenal reality. In another statement, quoted by V.V. Vinogradov in *Problema avtorstva i teoriia stilei*, Moscow, 1961, he says: "My critics understand only what goes on before their eyes, but because of nearsightedness, they themselves are not only unable to look ahead, but cannot even understand how for another person the future results of present events can be crystal clear" (p. 535).
The most famous formulation, of course, is: "They call me a psychologist, I am only a realist in the higher sense; that is, I depict all

the depths of the human soul" (Notebook, *Polnoe Sobranie*, Vol. 27, p. 65).

77. Ivan Kireevsky, "On the Necessity and Possibility of New Principles in Philosophy" (1856), in *Russian Philosophy* (op. cit.) Vol. 1, pp. 171–213. For the Russian text, see "O neobkhodimosti i vozmozhnosti novykh nachal v filosofii," in I.V. Kireevskii, *Polnoe Sobranie Sochinenii*, edited by M.O. Gershenzon, Moscow, 1911, pp. 223–264. Kireevsky's conception of European civilization is derived from the traditional Orthodox interpretation of the Great Schism of the eleventh century as the defection of the West from Christian unity, amounting to apostasy from the spirit of the Christ. By analyzing the addition of the *filioque* to the Nicene Creed as an arbitrary act of logic, backed by the authority of a single individual—the Pope—Kireevsky identifies autonomous reason with willfulness and the principle of individuation with self-assertion. This definition of the Roman Idea, posited as the presiding thesis of the Western historical dialectic, places the progression of European civilization under the evil sign of necessity, whose symptomatic manifestations are divisive strife and coercive violence. Implicit in this scheme is the notion of a demonic inversion of the Providential plan for humanity, which damns all Western values, be they conservative (reason/authority) or progressive (reason/rebellion). Dostoevsky, who shared Kireevsky's bias against Catholicism, found in him the right philosophical frame for his apocalyptic ruminations.

Frank, in *The Stir of Liberation* (op. cit.), p. 274, points out that Dostoevsky read the Slavophile ideologues while travelling in Italy with Strakhov in 1863. But long before that, in his explanation to the Investigative Commission in 1849, Dostoevsky had made the distinction between the "historical necessity" ruling French events, and what he foresaw as the Russian destiny (V.I. Semevskii, "Sledstvie i sud po delu Petrashevtsev," in *Russkie Zapiski*, 1916, pp. 9–11).

78. "Year LVII of the Republic, One and Indivisible" (op. cit.), p. 68.

79. "An Expired Force and the Forces of the Future," March 1876 issue of *A Writer's Diary* (op. cit.), p. 406. Jacques Catteau, in *La création littéraire* (op. cit.), pp. 321–324, notes that, while Dostoevsky was in Paris in 1862, the Russian Jesuit Gagarin published three of Chaadaev's *Philosophical Letters*: *Oeuvres choisies de Pierre Tchaadaief, publiées pour la première fois par le père Gagarin de la Compagnie de Jésus* (Librairie A. Franck), Paris-Leipzig, 1862. The first letter, which had appeared in *Teleskop* in 1836, contains the provocative statement: "We Russians, like illegitimate children, come to the world without

patrimony, without any links with people who lived on earth before us [p. 112].... we have given nothing to the world, we have not added a single idea to the mass of human ideas, we have contributed nothing to the progress of the human spirit." Quoted from Peter Chaadaev, "Philosophical Letters," *Russian Philosophy*, op. cit., Vol. I. p. 116. Chaadaev's exaltation of the Roman Idea, armed with the discipline of the syllogism, and his admonition to his fellow Russians to rejoin the universal Christian Unity from which Byzantium had defected, was the opening salvo of the historic debate that would divide the idealists of the forties—all Hegelians—into Westernizers and Slavophiles.

Catteau suggests that Chaadaev served as the model for Dostoevsky's type of alienated Russian aristocrat, the "eternal wanderer" whose roamings among foreign people and foreign ideas were the mythical stuff of the theme of "The Life of the Great Sinner," only partially realized in the character of Versilov.

80. This scenario may have been influenced by Herzen's account of Pius IX's political flirtation with the Roman populace during the winter of 1848 (Letter 6, dated from Rome, February 4, 1848 and Letter 8, dated from Rome, March 3, 1848, *Pis'ma*, op. cit.).

81. "Baal," pp. 90–91. Compare with Herzen's statement in Letter 6 of *Kontsy i nachala* (op. cit.), where he contrasts contemporary publicists with Biblical prophets: "Those prophets of yore would not lead the masses toward Baal" (p. 178).

82. Jacques Catteau, in "Du Palais de Cristal à l'âge d'or ou les avatars de l'utopie," in *Cahier de l'Herne*, No. 24, Paris, 1973, pp. 178–179, traces the evolution of the symbolic images of utopia in Dostoevsky's writings. I am indebted to him for the French derivation of the expression *"caserne-prison,"* as well as for the reference to "a palace of marble and gold" in *The House of the Dead*.

In *La création littéraire* (op. cit.) Catteau shows that Dostoevsky was familiar with the major works of French Utopian Socialism, as well as with Strauss's *La vie de Jésus* (1836). But he doubts if Dostoevsky read Marx's *La misère de la philosophie* (Paris, 1847), the only work by Marx in Petrashevsky's library.

83. Herzen's exchange with Pecherin first appeared in *Poliarnaia Zvezda*, in 1861. (Book 6, pp. 259–272) Subsequently, Herzen included it in *Byloe i dumy* (Vol. 11, *Sob. Soch.*, op. cit., pp. 391–403).

84. Lebedev's paradoxes and his ironic reference to Malthus as "that lover of humanity" are in Part III, chs. 4 and 5 of *The Idiot*.

85. "Baal," pp. 92–93. Geoffrey C. Kabat, in *Ideology and Imagination: The Image of Society in Dostoevsky*, Columbia U. Press, NY, 1978,

compares Dostoevsky's vision of the London proletariat with Friedrich Engels' *The Condition of the Working Class in England* (1844), which contains phrases like "the dissolution of mankind into monads" and "the brutal indifference, the unfeeling isolation of each individual person in his private interest." Kabat notes that in 1861, *Vremya* had published a Russian translation of Elizabeth Gaskell's novel, *Mary Barton: A Story of Manchester Workers*, as evidence that Dostoevsky's hellish vision of the condition of the English working class was already formed before he arrived in London (Kabat, Ch. 3, "Imagination and Society").

86. "Baal," p. 96.
87. Catteau, in *La création littéraire* (op. cit.), writes: "*Enfer social, instigatrice du crime, la ville saisit d'effroi les écrivains et poètes: alors remplis de crainte ils l'érigent en mythe*" (p. 81). In Dostoevsky's metaphoric language, "cannibalism" stands for the fundamental social law of capitalism, based on untrammelled self-assertion, and the "anthill" represents its historical nemesis of coercive socialism. Dolinin, in "*Dostoevskii i Gertsen*" (op. cit.), derives the image of the anthill from Wordsworth's *Prelude*, by way of Herzen. Andrzej Walicki, in *The Controversy over Capitalism*, Oxford U. Press, London, 1969, points out that conservative Slavophiles and radical Populists had both rejected capitalism in principle, long before Karl Marx's *Das Kapital* penetrated into Russia in the 1880s.
88. F.M. Dostoevskii, *Polnoe Sobranie Sochinenii* (op. cit.), Vol. 20, pp. 172–176. The quotation (translation mine): "*Masha lezhit na stole. Uvizhus' li s Mashei?*" is from p. 172, while my reference to the "great spiritual denial" goes back to "Baal" (p. 91).
89. *Pis'ma* (op. cit.) Vol. I, Letter 61 to F.M. Fonvizina, dated from *Omsk*, February 20, 1854, p. 142.
90. Frank, in *The Years of Ordeal* (op. cit.), observes that Western religious thinkers, from Tertullian and Augustine to Luther and Pascal, all dwelled on the opposition between reason and revelation. But the radical separation of Christian faith from reason, he argues, began with Kierkegaard's response to Hegel's *Phenomenology*. Frank sees a similarity between Kierkegaard's and Dostoevsky's "dialectical hovering" above the abyss of doubt (p. 162). Richard Gill, in "*The Rime of the Ancient Mariner and Crime and Punishment*," in *Philosophy and Literature*, Fall 1981, p. 145, observes that the strategy of emphasizing the irrationality of faith became prevalent only after the Renaissance ushered in the triumph of the geometrical model of reason.

91. *"...vseobchshaia kosnost' i mekhanizm veschestva znachit smert!"* *PSS*, Vol. 20 (op. cit.), p. 175.

92. Anna Dostoevsky, *Reminiscences*, translated by Beatrice Stillman, NY, 1975, p. 134: "His agitated face had a kind of dread in it, something I had noticed more than once during the first moments of an epileptic seizure." For the Russian text, see A.G. Dostoevskaia, *Vospominaniia*, edited by S.V. Belov and V. A. Tunimanov, Moscow, 1971.

93. "Looking at that picture you get the impression of nature as some enormous, implacable, and dumb beast, or, to put it more correctly, though it may seem strange, as some huge engine of the latest design, which has senselessly seized, cut to pieces, and swallowed up—impassively and unfeelingly—a great and priceless Being, a Being worth the whole of nature and its laws, worth the entire earth, which was perhaps created solely for the coming of that Being!" (F. Dostoevsky, *The Idiot*, translated by David Magarschack, Penguin Books, p. 447).

NOTES FROM THE UNDERGROUND — PART I

1. A. Gersten, *Polnoe Sobranie Sochinenii v 30. tomakh*, Tom XVI, "Russkim Ofitseram v Pol'she," pp. 251–256, Moscow, 1959.

2. Quoted by Joseph Frank, *Dostoevsky: The Stir of Liberation, 1860–65* (op. cit.), p. 274.

3. N.N. Strakhov, in *F.M. Dostoevskii v vospominanii sovremennikov*, Tom I, ed. by V.V. Grigorenko et al. (*Khudozhestvennaia literatura*), 1964, discusses his article "Rokovoi vopros" and the closing down of *Vremya*. In spite of Katkov's review in the June 1863 issue of *Russkii Vestnik*, explaining Strakhov's views, the government remained inflexible. After much lobbying, the censors authorized the publication of another journal by the Dostoevsky brothers. *Epokha* began in January 1864.

4. Both parts appeared in *Epokha* on June 4, 1864.

5. *F.M. Dostoevskii, Pis'ma* (1832–1867), ed. by A.S. Dolinin, *Moskva*, 1928, Letter 196, pp. 358–363. *"Budet veshch' sil'naia, i otkrovennaia; budet pravda. Khot' i durno budet pozhalui, no efekt proizvedet. Ia znaiu"* (p. 362).

6. See *Istochniki teksta*, in *F.M. Dostoevskii, Polnoe Sobranie Sochinenii v 30. Tomakh* (op. cit.), Tom V, pp. 374–383.

7. Ibid., p. 375.
8. I quote from "Notes from the Underground," in *Three Short Novels of Dostoevsky*, translated by Constance Garnett, Anchor Books, Doubleday, NY, 1960, Part I, ch. vii, p. 196. For the Russian text, see Tom V, of *Polnoe Sobranie...* (op. cit.) pp. 99–180.
9. Ibid.
10. Alexander Herzen, *From the Other Shore* (op. cit.), Ch. VI, "Omnia mea mecum porto," p. 139.
11. Ralph E. Matlaw (ed.), *Notes from the Underground and the Grand Inquisitor*, Dutton Paperback, NY, 1960, in his "Introduction" (pp. vii-xxii), identifies Rousseau and Hegel as the prime targets of the underground man's attacks on European rationalism.
    William J. Leatherbarrow, in *Fëdor Dostoevsky* (Twayne's World Authors Series), Boston, 1981, sees the *Notes* as "the greatest critique of narrow intellectualism and overrefined consciousness ever written, as well as a disturbing rejection of the ideals of the Enlightenment." He also notes that the underground man is a "captive of his own dialectical consciousness" (p. 67).
12. N.G. Chernyshevskii, *Chto delat'? Iz rasskazov o novykh liudiakh* (Ogiz), Moskva, 1949. I quote from Nikolai Chernyshevsky, *What Is To Be Done?* translated by Michael R. Katz, Cornell U. Press, 1989. See Michael Katz and William Wagner, "Introduction," pp. 21–27, for the history of the novel's composition.
13. Ralph E. Matlaw, in the "Introduction" to his edition of *NU* (op. cit.), details Dostoevsky's reaction to *Chto delat'?*, notably his criticism of the novel's form and ideas in the first issue of *Epokha*, to which *Sovremennik* replied by printing Schedrin's satirical fable, "The Swallows," directed at the editorial board of *Vremya* and *Epokha*. Dostoevsky rejoined with "Mr. Schedrin, or Schism among the Nihilists." Matlaw observes that while these polemics did provide the impetus and the direction of *The Notes*, the ideas thus advanced had long geminated in Dostoevsky's mind.
14. *NU*, Part I, p. 179. N.G. Chernyshevskii, in "Moi svidaniia s F.M. Dostoevskim" (1888), in *F.M. Dostoevskii v vospominanii sovremennikov* (op. cit.), describes a visit from Dostoevsky in early May 1862 at a time when fires, believed to be the work of revolutionary arsonists, had destroyed the Tolkuchii Market in Petersburg. Chernyshevsky reports that Dostoevsky urged him to use his influence with radical youth to put an end to the arsons. Realizing that he could not persuade Dostoevsky that he knew nothing about the fires, Chernyshevsky proceeded to treat

him as if he were a sick man beyond the reach of reason, gently leading him away from the inflammatory topic.
It is amusing to speculate on the effect this clinical forbearance
might have had on the hypersensitive Dostoevsky. Chernyshevsky
was arrested on July 7, 1862 and incarcerated in the Peter and Paul
Fortress.

15. Joseph Frank, in "Nihilism and *Notes from Underground*," *The
Sewanee Review*, vol. LXIX, 1961, pp. 1–33, sees *Notes* as "one mag-
nificent satirical parody" of Chernyshevsky's novel. He reads
Dostoevsky's intertextual strategy as an attempt "to undermine these
doctrines from within" (p. 4).

16. *What Is To Be Done?* (op. cit.), Ch. 4, ch. xvi, "Vera Pavlovna's Fourth
Dream," p. 361.

17. Ibid., ch. xvi, section 4, p. 365. In this section, Rousseau's *La Nouvelle
Héloise* is mentioned for its contribution to the cause of women's
sexual equality.

18. Ibid., ch. xvi., section 5, p. 367.

19. The insertion of *The Symposium* as intertext is deliberate and subversive, just as the allusion to Plato's myth of the cave in Vera
Pavlovna's first dream (ch. xii "Verochka's First Dream," pp.
129–131), in which she is delivered from being locked in a dark cellar. The radicals of the sixties decried Plato as the father of philosophical idealism. D.S. Pisarev, in "Plato's Idealism" (*Russian
Philosophy*, Vol. I, pp. 66–79), links Plato's lack of empiricism and his
preference for abstraction to his aristocratic approach to life and says
that he shows "no rational love for mankind, no respect for the individual" (p. 67). For the Russian text see D.I. Pisarev, *Sochineniia D.I.
Pisareva v 6. tomakh*, Tom I, pp. 275–280.

20. *Winter Notes*, Ch. 6, "Essay on the Bourgeoisie," p. 110.

21. *What Is To Be Done?*, Ch. xvi, section 8, p. 370.

22. Ibid.

23. Ibid., Ch. 2, "First Love and Legal Marriage," ch. xxiv, "Eulogy of
Marya Aleksevna," p. 167.

24. Jacques Catteau, in *La création littéraire* (op. cit.), notes that "the
acquisitive socialist" is a set type in Dostoevsky's writings and by no
means an exception (p. 250).

25. *NU*, Part I, ch. vii, p. 200.

26. Ibid., p. 201.

27. *NU*, Part I, ch. x, pp, 210–211.

28. *NU*, Part II, p. 221.

29. Leatherbarrow (op. cit.) treats the underground man as a quintessential Romantic, because of the flight from reason, his self-identification with literary heroes and his paradoxical mode of exposition (p. 66).
30. *NU*, Part i, ch. vii, p. 197.
31. *NU*, Part i, ch. ix, p. 208.
32. In Ch. V, "Consolatio," of Herzen's *From the Other Shore*, the ironic doctor who acts as his persona points out that Rousseau's famed aphorism "Man is born free" is an a priori declaration (p. 108).
33. *NU*, Part I, ch. xi, p. 209.
34. *NU*, Part I, ch. iii, p. 186.
35. Ibid., p. 189.
36. *NU*, Part I, ch. vii, p. 200.
37. *NU*, Part II, p. 297.
38. Mikhail Bakhtin, in *Problemy poetiki Dostoevskogo* (*Sovetskii Pisatel'*), Moskva, 1963, p. 310, suggests that the deliberate reversal of esthetic values in the opening lines: "I am a sick man.... I am a spiteful man. I am an unattractive man..." manifests something akin to *iurodstvo*, the religious practice of deliberate self-abasement aimed at confounding the wisdom of this world. But it seems clear to me that the underground man's habit of self-humiliation is an inverted form of self-assertion. The comparison with the holy fool can only be taken in a parodistic vein.

Alternately, one might read the underground man's negative self-presentation as a variation on the rhetorical paradox, a form of discourse that praises things and values held in common contempt. Gary Saul Morson, in "Paradoxical Dostoevsky," *Slavic and East European Journal*, Vol. 43, No. 3, Fall 1999, takes this approach. He writes that, "given his interest in menippaean satire, it is odd that Bakhtin never notices the profound importance in Dostoevsky's work of the rhetorical paradox" (p. 483). I too, like Morson, have drawn on Rosalie L. Cowlie's *Paradoxia Epidemica: The Renaissance Tradition of Paradox*, Princeton U. Press, 1966, for my understanding of the varieties of paradoxy.
39. *NU*, Part I, ch. viii, p. 203.
40. Lev Shestov, "Preodolenie samoochevidnostei, Otkroveniia smerti, Na Vesakh Iova," *Sovremennye Zapiski*, Paris, 1929, p. 54.
41. Lev Shestov, *Dostoevskii i filosofiia tragedii*, Berlin 1922 (originally written in 1901), p. 40.
42. Lev Shestov, "Preodolenie Samoochevidnostei..." (op. cit.), p. 50: "Dostoevsky is precisely attacking rational evidence. What we call

rationally self-evident is nothing but what we accept as such and, in the same way, he (Dostoevsky) tells us about it all the time — our life is not life, but death. And if you want to grasp Dostoevsky, you must constantly bear in mind that 2 by 2 is 4 means the beginning of death" (translation mine).

43. Letter 11, dated from Paris, June 1849, *Pis'ma iz Frantsii i Italii* (op. cit.), p. 80.

44. *NU*, Part I, ch. iii, p. 186.

45. Joseph Frank, "Nihilism and *Notes from Underground*," *Sewanee Review*, 1961 (op. cit.) quotes Apollinaria Suslova, who made the same mistake as Shestov in identifying the underground man's voice with Dostoevsky's own: "What kind of a scandalous tale are you writing?... I don't like it, when you write cynical things. It doesn't suit you" (p. 279).

N.N. Strakhov, in a letter to Leo Tolstoy, dated November 28, 1883, where he repeats the unsubstantiated rumor about Dostoevsky's rape of a little girl, writes, "The characters whom he most resembles are the hero of *Notes from the Underground*, Svidrigailov in *Crime and Punishment* and Stavrogin in *The Devils*. Katkov did not want to print one scene from Stavrogin (debauchery and other things), but Dostoevsky read it to many at the time...." (*Perepiska L.N. Tolstogo s N.N. Strakhovym*, 1870–1894, St. Petersburg, 1914, p. 378).

For the refutation of the rape slander see V.N. Zakharov, "Fakty protiv legendy," *Problemy izucheniia Dostoevskogo*, Petrozavodsk, 1978, pp. 79–109. He shows that the rumor surrounding the suppressed chapter "At Tikhnon's" was fuelled by Turgenev in the late 1870s and D.V. Grigorovich in early 1880s. Anna Grigorievna defended her husband in "Conversation with Tolstoy." See *Vospominaniia A.G. Dostoevskoi* (op. cit.) pp. 391–395.

Robert Louis Jackson, in "A View from the Underground," in *Dialogues with Dostoevsky: The Overwhelming Questions*, Stanford U. Press, 1993, pp. 104–120, suggests that Strakhov's motive for circulating the slander may have been revenge for Dostoevsky's sketch of Strakhov as "the purest strain of the seminarian, a type lacking all civic duty with a taste for a cushy life and a greed for fame" (Notebook for *A Writer's Diary*, 1877).

46. *NU*, Part I, p. 179. In the editorial announcement for Epokha, Dostoevsky notes the passing of that generation in these terms: "*My vidim, kak ischezaet nashe sovremennoe pokolenie, samo soboiu, vialo i bessledno, zaiavliaia sebia strannymi e neveroiatnymi dlia potomstva priznaniiami svoikh 'lishnikh liudei' *" (*Istochniki teksta*, p. 376).

47. Robert Louis Jackson, *Dostoevsky's Underground Man in Russian Literature* (Mouton), The Hague, 1958, p. 14.

48. Joseph Frank, "Nihilism and *Notes from Underground*" (op. cit.), p. 4. Later, in *The Stir of Liberation* (op. cit.), Frank will draw attention to the parallel that exists between the situation of the underground man— a man trapped within a deterministic system that his reason accepts even while his will rejects it— and the lead character in Diderot's *Le neveu de Rameau* (1765), who, too, exemplifies the consequences of accepting radical materialism as a philosophical system. The comparison between the underground man and Rameau's nephew was first made by Vasili Rozanov, in *Legenda o Velikom Inkvizitore*, St. Petersburg, 1894, p. 27. See also A. Grigoriev, "Dostoevskii i Didro," *Russkaia Literatura*, 4, 1966, pp. 88–102.

In *Phenomenology of the Spirit* Hegel analyzed the case of Rameau's nephew as a negative character, the master of the dialectic of irony, who pits his act of negation against the stagnant thesis of physiological materialism and, in the process, revitalizes the ideas of "good" and "evil."

Michel Foucault, in *Histoire de la folie à l'âge classique*, 3ᵉ partie (Gallimard), Paris, 1972, identifies buffoonery as a common strain in the discourse of both Rameau's nephew and the underground man. In Foucault's theory, buffoonery is the self-caricatural form that madness assumes, once it is radically marginalized and driven out of society.

More recently, Jacques-Jude Lepine, in "Le neveu souterrain: la conscience subjective dans *Le Neveu de Rameau et Les Mémoires Ecrites dans un Souterrain*," *Constructions*, Saratoga, Ca. (Anma Libri & Co), 1986, pp. 53–64, sees Diderot's character as an embryonic underground man, a little man devoured by envy of his genial uncle, inaugurating the lineage of Nietzschean resentment.

49. *Letter to Michelet* (op. cit.), p 180.

50. *NU*, Part I, ch. iii, p. 189.

51. *Istochniki teksta* (op. cit.) p. 377.

52. Joseph Frank, "Nihilism and *Notes from Underground*" (op. cit.), p. 7.

53. *NU*, part I, ch. iii, p. 189. "*Razumeetsia, ia ne prob'iu takoi steny lbom, esli i v samom dele sil ne budet probit', no ia ne promirius' s nei potomy tol'ko, chto u menia kamennaia stena i u menia sil ne khvatilo*" (pp. 105–106) *PSS*, Tom 5.

54. *NU*, Part I, ch. ii, p. 184.

55. Ralph E. Matlaw, in his "Introduction" (op. cit.), made that point.

154 THE SCANDAL OF REASON

56. *NU*, Part I, ch. ii, p. 183. The underground man's throwaway, dismissive allusion to Kant's fusion of moral and esthetic values in the essay "Of the Lofty and the Beautiful" highlights the gap in sensibility that separates this nineteenth-century Romantic dialectician from the rationalists of the Enlightenment, who believed that man could live in harmony with his conscience and with nature.

57. *NU*, Part I, ch. ii, p. 189.

58. Ibid., p. 184. Malcolm Jones, in *Dostoevsky: The Novel of Discord* (Harper and Row), NY, 1976, emphasizes the underground man's "cult of perversity" and his propensity for self-contradiction, which entraps him in the procedures of reason that he so vehemently denounces. William J. Leatherbarrow (op. cit.) points out that the underground man "uses reason, but never transcends it" (p. 67).

59. *PSS*, Tom 20 (op. cit.), p. 175.

60. "The slave's revolt in morals begins with this, that *ressentiment* itself becomes creative and gives birth to values: the *ressentiment* of those who are denied the real action, that of the deed, and who compensate with an imaginary revenge" (From *Toward a Genealogy of Morals*, 1887, in *The Portable Nietzsche*, edited and translated by Walter Kaufmann [Penguin Books] 1982, p. 451). About Dostoevsky, Nietzsche wrote in a letter to Overbeck, dated from Nizza, February 23, 1887: "...I did not even know the name of Dostoevski just a few weeks ago—uneducated person that I am, not reading any journals. An accidental reach of an arm in a bookstore brought to my attention *L'esprit souterrain*, a work just translated into French.... The instinct of kinship (or how should I name it?) spoke up immediately; my joy was extraordinary... (it is two novellas, the first really a piece of music, *very* strange, very *un*-German music; the second, a stroke of genius in psychology, a kind of self-derision of the *gnosi auton*)" (p. 455). Somewhat later, in a letter to Georg Brandes, dated November 20, 1888, he nuanced his judgment: "Dostoevsky's work was the most valuable psychological material known to me—I am grateful to him in a remarkable way, however much he goes against my deepest instincts" (*Selected Letters of Friedrich Nietzsche*, edited and translated by Christopher Middleton, Chicago, 1969, p. 327). Robert Louis Jackson has analyzed this complex relationship of affinity and contrast in his brilliant essay, "Counter-point: Nietzsche and Dostoevsky," *Dialogues with Dostoevsky* (op. cit.), pp. 237–250. Jackson argues that both thinkers recoil from the nature of man as they find him in raw reality—Nietzsche seeks a redeeming vision in the Apollonian illusion of esthetic experience, in the poetry of

self-transcendence, whereas Dostoevsky finds redemption in the poetry of ecstatic populism.

61. Albert Camus, *L'homme révolté, Essais*, Paris, 1967, p. 427: *"Le ressentiment est très bien défini par Scheler comme une auto-intoxication, la sécrétion néfaste en vase clos d'une impuissance préconçue."*

62. *NU*, Part I, ch. vi., p. 195.

63. *From the Other Shore* (op. cit.), p. 3. In Kirilov's suicide note, in Part III, Ch. VI, "A Busy Night," ch. ii of *The Devils* (op. cit., p. 632), at a moment when the "bridge-builder's" supreme emancipatory gesture is about to collapse into mockery, Dostoevsky delivers his not so well-concealed barb at Herzen the man: "I'll sign it again in French, you know. *De Kiriloff, gentilhomme russe et citoyen du monde civilisé...*" and at his Western values: *"Liberté, égalité, fraternité, ou la mort!"*

64. Alexander Herzen, *My Past and Thoughts* (op. cit.), "Moscow, Petersburg and Novgorod (1840–47)," p. 237.

65. *The Reaction in Germany* (op. cit.), p. 397.

66. *NU*. Part II, ch. i, p. 217.

67. "Unglückliches Bewusstein" in Hegel's *The Phenomenology of the Spirit* characterizes the state of isolation from the stream of life, which the Spirit experiences when it first pits itself against Nature. For Hegel, this marks the lowest stage of emerging consciousness. The true philosopher is not divorced from the external world, but comprehends himself in the act of his mind's manifestation outside the confines of his own self. In Hegel's system, Nature and Mind share the same origin but are not co-equal branches.
   V.V. Kirpotin, in *F.M. Dostoevskii, Tvorcheskii Put', 1821–59* (Gostizdat), Moskva, 1960, pp. 482–497, has argued that the underground man's consciousness demonstrated that Hegel's absolute idealism negates freedom, leading to fatalism.

68. *A Writer's Diary.* (op. cit.), 1873, "Old People," p. 126.

69. Ibid. pp. 126–127.

70. *NU*, Part II, ch. i, p. 218–219.

71. "Vixerunt!" (op. cit.) p. 74.

72. Ibid. p. 75.

73. "Before the Storm" (op. cit.) p. 74.

74. Ibid., p. 36.

75. *NU*, Part II, ch. ix, p. 290.

76. "...puskai otsa zastavliat/ menia derzhat', kak syna, ne kak, mysh/ rozhdennuiu v podpol'e...". See A.L. Bem, O Dostoevskom, Vol. ii, Prague, 1933, p. 17.

77. *NU*, Part I, ch. iii, p. 168.
78. *Kontsy i nachala* (op. cit.), p. 176.
79. A.S. Pushkin, *Izbrannye Proizvedeniia* (Lenizdat), 1973, pp. 180–181.
80. *The Reaction in Germany* (op. cit.), pp. 404 and 405.
81. Ibid., p. 406.
82. *NU*, Part II, ch. x, p. 297.

NOTES FROM THE UNDERGROUND — PART II

1. Letter to Mikhail, dated April 13, 1864, in Pis'ma (op. cit.) Letter 198, p. 365.
2. NU, Part II, ch.i, p. 180.
3. P.V. Annenkov, in "Zametki o russkoi literature," *Sovremennik*, No. 1, otd. III, 1849, p. 10, noted that *"syroi dozhdik i mokryi sneg"* were characteristic of the Petersburg landscape favored by the practitioners of the natural school.
4. *NU*, Part II, ch. 1, p. 216.
5. *What Is To Be Done?*, Ch. 3, "Marriage and Second Love," ch. viii, pp. 209–210.
6. *NU*, Part II, ch. iv, p. 250.
7. *NU*, Part II, ch. v, p. 52.
8. Ibid., p. 255.
9. *A Writer's Diary*, "The Russian Society for the Protection of Animals," January 1876, pp. 327–328.
10. *NU*, Part II, ch. vi, p. 267.
11. *NU*, Part II, ch. ix, p. 289.
12. Ibid.
13. Ibid., p. 291. Robert Louis Jackson has drawn attention to Dostoevsky's use of the word "suddenly" (*vdrug*), which often signals the crumbling of the outer wall of reality and the opening out to the time of *kairos*. In this transformational moment, suddenly, the leap of faith into the true freedom of the spirit has become possible. Jackson writes: "...and *suddenly* (*vdrug*) is one of his favorite words..." leading up to "a poetry that in spiritual-religious terms is revelation but in purely esthetic terms for Dostoevsky means a triumph over naturalistic surface reality, a disclosure of the rich but usually masked interiority of man and human reality" ("Counterpoint: Nietzsche and Dostoevsky," op. cit., p. 240).

14. *NU*, Part II, ch. ix, p. 291.
15. *NU*, Part II, ch. x, p. 292.
16. *PSS*, Tom 20, pp. 191–194.
17. Ibid., p. 172: "*Mezhdu tem posle poiavleniia Khrista, kak ideala che-loveka vo ploti, stalo iasno kak den', chto vysochaishee, poslednee razvi-tie lichnosti imenno i dolzhno doiti do togo (vo samom kontse razvitiia, v samom punkte dostizheniia tseli) chtob chelovek nashel, soznal i vsei siloi svoei prirody ubedilsia, chto vysochaishee upotreblenie, kotoroe mozhet sdelat' chelovek iz svoei lichnosti, iz polnoty razvitiia svoego ia —eto kak by unichtozhit' eto ia, otdat' ego tselikom vsem i kazhdomu bezrazdel'no i bezzavetno. I eto velichaishee schastie. Takim obrazom, zakon ia slivaetsia s zakonom gumanizma, a v slitii, oba, i ia i vse (po-vidimomu, dve krainie protivopolozhnosti) vzaimno unichtozhennye drug druga, v to zhe samoe vremia dostigaiut i vysshei tseli svoego indi-vidual'nogo razvitiia kazhdyi osobo.*"
18. *Pis'ma* (op. cit.) Vol. I, p. 353.
19. "Introduction" (op. cit.) p. xvi. Jacques Catteau, in *La création lit-téraire* (op. cit.), puts the same idea in philosophical terms: "*L'affirmation est posée par la double négation du déterminisme et de la liberté totale, illimitée...*" (p. 114). Catteau sees Dostoevsky's mind as fundamentally dialectical but tempted by "*la conciliation des inc-onciliables*" (p. 118). I agree that Dostoevsky thinks dialectically and creates voices he pits against each other in a polyphonic manner, cre-ating what Catteau calls "*une polyphonie qui s'oppose à la nécéssité de conclure,* sinon par l'expérience tragique..." (emphasis mine).
20. *NU*, Part I, ch. x, p. 211.
21. Ibid., p. 212.
22. Camus' intertextual dialogue with Dostoevsky's *Notes* has been noted and analyzed by many critics. Elizabeth Trahan, in her pio-neering essay "Clamence vs. Dostoevsky: An Approach to *La Chute*," vol. XVIII of *Comparative Literature*, 1966, draws attention to Camus' lifelong interest in and his many references to Dostoevsky. She particularly notes the parallels between the uses of "expansive monologue" in both texts (p. 339). Ernest Sturm, *Conscience et impuissance chez Dostoievski et Camus, Parallèle entre 'Le sous-sol' et 'La Chute'* (Librairie A.G. Nizet), Paris, 1967, compares the under-ground man and Clamence as two types who exemplify the moral malaise of their time. He also explores the uses of the first-person narrative in the two texts.
    More recently, Krisztine Horvath, in "Dostoievski et Camus, Introduction à une analyse comparée," *Acta Litteraria Academiae*

Scientiarum Hungaricae, Budapest, 1983, Vol. XXX, Nos 3 and 4, offered a Christian existentialist interpretation of both texts, linking them to Kierkegaard.

Shoshana Felman, in "The Betrayal of the Witness: Camus' *The Fall*," *Testimony* (Routledge), NY and London, 1992, discusses the ambiguity of Clamence's moral posture against the background of the Holocaust. She notes that the false confessor repeats his testimony in a deceptive game of confession, tracing a pattern of repetition in the shape of concentric circles. The implied allusion to Dante in the portrayal of the stagnant, circular time of the damned is picked up in Nola M. Leov, "Thalassa, Thalassa: Camus' Use of Imagery in *La Chute*," *New Zealand Journal of French Studies*, November 1993, p. 5–29, as well as in Adrian Van Den Hoven and Basil D. Kingstone, in "Amsterdam as a Source of Symbols for Camus' *The Fall*," *Canadian Journal of Netherlandic Studies*, Fall 1993.

23. *La Chute*, p. 86: "un enfer mou," and also, on pp. 19–20: "*l'enfer bourgeois, naturellement peuplé de mauvais rêves.*"

24. Ibid., p. 15: "*Mon métier est double—je suis juge-pénitent.…*" The term "*vocation des sommets*" is used by Clamence in reference to his former career as a lawyer in Paris, a defender of victims (p. 32).

25. Interestingly, Clamence places himself in the First Circle of the Inferno, among the Neutrals.

26. Clamence compounds his rhetorical act of dominance with the addition of a hyperbolic abstraction, whereby the transference of guilt to the shadowy "other" in front of him comes to encompass all of Europe. "*Tout ce continent m'est soumis sans le savoir*" (p. 158).

27. *NU*, Part II, p. 297. In her insightful essay "Dora and the Underground Man," *Russian Literature and Psychoanalysis*, Vol. 31, ed. by Daniel Rancour-Laferrière (John Benjamin's Publishing Co.), Amsterdam/Philadelphia, 1989, pp. 417–429, Harriet Muraw treats the text's lack of closure as a device that reveals the underground man to be a "melancholic," subject to a form of neurosis Freud analyzed in his paper "Mourning and Melancholy" (1917). Muraw explains: "The melancholic is someone whose masochistic pleasure in self-torment never permits the work of mourning to come to a close" (p. 421). Further, she says: "Dostoevsky would permit us to discern the symptoms of melancholy in the *Notes*, but only if we recognize that the lost object is God" (p. 427).

28. Gary Rosenfeld, "The Fate of Dostoevsky's Underground Man: The Case for an Open Ending," *SEEJ*, Vol. 28, no. 3, Fall 1984, pp. 87–100.

29. Robin Feuer Miller, "Rousseau and Dostoevsky: The Morality of the Confession Reconsidered," *Western Philosophical Systems in Russian Literature*, ed. by M. Mlikotin, U. of Southern California Press, 1979, pp. 91–93.

30. Irene Kirk, "Dramatization of Consciousness in Albert Camus' *La Chute* and Dostoevsky's *Notes from Underground*," *Bucknell Review*, No. 16, 1968.

Rousseau prefaces his *Confessions* (1770) with a declaration that insists on the uniqueness of his project: *"En guise de prologue: Voici le seul portrait d'homme peint exactement d'après nature, et dans toute sa vérité, qui existe et qui probablement existera jamais."* Again, in *"Livre premier"* (1712–1728): *"Je forme une entreprise qui n'eut jamais d'exemple et dont l'exécution n'aura point d'imitateur. Je veux montrer à mes semblables un homme dans toute la vérité de la nature; et cet homme sera moi...."* (Quoted from *Les Confessions* de Jean-Jacques Rousseau (J.J. Pauvert), Paris, p. 61.) It is obvious that Dostoevsky understood the psychological mechanism at work here as a particularly noxious form of self-assertion. The underground man, whose own performance offers a comeuppance to Rousseau's claim of inimitable uniqueness, says: "I will observe, in parenthesis, that Heine says that a true autobiography is almost an impossibility, and that man is bound to lie about himself. He considers that Rousseau certainly told lies about himself in his confessions, and even intentionally lied, out of vanity. I am convinced that Heine is right...." (*NU*, Part I, ch. xi, p. 213).

The story of *"le ruban volé"* (1728) from *Livre Deuxième of Les Confessions* (1770) is plagiarized by Ferdyshchenko in Part I, ch 4 of *The Idiot*, where the article stolen by the confessor is a three-ruble note, instead of an old ribbon. But in both stories, the crux of the matter lies in the victimization of a servant girl (Marion in Rousseau's tale and Darya in Fredyshchenko's imitation) who is publicly denounced for the theft as the real perpetrator stands by in silence.

Rousseau treats his "crime" with the full weight of moral self-reproach it deserves: *"Ce poids est donc resté jusqu'à ce jour sans allègement sur ma conscience, et je puis dire que le désir de m'en délivrer en quelque sorte a beaucoup contribué à la résolution que j'ai prise d'écrire mes confessions"* (p. 166). By contrast, Ferdyshchenko's retelling of Rousseau's memory is intended as light entertainment, a token he antes up in a social game of competing vanities. When Nastasya Filipovna unmasks Ferdyshchenko's strategy of inverted self-praise, she indirectly implicates Rousseau's profession of shame in her exposure.

The *"ruban volé"* episode, used as intertext in a trite performance by an obvious liar, thus completes the destruction of Rousseau that began with the underground man's jibe at *"l'homme de la nature et de la vérité,"* in Part I, ch. iii, of *Notes* (p. 187).

31. *NU*, Part I, ch. xi, pp. 213–214. Bernard I. Paris, in *"Notes from the Underground*: A Horneyan Analysis," *PLMA*, 1973, pp. 511–522, interprets the irrationalist philosophy in Part I as the underground man's attempt to rationalize his past behavior.

32. *NU*, Part I, ch. xi, p. 213: "I write only for myself, and I wish to declare once and for all that if I write as though I were addressing readers, that is simply because it is easier for me to write in that form —I shall never have readers. I have made this plain already...."

33. *NU*, Part II, ch. x, p. 297.

34. *Pis'ma* (op. cit.), Vol. I, Letter 61, dated from Omsk, February 20, 1854, p. 142: *"Malo togo, eslib kto mne dokazal, chto Khristos vne istiny, i deistvitel'no bylo by chto istina vne Khrista, to mne luchshe khotelos' by ostavat'sia so Khristom, nezheli s istinoi."*

35. Robert Louis Jackson, in "Bakhtin's Poetics of Dostoevsky and Dostoevsky's Declaration of Religious Faith," *Dialogues With Dostoevsky* (op. cit.) pp. 251–269, writes in Note 77 to his text that the underground man is "lost in the logical tangle of his rationalistic consciousness, his vicious circle made of his desire to have faith and his unwillingness to accept his faith" (p. 334). Earlier in the same essay he refers to "the tragic *perpetuum mobile* of the underground man" (p. 290).

36. Quoted by Jacques Catteau, in *La création littéraire* (op. cit.), p. 477, in the context of a discussion of Dostoevsky's device of supercharging narrative time to the point of explosion. Catteau, along with Bakhtin, recognizes the cataclysmic condensation of events and the fracturing of the narrative line as characteristic features of Dostoevsky's novelistic style. And, not unlike Jackson, he sees the feverish motion of Dostoevskian time as an upward spiral, surging towards the transformational moment of *kairos*, which he calls *"le temps de puissance"* (p. 472).

37. *The Portable Nietzsche* (op. cit.), pp. 454–455.

38. Nikolai Berdiaev, *Mirosozertsanie Dostoevskogo*, Paris, 1968, p. 59. Jackson, who quotes this saying by Berdiaev in his essay on Nietzsche and Dostoevsky, "Counterpoint" (op. cit.), counters that it is equally true when turned around.

THE BROTHERS KARAMAZOV

1. In his letter to the editor, N. A. Liubimov, dated from Petersburg, November 8, 1880, Dostoevsky writes: "I am sending off to the *Russian Herald* the concluding Epilogue of the Karamazovs, which ends the novel.... Well, and now the novel is finished! I worked on it for three years, published it for two—a great moment for me. Toward Christmas I want to issue a separate edition." Quoted from *The Brothers Karamazov*, ed. Ralph E. Matlaw (Norton) New York 1976, "Background and Sources," pp. 768–769. Unless otherwise indicated I cite from this edition of the novel, in the Constance Garnett translation, revised by Ralph E. Matlaw. For the Russian text, I have used F. M. Dostoevskii, Vol. 14 and 15, *Polnoe Sobranie Sochinenii v 30. tomakh*, ed. G. M. Fridlender (Nauka), Leningrad, 1976.

2. "This is the most 'constructed' and ideologically complete of all Dostoevsky's works," notes Konstantin Mochulsky in *Dostoevsky: His Life and Work*, Princeton, 1967. I quote from "Essays in Criticism," p. 776, in the Matlaw edition of *BK*. See Victor Terras, *A Karamazov Companion: Commentary on the Genesis, Language and Style of Dostoevsky's Novel*, U. Wisconsin, 1981, pp. 43–47, for a discussion of the allegorical dimension of the novel. Terras credits Vyacheslav Ivanov for being the first to read *BK* as an allegory.

3. L. M. Reynus, in *Dostoevskii v Staroi Russe*, Leningrad, 1971, establishes Staraia Russa, a spa town to the south of Petersburg, where Dostoevsky vacationed with his family from 1872 on, as the model for the fictional Skotoprigonevsk. He points out that in 1874 Dostoevsky moved to Iliinskii Street, a name that resurrected in his mind the memory of Dmitri Iliinskii, a fellow convict in Omsk—a nobleman condemned for ten years for the murder of his father and later found to be innocent. On September 13, 1874, Dostoevsky jotted down in his Notebook: "Plot. In Tobolsk, twenty years ago, like Ilinsky's case. Two brothers, an old father, one is engaged to a girl with whom the second is secretly and enviously in love. But she loves the older. But the older, a young lieutenant, carouses and plays the fool, quarrels with the father. The father disappears. For several days neither hide nor hair of him. The brothers discuss the inheritance. And suddenly the authorities: the body is dug out of the cellar. Evidence against the older (the younger does not live with him). The older is tried and sentenced to penal servitude...." (Quoted in "Background and Sources," the Matlaw edition of *BK*, p. 749).

4. *BK*, Part II, Book 5, Ch. vi, "For a While a Very Obscure One," p. 245.

5. Ibid., ch vii, "It's Always Worthwhile Speaking to a Clever Man," p. 255.
6. The facts and circumstances surrounding the violent death were never legally established. V.S. Nechaeva, in *Rannii Dostoevskii*, Moscow, 1979, having examined the evidence, supports the family lore about the murder as an act of revenge by the serfs against a despotic, sexually predatory master. That lore was made public in L.F. Dostoevskaia's biography of her novelist father, published in Germany, *Dostojewski*, München, 1920.
7. Part II, Book 5, ch. vii, p. 257.
8. Ibid, p. 258.
9. Ibid, p. 259.
10. Freud's article, "Dostoevsky and Parricide," was begun in June 1926 and published in 1928. The biographical data used by Freud to construct the theoretical model of Dostoevsky's psyche are based on René Fülöp-Miller, *Dostojeewskijs heilige Krankheit*, Zurich, 1926. The latter relies on L.F. Dostoevskaia. See Sigmund Freud, *Standard Edition of the Collected Psychological Works*, ed. James Strachey (Hogarth Press) London, 1961, pp. 177–194. I quote from *Dostoevsky: A Collection of Critical Essays*, ed. René Wellek, Englewood Cliffs, NJ, 1962, p. 102.
11. Ibid., p. 108.
12. Slobodanka Vladiv-Glover, in "Dostoevsky, Freud and Parricide: Deconstructive Notes on *The Brothers Karamazov*," *New Zealand Slavonic Journal*, 1993, pp. 7–34, argues that Freud proceeded from an a priori assumption that Dostoevsky's epilepsy was a hysterical and not a physical phenomenon, which required no proof beyond what could be found in his artistic self-expression. She points out that Freud does not offer a detailed analysis of *The Brothers Karamazov* and approaches Fyodor's murder as a psychic act, shared by all four brothers, rather than an actual event.
13. Joseph Frank, in *Dostoevsky: The Seeds of Rebellion*, (1821–1849), Appendix: "Freud's Case History of Dostoevsky," pp. 379–391, undermines Freud's linkage of Dostoevsky's epilepsy to the Oedipal trauma, presumably unleashed by the news of the father's sudden and violent death in June 1839. Frank places Dostoevsky's first epileptic fit in 1846. He also rejects the "legend" of Dostoevsky's adolescent hatred of his father, tracing it back to Strakhov-Miller's biography, which was repudiated by Dostoevsky's widow, Anna Grigorievna (Orest Miller i Nikolai Strakhov, *Biografiia, Pis'ma i Zametki iz Zapisnoi Knizhki F.M. Dostoevskogo*, St. Petersbrug, 1883).

More recently, Emmanuel Filhol in "Freud, lecteur de Dostoievski: épilepsie et rivalité oedipienne," *Neophilologus*, April 1993, accepts Freud's linkage of Dostoevsky's epilepsy with his parricidal desire and traces the first attack to age seven, when the boy heard his mother cry out at night from her bedroom. Filhol bases his "primal scene" scenario on a report by Leonid Grossman, who cites Anna Grigorievna as the original source. In Filhol's variation on the classical pattern of a son's desire to possess his mother and kill his father (a desire that must be repressed for fear of castration), the Oedipal subject identifies himself with the femininity of the mother as the object of the father's love. Freud himself had drawn attention to the symptom of latent homosexuality as a secondary manifestation of the Oedipal trauma. But unlike Freud, Filhol treats Dostoevsky's epilepsy as a physical phenomenon. More importantly, he criticizes Freud for giving a partial reading of the Oedipal myth as we know it from Sophocles, by ignoring the father Laius's guilt in ordering the death of his infant son: *"Les premières fautes de cette histoire ne sont pas celles du fils Oedipe, meurtrier de son père, époux de sa mère Jocaste, mais bien celles du père.... L'histoire d'Oedipe n'est pas qu'une histoire du parricide et d'inceste, mais celle d'un enfant sans place, d'un enfant déplacé, qui n'a pas su s'inscrire, à cause des fautes du père, dans une place clairement située, à la vraie place qui aurait dû légitimement lui être reconnue"* (p. 176). Seen in this light, the parricidal act is also an act of retribution against a tyrannical father, which assimilates it to the Schillerian script of righteous rebellion.

14. Louis Breger, *Dostoevsky: The Author as Psychoanalyst*, New York U. Press, 1989, p. 89. Breger's thesis is that "Dostoevsky's life and art are intermingled.... My position is that Dostoevsky's fiction is a literary transformation of his personal experience" (p. 68). In retracing Dostoevsky's childhood and family life Breger draws on the younger brother Andrei's reminiscences, written down in 1875 and revised in 1895–96. Breger works with a translation from the Russian edition of 1930, prepared for him by Karen Makoff.

15. "Onomastics (the study of the form of proper names) are crucial. The family name, the given names, the names of other characters always point to something significant. Dostoevsky distributed his spiritual and intellectual strivings and shortcomings, his physical drives and his disease among the four brothers. He endowed his favorite character with the name of his recently deceased young boy, Alexey; to Dmitri he gave his sensuality, to Ivan his dialectical and rational skills, to Smerdyakov his epilepsy; and to old Karamazov, the

source from which the novel turbulently flows, the father of us all, the creator of the novel, he assigned his own name, Fyodor— Theodore, 'the gift of God'! Indeed!" p. 763, Ralph E. Matlaw, "On Translating *The Brothers Karamazov*," the Norton edition of *BK*.

16. "Dostoevsky and Parricide," p. 105.

17. *BK*, Part I, Book 1, ch. v, "Elders," p. 21.

18. "Verily, verily, I say unto you, except a corn of wheat fall into the ground and die, it abideth alone: but if it die, it bringeth forth much fruit" (John 12:24).

19. See Dostoevsky's letter to his brother Nikolai, dated May 16, 1878 from Petersburg: "My very dear brother Nikolay Mikhaylovich, today our Alyosha died from a sudden attack of epilepsy, which he had never had before" (Letter No. 632, p. 756, "Backgrounds and Sources," *BK*). Breger (op. cit.) writes: "This was further stimulus to guilt that could be worked over in the writing of *The Brothers Karamazov*" (p. 224). Breger describes the two journeys Dostoevsky undertook at this time—the pilgrimage to Optina Pustyn' with Vladimir Soloviev and the solitary return to Darovoe with the nearby copse of Chermashnya as pivotal to the process of his final "disidentification" from the father (p. 228).

20. The transformational moment when bitter grief passes into gentle sorrow is reflected in the novel, in Part I, Book 2, ch. ii, "Peasant Women Who Have Faith." William J. Leatherbarrow, in *Fëdor Dostoevsky* (Twayne), Boston, 1981, reads this experience as a transformation of the complex guilt feelings surrounding the father-and-son relationship into a passionate sense of mutual obligations between father and son. Leatherbarrow considers *BK* as Dostoevsky's "final statement of faith in the existence of some higher, absolute, unifying harmony, which lies beyond man's rational awareness and which promises the ultimate reconciliation of man's discords and moral despair in the 'vale of tears' of earthly existence" (p. 146).

21. Part I, Book 2, ch. vii, "A Seminarian Bent on a Career," p. 69.

22. Part III, Book 8, ch. iv, "In the Dark," p. 370.

23. "It can scarcely be owing to chance that the masterpieces of the literature of all time—the *Oedipus Rex* of Sophocles, Shakespeare's *Hamlet* and Dostoevsky's *The Brothers Karamazov*—should all deal with the same subject: parricide. In all three, moreover, the motive for the deed, sexual rivalry for a woman, is laid bare." p. 107, "Dostoevsky and Parricide."

The reference to the "primal horde" of brothers who murdered their father, on p. 105 of this essay, reiterates the paradigm originally described by Freud in *Totem and Taboo* (1912–1913).

24. Part I, Book 3, ch. ix, "The Sensualists," p. 129.
25. "Dostoevsky and Parricide," p. 108.
26. The motif of "the tragedy of reason" was noted by Helen Muchnic, "Ivan Karamazov: The Tragedy of Reason," *Transactions of the Association of Russian-American Studies*, XIV, pp. 138–157.
27. "Dostoevsky and Parricide," p. 108.
28. Part I, Book 3, ch. ix, "The Sensualists," p. 131.
29. The phrase "But a man always talks of his own ache" is uttered by Dmitri, when he is about to reveal to Alyosha the particulars of his tortuous relationship with Katerina Ivanovna (Part I, Book 3, ch. iii, "The Confession of an Ardent Heart-in Verse," p. 97).
30. This point was made by F.F. Seelye, "Ivan Karamazov," Malcolm V. Jones and Garth M. Terry (eds.), *New Essays on Dostoevsky*, Cambridge U. Press, 1983, pp. 115–136.
31. Throughout this chapter I quote from David Grene's translation of Sophocles' *Oedipus the King*, in the University of Chicago edition of the text.
32. The narrator describes Fyodor as "a trashy and depraved type and, in addition, senseless." Part I, Book 1, ch. i, "The History of a Certain Family," p. 2.
    Jan M. Meijer, in "The Author of *Bratiia Karamazovy*," *The Brothers Karamazov* by F.M. Dostoevskij, *Dutch Studies in Russian Literature 2* (Mouton) The Hague, 1971, analyzes the persona and the function of the novel's narrator and the various voices he uses. Also see Robert L. Belknap, *The Structure of* The Brothers Karamazov (Mouton), The Hague, 1967.
33. Part I, Book 2, ch. vi, "Why is Such a Man Alive?" p. 65.
34. Part I, Book 3, ch. ix. "The Sensualists," p. 127.
35. Part I, Book 1, ch. v, "Elders," p. 25.
36. Part I, Book 2, ch. v, "So Be It! So Be It!," p. 52.
37. Ibid.
38. Ibid., p. 54. Ivan's presentation of the Roman Church's engagement with the secular State as a contest over authority recalls Kireevsky's conception of the Roman Idea. But while Kireevsky and other Slavophiles demonized the dialectics of Western Christianity, Ivan appears to speak in their praise.
39. Part I, Book 1, ch.v, "Elders," p. 26.

40. See Sergei Hackel, "The Religious Dimension: Vision or Evasion?" in Jones and Terry, *New Essays on Dostoevsky*, op. cit. pp. 73–77.

41. Part I, Book 2, ch.vi, "Why Is Such a Man Alive?" p. 65.

42. Ibid., p. 60.

43. Ibid., p. 61.

44. Ibid.

45. Pascal, *Pensées*, "Misère de l'homme sans Dieu," pp. 39–43 (Collection Internationale, Doubleday), NY 1961.

46. Friedrich Nietzsche, *The Will to Power*, edited and translated by W. Kaufmann and R. J. Hollingdale, NY 1968, p. 326.

47. The original Russian, *"vse budet pozvoleno"* (p. 65, Vol. 14 of the Nauka edition, op. cit.), has been translated by Magarshack as "everything would be lawful," on p. 60, Part I, Book 2, ch. vi).
Albert Camus, in *Le Mythe de Sisyphe*, Paris, 1942, comments on Ivan's formula of license: *"Cette innocence est redoutable.... Il ne s'agit pas d'un cri de délivrance et de joie, mais d'une constatation amère"* (p. 94).
Robert Louis Jackson, in "Last Stop: Virtue and Immortality in *The Brothers Karamazov*," *The Art of Dostoevsky: Deliriums and Nocturnes*, Princeton, 1981, notes that Ivan's social thinking, rooted in his inability to see the good in man, resembles the ideas of Thomas Hobbes, who also recognized the existence of moral law founded on God, but saw that law as contrary to human nature. Jackson points out that Dostoevsky shared Ivan's premise, citing from a passage in *A Writer's Diary*, 1876: "I declare (once again for the time being) without proof that love for humanity is even quite unthinkable, incomprehensible and quite impossible without con-current faith in the immortality of the human soul" (*Polnoe Sobranie Sochinenii*, vol. 24, p. 49). But unlike Dostoevsky, Ivan is unable to make the leap of faith. As Jackson puts it, Ivan is "a victim of the fatal logic of his proposition: believing absolutely in the concrete as it were, day-to-day interdependence of virtue and faith, but lacking personal belief in immortality, he arrives at the intellectual position that 'all is permissible' " (p. 295).

48. Part II, Book 5, ch. iii, "The Brothers Get Acquainted," p. 217.

49. Letter to N. A. Liubimov, dated from Staraia Russa, May 10, 1879: "...this fifth book is in my view the culminating point of the novel and must be finished with particular care. Its meaning, as you will see from the text I sent, is the depiction of extreme blasphemy and the kernel of the idea of destruction of our time, in Russia, among our youth who have broken away from reality.... My hero chooses a theme I consider irrefutable: the senselessness of children's suffering,

and develops from it the absurdity of all historical reality." Quoted from the Matlaw edition of *BK*, "Background and Sources," Letter No. 660, pp. 757–758.

50. Ibid., Letter No. 604 to K. P. Pobedonostsev, dated from Ems, August 24, 1879: "For I proposed to make the sixth book, 'The Russian Monk,' which will appear August 31, the answer to that whole *negative side*. And for that reason I tremble for it in this sense: will it be answer *enough*? The more so as it is not a direct point by point answer to the propositions previously expressed (in the Grand Inquisitor and earlier) but an oblique one" (pp. 761–762).

51. Part II, Book 5, ch. iii, "The Brothers Get Acquainted," p. 215.

52. Ibid.

53. Ibid. "You know, dear boy, there was an old sinner in the eighteenth century who declared that, if there were no God, he would have to be invented. *S'il n'existait pas Dieu, il faudrait l'inventer*. And man has actually invented God." Quoting from Voltaire's *Epitre* CXI, "*A l'auteur d'un nouveau livre sur les trois imposteurs*" (1769), Ivan clearly identifies himself with "the old sinner."
Leonid Grossman, in "Russkii Kandid," *Vestnik Evropy*, May 1914, pp. 192–203, presents Ivan Karamazov as a convinced Voltairean.
Victor Terras, in *A Karamazov Companion* (op. cit.), notes that Ivan's proposition about man's invention of God was a popular notion among the Russian radicals of the 1860s, derived from Ludwig Feuerbach (1804–1872).

54. Claude Bernard's *Introduction à la médicine experimentale* was published in 1865, just a year before the fictional events of *BK* unfold. Claude Bernard died in 1878, while Dostoevsky was at work on *BK*, and his death occasioned numerous commentaries in the Russian press. Dostoevsky was certainly familiar with his friend N.N. Strakhov's review of Bernard's book *Zapiski Otechestva*, 1866. In the novel, Dmitri makes several contemptuous references to the "Bernards" of modern science and calls Rakitin, who is reporting on his trial a "Bernard."

55. Part II, Book 5, ch. iii, p. 216.

56. Ibid.

57. Ibid. The allusion is to the great Russian mathematician N. I. Lobachevsky, who developed his spatial geometry in the 1820s and died in 1856.

58. " 'God is necessary and so must exist.... But I know He doesn't and can't.... Surely you must understand that a man with two such ideas

can't go on living?'" *The Possessed* (Modern Library) op. cit., Part III, Ch. VI, ch. ii, p. 626.

59. Malcolm V. Jones, in *Dostoevsky: The Novel of Discord*, NY, 1976, observes that Dostoevsky was equally opposed to the spirit of scientific humanism and to Promethean Romanticism. "The first was characterized by the elevation of Reason, the second by the elevation of Will.... Worst of all in Dostoevsky's world were solutions which combined Reason and the Will in the quest for emancipation" (pp. 194–95).

60. In Part IV, Book 11, ch. ix, "The Devil. Ivan Fyodorovich's Nightmare," p. 610, the devil quotes that legend back at Ivan. See F. F. Seeley, "Ivan's Writings," in Jones and Terry, *New Essays* (op. cit.) for the reconstruction of the chronological sequence of Ivan's writings.

61. Part II, Book 5, ch. iii, p. 216.

62. Part II, Book 5, ch. iv, "Rebellion," p. 226.

63. Vissarion Belinsky, "Letters to V.P. Botkin," in *Russian Philosophy*, Vol I (op. cit.),
Letter I, dated March 1, 1841 from St. Petersburg, pp. 304–305. For the Russian text, see *Polnoe Sobranie Sochinenii*, Moscow 1953.
Victor Terras, in *Belinskij and Russian Criticism*, U. of Wisconsin Press, 1974, noted the intertextual link: "In a spirited tirade, which reminds one of Ivan Karamazov's 'return of his ticket' to the Creator of this world, Belinski returns his ticket to Hegel" (pp. 87–88).
Nikolai Berdiaev was one of the first to draw attention to the intellectual kinship between Ivan Karamazov and Belinsky (*Russkaia Ideia*, YMCA Press, Paris, 1946, p. 78).

64. Vissarion Belinsky, "The Russian Nation and the Russian Tsar," *Russian Philosophy*, Vol. I, pp. 296–299. This article was inspired by Belinsky's reading of Zhukovsky's poem about the battle of Borodino.

65. Part II, Book 5, ch. iii, p. 216.

66. Leibniz, *Opera philosophica*, ed. J.E. Erdmann, Berlin 1840, I, "De rerum originatione radicali," p. 149. I quote the English translation from Richard A Brooks, *Voltaire and Leibniz* (Librairie Droz), Geneva, 1964, p. 12.

67. "Letter to Botkin," dated September 4, 1841, pp. 310–11.

68. *Poème sur le désastre de Lisbonne* was published in 1756, along with *Poème sur la loi naturelle*, which Voltaire had composed a few years earlier. I quote from *Oeuvres complètes de Voltaire*, ed. Louis Moland, Paris, 1877, Vol. 9, pp. 465–479.

In eighteenth-century Russia, between 1760 and 1790, Voltaire was systematically translated and acclaimed as the leading progressive thinker. A reaction against Voltaire's thought was sponsored by Catherine II, in the wake of the French Revolution. A lively polemic about Voltaire, which included Vasilii Levshin's "Pis'mo Vasiliia Levshina o poeme: Na razrushenie Lissabona" (1788), lasted into the reign of Alexander I. By that time, the diffusion of Voltaire's ideas was marked by a distinct process of vulgarization and had become associated with the spirit and lifestyle of aristocratic licentiousness and petty anticlericalism. Fyodor Karamazov, who likes to quote Voltaire and who sometimes invents spurious anecdotes about other figures of the Enlightenment, such as his story about Diderot in Russia, is a throwback to the type of the Russian Voltairean, albeit in a heavily parodistic form. Ivan Karamazov, on the other hand, restores the intellectual tone of irony to the Voltairean archetype.

See D. D. Iazykov, "Vol'ter v russkoi literature," *Festschrift* for Nicholas Storozhenko (*Pod znameniem nauki*), Moscow, 1902. For a treatment of the relation between Dostoevsky and Voltaire, consult A. Rammelmayer, "Dostoevskij und Voltaire," *Zeitschrift für Slavische Philologie*, XXVI, 2, pp. 252–278, Leipzig, 1958.

69. See T. D. Kendrick, *The Lisbon Earthquake*, Philadelphia, 1957.

70. "*J'ose prendre le parti de l'humanité contre ce misanthrope sublime*" declares Voltaire (p. 141), as he proceeds with his point-by-point refutation of Pascal's Augustinian pessimism. "*Pour moi, quand je regarde Paris ou Londres, je ne vois aucune raison pour entrer en ce désespoir dont parle M. Pascal; je vois une ville qui ne ressemble en rien à une île déserte, mais peuplée, opulente, policée, et où les hommes sont heureux autant que la nature humaine le comporte*" (p. 148). I quote from Voltaire, Lettres philosophiques (Garnier), Paris, 1956.

71. Alexander Pope, *An Essay on Man*, ed. by Maynard Mack, London, 1950, p. 51.

72. Quoted by George R. Havens, "The Conclusion of Voltaire's *Poème sur le désastre de Lisbonne*," *Modern Language Notes*, LVI, 1941, p. 423.

73. "Besides, too high a price is asked for harmony; it's beyond our means to pay so much to enter on it. And so I hasten to give back my entrance ticket, and if I am an honest man I am bound to give it back as soon as possible. And that I am doing. It's not God that I don't accept, Alyosha, only I most respectfully return Him the ticket" (p. 226, Part II, Book 5, ch. iv, "Rebellion").

74. Ibid., p. 219.

75. Ibid., p. 217: " 'I must admit one thing to you,' Ivan began, 'I could never understand how one can love one's neighbors. It's just one's neighbors, to my mind, that one can't love, although one might love those at a distance.' "

76. Richard Brooks, *Voltaire and Leibniz* (op. cit.), writes: "Leibniz's faith convinced him that a priori argument was sufficient, and his inability to rationalize the concomitance of evil and a good God in detail was not a stumbling block, precisely because of that faith" (p. 95).

77. Part II, Book 5, ch. iii, p. 216.

78. Ibid.

79. ch. iv, p. 224.

80. ch. iii, p. 212.

81. I.I. Golosovker, in *Dostoevskii i Kant* (Akademiia Nauk), Moscow, 1963, writes that Ivan's formula "all is allowed," which he rightly sees as the core of his destructive atheism, is an idea that "reeks of blood and covers the scene with corpses" (p. 92). Golosovker argues that Ivan's tragedy of reason represents Dostoevsky's "duel with Kant" (p. 93). Even though Gudzii, in his introduction to Golosovker's book, affirms Dostoevsky's familiarity with Kant's *Critique of Pure Reason* (based on the reference in Dostoevsky's letter to his brother Mikhail, dated February 22, 1854), the real question is how much of Kant there is in Ivan's mind. The passage about a world where "cause follows effect, simply and directly" (ch. iv, p. 224) may suggest a familiarity with the first of Kant's four antinomies: the world is either created and finite or not created and eternal. But the model of an enduring material universe without a presiding will and responsibility is irrelevant to Ivan's argument. Golosovker is much more to the point in saying that Ivan has opted for the negative pole of Kant's second antinomy, about the immortality of the soul or the lack thereof.

82. See Dmitry Tschizewskij, "Schiller and *The Brothers Karamazov*," Norton edition of *BK*, "Background and Sources," pp. 794–807.

83. ch. iii, p. 211. The allusion to Pushkin's poem "Chill Winds Still Blow" (*Esche veiut kholodnye vetry*, 1828) is a concession to his submerged idealism and love of poetry.

84. ch. iv, p. 225.

85. "Letters to Botkin" III, p. 307, and II, June 28, p. 397. In his passion for justice, Ivan is reminiscent of Cimourdain, the pitiless revolutionary in Victor Hugo's novel *Quatrevingt-Treize* (1874). A defrocked priest turned ideologue of the Revolution, Cimourdain is

a *commissaire délégué of the comité du salut public* sent to the war in Vendée in the summer of 1793. He casts the decisive vote that condemns to the guillotine his beloved pupil Gauvain, who as a commander of a revolutionary regiment has shown mercy to the enemy. Cimourdain will kill himself at the moment when Gauvain's head falls into the basket. The night before the execution, the two friends exchange views about the Revolution:

—*Tu te perds dans le nuage.* [Cimourdain to Gauvain]
—*Et toi dans le calcul.*
—*Il y a du rêve dans l'harmonie.*
—*Il y en a aussi dans l'algèbre.*
—*Je voudrais l'homme fait par Euclide.*
—*Et moi, dit Gauvain, je l'aimerais mieux fait par Homère.*

Victor Hugo, *Quatrevingt-Treize* (Gallimard), Paris, 1979, p. 467. This dialectical exchange between the idealist and the realist has been noted by Victor Terras, in *A Karamazov Companion*, as a secular parallel to the confrontation between the Christ and the Grand Inquisitor. Even more striking is Cimourdain's use of Euclid as a metaphor for the ideal society based on the perfect symmetry of justice. There is undoubtedly an echo of Hugo in Ivan's use of the word "harmony" (op. cit., p. 15).

86. ch. iv, p. 224.
87. Ibid., p. 226.
88. In Schiller's drama *Don Carlos* (1785), the Grand Inquisitor confronts a mere human, King Philip II, and not the Christ (Act V, Scene 10). But as Victor Terras points out, the Grand Inquisitor offers Philip the same bargain as that presented by Dostoevsky's satanic priest to Christ: freedom and exposure to sin, or giving up freedom and surrendering all responsibility and the burden of sin, which the priest will assume instead (Victor Terras, *A Karamazov Companion*, op. cit., p. 16).
89. Part I, Book 2, ch. vi, p. 61.
90. Part II, Book 5, ch. v, p. 230.
91. Leatherbarrow, op. cit., p. 157.
92. "At Tikhon's," *The Possessed* (p. 691–730). Stavrogin's confession to the elder Tikhon was first published in Moscow in 1927. See Vol. VII of the Nauka edition of F. M. Dostoevskii, in 30 volumes.
93. Part II, Book 5, ch. v, p. 238.

94. See Rostislav Pletnev, "Ob iskushenii Khrista v pustyne i Dostoevskom," *Russian Language Journal*, XXXVI, Nos. 123–124, pp. 66–73, 1982.
95. Part II, Book 5, ch. v, p. 241.
96. Ibid., p. 242.
97. Ibid., p. 236: "Thou didst proudly and well, like God; but the weak, rebellious race of men, are they gods?"
98. Ibid., p. 241.
99. Ibid., p. 243.
100. The Catholic scholar Romano Guardini, in *Religiöse Gestalten in Dostoevskijs Werk*, Munich, 1947, does not accept the image of the Christ in the Legend as a canonical representation. E. Sandoz, *Political Apolcalypse*, Baton Rouge, 1971, also questions the image: "The Christ of the Legend is the triumphant figure of the Palm Sunday entry into Jerusalem, not the Christ of the Passion, nor the Resurrected Christ, nor the eternal Word whose place is at the right of the Father. He is the humanist's Christ whose revelation is of the God in man" (pp. 184–85).
101. Part II, Book 5, ch. v, p. 243.
102. Robert Louis Jackson, in "Bakhtin's Poetics of Dostoevsky and Dostoevsky's Declaration of Faith," pp. 269–292 of *Dialogues with Dostoevsky: The Overwhelming Questions*, Stanford U. Press, 1993, argues that Bakhtin understood the importance of Dostoevsky the author as a participating player in the polyphonic world that he created. This can be seen in the way he threw into his text the image of the Christ, which represented for him the resolution of all ideological conflicts. The Christ figure comes alive only after Alyosha's questions open up the Grand Inquisitor's monologic, finalizing discourse about man, into a brotherly dialogue between despair and faith.
103. Part II, Book 5, ch. v, p. 240.
104. Ibid., p. 243.
105. Ibid., p. 244.
106. Robert Louis Jackson, "States of Ambiguity: Early Shakespeare and Late Dostoevsky, the two Ivans," pp. 228–236 of *Dialogues with Dostoevsky: The Overwhelming Questions*, op. cit., p. 234. Jackson compares Ivan's winking complicity with his father's murder to two episodes of Shakespeare's *King John*. In the first episode (Act III, Scene 2) King John, the usurper, instigates Hubert, a citizen of Angers, to kill the young Arthur, Duke of Brittany, who is the legitimate claimant to the English throne. In the second episode (Act IV,

Scene 2) King John, believing the murder to have been accomplished, accuses Hubert of provoking him to commit the crime. Jackson notes that Ivan, just like King John, is reluctant to admit the link between his wish and the hand that does the deed.

V. E. Vetlovskaia, in "Ritorika i poetika: utverzhdenie i oproverzhenie mnenii v *Bratiiakh Karamazovykh*," *Issledovaniia po poetike i stilistike*, Leningrad, 1972, pp. 163–184, has demonstrated how Dostoevsky uses this scene, among others, to develop his *ad hominem* refutation of Ivan's ideas.

107. Part II, Book 5, ch. iii, p. 213.

108. Part II, Book 5, ch. ii, "Smerdyakov with a Guitar," p. 208.

109. Ibid., p. 206.

110. p. 296, "Last Stop: Virtue and Immortality in *The Brothers Karamazov*," *The Art of Dostoevsky: Deliriums and Nocturnes*, op. cit.

111. "'Sit still. Now we've a treat for you, in your own line, too' [says Fyodor to Alyosha]. 'It'll make you laugh. Balaam's ass has begun talking to us here—and how he talks! How he talks!' Balaam's ass, it appeared, was the lackey" (p. 112, Part I, Book 4, ch. vi, "Smerdyakov"). Fyodor is apparently unaware of the dramatic irony lurking in his Biblical reference to Numbers 22 (21–34), where the Lord opens the mouth of the she ass after her master Balaam has smitten her three times for resisting him. When Balaam's ass speaks with a human voice, she becomes the instrument of the Lord's will, leading Balaam back to the righteous path.

112. Part I, Book 3, ch. viii, "Over the Brandy," p. 120.

113. Part I, Book 3, ch. vii, "The Controversy," p. 117.

114. "*Forse/ tu non pensavi ch'io loico fossi!*'" says the devil to Guido as he drags his soul to hell.

115. Part I, Book 3, ch. vii, p. 118.

116. Ibid., p. 119.

117. Part III, Book 8, ch. iv, "In the Dark," p. 370. This is an instance of Dostoevsky's cunning use of the chronicle mode, which allows him to pit the myopic view of the actual narrator against the stereoscopical overview of the author. Catteau calls this method of composition a *chronique à chaud*, and he argues that it preserves the hero's freedom, no less than the author's. (See Jacques Catteau, *La création littéraire chez Dostoivski*, Paris 1978.)

The effect of suspense on the first readers, who were exposed to the text serially, can be gauged by Dostoevsky's response to E. N. Lebedeva, who was confused by the suspension points in Chapter 4.

"Dear Madame: The servant Smerdyakov killed old Karamazov. All the details will become clear as the novel progresses. Ivan Fyodorovich participated in the murder only obliquely and remotely, only by failing (intentionally) to inform Smerdyakov during their conversation before his departure for Moscow and clearly and categorically expressing his repugnance for the crime Smerdyakov conceived (which Ivan Fyodorovich clearly saw and had a presentiment of) and thus *seemed to permit* Smerdyakov to commit the crime. Smerdyakov had to have that *permission*, the reason for which will again become clear in the rest of the novel. Dmitri Fyodorovich is completely innocent of his father's murder" (Letter No. 701, dated from Petersburg, November 8, 1879), p. 763, The Matlaw edition of *BK* (op. cit.).

118. ch. iv, p. 370.

119. V. V. Vetlovskaia, in *Poetika romana Bratiia Karamazovy*, Leningrad, 1977, calls attention to the predominance of the number three in the composition of the novel, identifying the ternery pattern of organization as the sign of the novel's mytho-poetic structure, which she relates to the fairy tale. The same could be said of the structure of Sophocles' *Oedipus the King*.

120. Part II, Book 5, ch. vii, "It's Always Worthwhile Speaking to a Clever Man," p. 259.

121. Part IV, Book 11, ch. vi, "The First Interview with Smerdyakov," p. 576.

122. Ibid., p. 574.

123. Ibid., p. 577.

124. Part IV, Book 11, ch. vii, "The Second Visit to Smerdyakov," p. 583.

125. Ibid.

126. Ibid., p. 586.

127. Part IV, Book 11, ch. viii, "The Third and Last Interview with Smerdyakov," p. 590.

128. Ibid., p. 588.

129. Ibid., p. 591.

130. Robert Louis Jackson, in "States of Ambiguity..." op. cit., comments that Smerdyakov, like King John who projects his vileness on Hubert, "mistakenly sees in Ivan the mirror image of himself" (p. 235). But Jackson reminds us that it is John, not Hubert, who has the soul of a slave and thus resembles Smerdyakov. When Smerdyakov realizes that Ivan was at least partially unaware of his complicity, "his idol crumbles" (p. 235).

131. Rostislav Pletnev, in "Zemlia," Vol. I of *O Dostoevskom: Sbornik statei*, ed. A. L. Bem, Prague, 1929, established that Dostoevsky possessed a contemporary Russian edition of the seventh-century Greek text, *Slova podvizhnicheskaia*. Pletnev also argued that Zosima's practice of ecstasy was based on Isaac's theory of tearful worship. This would align Grigory, with his harsh, earthly practice of Orthodoxy, with Zosima's gentle spirituality, in a paradoxical coincidence of opposites.
    Victor Terras, pp. 22–23 of *A Karamazov Companion*, op. cit., notes that the Russian text of Isaac's sayings in Dostoevsky's possession had been prepared by Paissy Velichkovsky in 1787.

132. viii, p. 599.

133. Smerdyakov's rejection of the feminine can be traced to his revulsion of shame against the womb that gave him birth: "Grigory Vasilyevich blames me for rebelling against my birth. 'You rent her womb,' he says, but I would have sanctioned their killing me before I was born that I might not have come into the world at all, ma'am" (p. 206, Part II, Book 5, ch. ii). Smerdyakov's choice of the paternal world of tyranny to which he aspires places him outside the pale of the nurturing, deeply maternal spirituality that Dostoevsky embraces in this novel, which he dedicated to the grieving mother of the dead infant Alyosha, his wife Anna Grigorievna.
    Louis Breger, in *Dostoevsky: The Author as Psychoanalyst*, op. cit., links that spirituality to Dostoevsky's meditation over Marya Dmitrievna's dead body in 1864. He comments: "Here, Dostoevsky outlines a religious way of life that is far from the Judeo-Christian mainstream.... It is linked to that minor voice in Christianity that goes back to the Gnostics and that reappeared in the nineteenth-century Romantic movement. While one can connect it to various sources such as these, I believe Dostoevsky worked it out for himself. In addition to the image of merger, this vision stresses process or being; it contrasts with the more familiar Christian doctrine, which defines earthly life as a means to a higher end. Significantly absent from Dostoevsky's view is the image of a judgmental, patriarchal God" (pp. 188–89).

134. Part IV, Book 11, ch. x, "It Was He Who Said That!" p. 618.

135. Part IV, Book 11, ch. viii, p. 600.

136. Part IV, Book 12, ch. v, "A Sudden Catastrophe," p. 652.

137. E. Sandoz, *Political Apocalypse*, op. cit., notes on p. 113 that "simple atheism is not his [Ivan's] true affliction, if indeed it is the affliction

of any man: men always worship God, and if they cannot relate themselves to the transcendent ground of being, then they must inevitably fall back upon substitute grounds."

138. *The Possessed*, Book III, Ch. VI, ch. ii, p. 626.

139. Part IV, Book 11, ch. ix, p. 603.

140. Ibid.

141. Ibid., p. 607.

142. Part I, Book 1, ch. iv, "The Third Son, Alyosha," p. 18. Robert L. Belknap, in *The Structure of* The Brothers Karamazov, op. cit., pp. 41–47, shows how the persona of the babbling buffoon, which Fyodor shares with his sidekick Maximov, is incorporated into the figure of Ivan's devil.

143. ch. ix, pp. 602–603.

144. Ibid., p. 613.

145. From Ivan's juvenilia the devil cites "The Legend of the Unbelieving Philosopher" (pp. 610 and 614) and "The Geological Cataclysm" (pp. 615 and 616), wrapping up with the formula "all things are lawful" (p. 616).

146. "Well, if you like, I have the same philosophy as you, that would be true. *Je pense, donc je suis*. I know that for a fact, all the rest, all these worlds, God and even Satan—all that is not proved, to my mind. Does all that exist of itself, or is it only an emanation of my ego which alone has existed forever..." (pp. 609–610).

    In *The Bounds of Reason: Cervantes, Dostoevsky, Flaubert*, Columbia U. Press, 1986, Anothony J. Cascardi draws on Kierkegaard's critique of the primacy of logic ("What reality is cannot be expressed in the language of abstraction. Reality is *interesse*") to highlight the solipsism inherent in Descartes' formula. "The 'abstract thinker,' the professional skeptic or epistemologist, wants to found existence on pure cognition (e.g., as in Descartes' *cogito* argument), but in so doing he denies existence; he fails to fashion an actual response to the world" (p. 127).

147. Part II, Book 6, ch. iii, "Conversations and Exhortations of Father Zosima," p. 301.

    Jackson, in "Last Stop: Virtue and Immortality in *BK*," op. cit., draws attention to the fact that Dostoevsky had marked out the lines from the First Epistle of John in his personal Bible: "He who does not love, remains in death.... If a man say 'I love God' and hateth his brother, he is a liar." The link between love of humanity and faith is organic and cannot be separated or approached logically as an either/or.

148. Part IV, Book 11, ch. ix, p. 615.
149. Ibid., p. 614.
150. Ibid., p. 615.
151. Ibid., p. 605.
152. Ibid., 608.
153. Ibid., p. 604.
154. Ibid., p. 606. The Terence line *"Homo sum et nihil humanum a me alienum puto"* comes from the play *The Self-Tormentor.*
155. I have drawn on Bernard M. W. Knox's luminous reading: "The Last Scene," pp. 90–98, *Twentieth-Century Interpretations of Oedipus Rex,* ed. by Michael Y. O'Brien (Spectrum Books) 1968.
156. *Oedipus at Colonus,* translated by Robert Fitzgerald, in The U. of Chicago edition of the Theban trilogy, *Sophocles I.*
157. "Epilogue," Ch. I, "Plans to Save Mitya," pp. 717–721, and Ch. II, "For a Moment the Lie Becomes Truth," pp. 721–727.
158. "Epilogue," Ch. III, "Ilyushechka's Funeral. The Speech at the Stone," p. 735. Jackson points out that Alyosha speaks not of God but of the brotherhood of love, consecrated by the memory of Ilyusha, the suffering son of a loving but ineffectual father. See "Last Stop: Virtue and Immortality in *The Brothers Karamazov,*" op. cit.
159. Dostoevsky's hopes for a revival of a socially active, spiritual Christianity in Russia may have been rekindled by his friendship with the young philosopher and mystic of Divine Sophia, Vladimir Soloviev (1853–1900). To Dostoevsky, Soloviev's decision to quit the faculty of natural sciences to enter the theological seminary (1873) seemed to augur a vaster shift from disbelief to faith in the rising generation of the intelligentsia. In 1878, Dostoevsky was in the audience that heard Soloviev's "Lectures on God-Manhood," and that same year the two of them undertook the pilgrimage to Optyn'. See Ch. III, pp. 31–60 of Maria Nûmcová Banerjee, *The Religious and Metaphysical Interpretation of Dostoevskij from Vladimir Solov'ev to Berdjaev: A Study of Six Great Commentaries* (PhD Thesis, Harvard 1962).
   Marina Kostalevsky, *Dostoevsky and Soloviev: The Art of Integral Vision,* Yale U. Press, 1997, offers a comprehensive treatment of the subject.
160. Part IV, Book 12, ch. v, "A Sudden Catastrophe," p. 650.
161. Part IV, Book 11, ch. ix, p. 608.
162. Since names are meaningful in this novel, it is noteworthy that fetya, in Russian, is the obscene word for the female sexual organ. This

point was made by Marina Kostalevsky, in "The Pleasure and Pain of Thinking," a paper read on October 2, 1999 at the Symposium on *The Brothers Karamazov*, in Honor of Robert L. Jackson, held at Yale University. Fetyukovich, who deploys systematic skepticism to deconstruct the *arche* of fatherhood, is an adulterer of thought. Dmitri rejects his defense counsel's sophistical argument, even though it could serve to prove him innocent.

163. Part IV, Book 12, ch. v, p. 651.

164. Ibid.

165. Ibid., pp. 651–652.

166. Cascardi, in *The Bounds of Reason*, op. cit., compares Dmitri to Socrates: "Like Dmitri, Socrates refused to defend himself by the shameless effrontery and sophistical arguments common in the courts of law. This refusal is his defense, and it is his conviction as well..." (pp. 120–121).

167. ch. v, p. 654.

168. The prosecutor's speech occupies four chapters: Part IV, Book 12, Ch. 6 "The Prosecutor's Speech. Sketches of Character"; Ch. 7, "An Historical Survey"; Ch. 8, "A Treatise on Smerdyakov" and Ch. 9, "Psychology at Full Steam. The Galloping Troika. The End of the Prosecutor's Speech." Kate Holland, in "The Legend of the *Ladonka*," a paper read on October 3, at the Symposium on *The Brothers Karamazov*, at Yale University, pointed out that both legal discourses—Fetuykovich's display of skepticism as well as Ippolit Kirilovich's cause and effect exposition, operate within the framework of determinism, where inertia (*kosnost*) rules.

169. Part IV, Book 12, ch. xiv, "The Peasants Stand Firm," p. 716.

170. For this, Robert Louis Jackson dubs him "the nineteenth-century Oedipus" in "States of Ambiguity..." op. cit., p. 228.

171. Alan Woolfolk, in "The Two Switchmen of Nihilism: Dostoevsky and Nietzsche," *Mosiac*, Vol. 22, No. 1, Winter 1989, draws on René Girard's concept of "mimetic desire" to describe the violence inherent in the intellectual gesture of stripping the world of its sacred *arche*: "...the effort to achieve godlike autonomy, of which Nietzsche is the supreme symbolist, always moves toward the denial of limits, esthetic and otherwise, upon the self, and ultimately results in self-destruction. Zarathustra authorizes his underground shadow, just as Ivan Karamazov serves as a mediator for Smerdyakov, and Stavrogin is a model for the possessed. Whatever tragic greatness there is in the model fades in the mimesis. The nobility of evil

becomes, in Hannah Arendt's fine phrase, 'the banality of evil,' because the initiator recognizes only the intentions, desires, wishes, dreams of the self as genuine, not limits upon them. According to Girard, through Dostoevsky's eyes 'Nietzsche's superhumanity would have been merely an underground dream.' One might add that for those who would attempt to become supermen, Dostoevsky's Underground Man would seem to be more than merely a nightmare" (pp. 78–79).